THE

# MIAMI

**read Rough Guides online**

www.roughguides.com

## Rough Guide Credits

Text editor: Hunter Slaton
Series editor: Mark Ellingham
Production: Zoë Nobes, Andy Turner
Proofreading: Diane Margolis
Cartography: Ed Wright

## Publishing Information

This second edition published November 2002
by Rough Guides Ltd,
80 Strand, London WC2R 0RL.

### Distributed by the Penguin Group:

Penguin Books Ltd, 80 Strand, London WC2R 0RL.
Penguin Putnam, Inc. 375 Hudson Street, New York 10014, USA
Penguin Books Australia Ltd, 487 Maroondah Highway,
PO Box 257, Ringwood, Victoria 3134, Australia
Penguin Books Canada Ltd, 10 Alcorn Avenue,
Toronto, Ontario, Canada M4V 1E4
Penguin Books (NZ) Ltd,
182–190 Wairau Road, Auckland 10, New Zealand

Typeset in Bembo and Helvetica to an original design by Henry Iles.
Printed in Spain by Graphy Cems.

No part of this book may be reproduced in any form
without permission from the publisher except for the
quotation of brief passages in reviews.

© Rough Guides, 2002
336pp, includes index
A catalog record for this book is available from the British Library.

### ISBN 1-84353-137-2

The publishers and authors have done their best to ensure
the accuracy and currency of all the information in
*The Rough Guide to Miami*; however, they
can accept no responsibility for any loss, injury or
inconvenience sustained by any traveller as a result of
information or advice contained in the guide.

# THE ROUGH GUIDE TO

# MIAMI

## by Mark Ellwood

ROUGH GUIDES

**W**e set out to do something different when the first Rough Guide was published in 1982. Mark Ellingham, just out of university, was traveling in Greece. He brought along the popular guides of the day, but found they were all lacking in some way. They were either strong on ruins and museums but went on for pages without mentioning a beach or taverna; or they were so conscious of the need to save money that they lost sight of Greece's cultural and historical significance. Also, none of the books told him anything about Greece's contemporary life – its politics, its culture, its people and how they lived.

So with no job in prospect, Mark decided to write his own guidebook, one which aimed to provide practical information that was second to none, detailing the best beaches and the hottest clubs and restaurants, while also giving hard-hitting accounts of every sight, both famous and obscure, and providing up-to-the-minute information on contemporary culture. It was a guide that encouraged independent travelers to find the best of Greece and was a great success, getting shortlisted for the Thomas Cook Travel Guide Award, and encouraging Mark, along with three friends, to expand the series.

The Rough Guide list grew rapidly and the letters flooded in, indicating a much broader readership than had been anticipated, but one which uniformly appreciated the Rough Guide mix of practical detail and humor, irreverence and enthusiasm. Things haven't changed. The same four friends who began the series are still the caretakers of the Rough Guide mission today: to provide the most reliable, up-to-date and entertaining information to independent-minded travelers of all ages, on all budgets.

We now publish more than 200 titles and have offices in London and New York. The travel guides are written and researched by a dedicated team of more than 100 authors, based in Britain, Europe, the USA and Australia. We have also created a unique series of phrasebooks to accompany the travel series, along with an acclaimed series of music guides, and a best-selling pocket guide to the internet and World Wide Web. We also publish comprehensive travel information on our website: **www.roughguides.com**

## Help us update

We've gone to a lot of trouble to ensure that this Rough Guide is as up-to-date and accurate as possible. However, things do change. All suggestions, comments and corrections are much appreciated, and we'll send a copy of the next edition (or any other Rough Guide if you prefer) for the best letters.

Please mark letters **"Rough Guide Miami Update"** and send to:
Rough Guides, 80 Strand, London WC2R 0RL or
Rough Guides, 4th Floor, 345 Hudson St, New York NY 10014.
Or send an email to mail@roughguides.com
Have your questions answered and tell others about your trip at
www.roughguides.atinfopop.com

## Acknowledgments

In Miami and around, thanks to Herb Sosa at the Miami Design Preservation League for everything architectural; Jennifer Rubell for insight and accommodation; Erica Freshman, Zack Bush and crew (Julie, Dina, Erica, Jourdan, Alexis) for nights on the town; Charlie Herman; Helen Gill Blank for the history of Key Biscayne; Mariela Ferretti and Ramon Bonachea at the Cuban-American National Foundation; the infectiously enthusiastic Ginny Gutierrez; Jacquelynn D. Powers; Didi Bushnell and team at Stuart Newman Assos. for shepherding my trip through the Keys, plus Nicola Tomlinson and Rob Muraskin for company there.

In New York and London, thanks to Hunter Slaton for his patient editing and sense of humor; to Yuki Takagaki for her help during my trip to Miami; to Ed Wright for his excellent maps; to Andy Turner for his skilled typesetting; to Diane Margolis for her meticulous proofreading; and to Andrew Rosenberg for sending me to Miami in the first place. Thanks, too, to Maureen, Clare, Karen and Ben for keeping the home fires burning.

## Cover credits

Main front picture Living Room Building ©Rosario Marquardt & Roberto Behar; Front small picure ©Stone
Back top picture South Beach ©Robert Harding;
Back lower picture Colony Hotel, Miami Beach ©Robert Harding

# CONTENTS

# MAP LIST

# Introduction

**M**iami is a gorgeous, gaudy city, resting on the edge of the Caribbean like a tropical paradise, at least climate-wise. The people on the beach are as tan and toned as they are on TV, and the weather rarely dips below balmy; there are lazy palm trees everywhere, and wide, golden beaches spacious enough to seem empty even on a sweltering Sunday in high season. And, for a place built on holidays and hype, Miami lives up to, and revels in, every cliché: sleek Art Deco hotels; pumping, hedonistic nightlife; cafés full of aspiring models – you'll likely see all these things even during a brief stay. Miami's not all beaches and beautiful people, though; what few visitors expect is the city's diversity, exhibited in its glorious tropical gardens and excellent modern art museums, plus vibrant Cuban and Haitian immigrant communities.

Founded little more than a century ago, Miami has grown up fast from its beginning as a humble trading post, first losing its backwater feel with the extension of Henry Flagler's railroad in 1896. In the 1920s, local businessmen aggressively seized the chance to capitalize on the new vogue for vacations in the sun, and a hotel building boom in Miami Beach ensued, producing some of the greatest Art Deco masterpieces in the country. Aside from a brief period during World War II, Miami remained a prime vacation

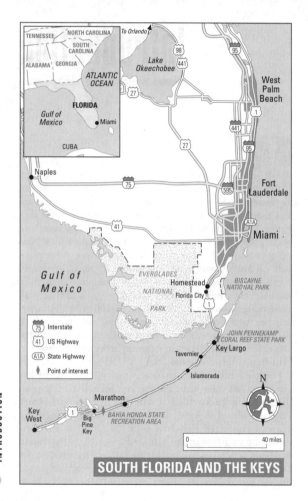

SOUTH FLORIDA AND THE KEYS

destination until the early 1960s, when the first wave of Cuban refugees arrived, fleeing a newly installed Fidel Castro and his communist regime. This set the stage for a further flood of immigrants from Cuba and other Latin American countries; indeed, more than half of Miami-Dade County's current population was born overseas. Because of this, to many further north, Miami is seen as barely part of the US, a place that's tropically lawless and suspiciously bilingual. Yet at the heart of the city is a glorious contradiction: to Venezuelans, Peruvians and other new Latin arrivals, it's a quintessentially American town, ordered, safe and filled with opportunity.

In some ways, both sides are right. In addition to dealing with its transformation into a multi-ethnic metropolis over the course of a few furious decades, Miami endured violent, headline-grabbing race riots, an alarming murder rate that was at one point the nation's highest, and a role as a prominent port-of-entry for the drug trade. However, by the 1990s the situation was improving, thanks to a stronger local economy and a number of city revitalization projects. Miami's makeover as a hip, hot city was cemented when South Beach was "discovered" by fashion photographers, bringing swarms of beautiful people, both models and visitors, in their wake. Some of that glamorous sheen has already, perhaps inevitably, worn off, but so have some of the more damaging parts of the city's reputation – making for a constant and welcome defying of expectations for the casual visitor.

## Neighborhoods and orientation

Radiating out from the mouth of the Miami River and stretched along the sandbanks sheltering Biscayne Bay from the ocean, Miami is an enormous city, comprised of dozens of small, dense districts. While its central neighborhoods are minutes' drive from each other, Greater Miami is a large city that's only getting larger. In fact, Metro–Dade County is the size of Rhode Island, and the sprawling suburbs in its western district are some of the fastest-growing in America.

Miami's most famous district is **South Beach**, where Art Deco buildings and decadent lifestyle made headlines and much money for the city during the 1990s. It's still likely to be the place where you spend the most time: a huge number of the city's hotels are grouped together here, and the strip of Art Deco buildings along Ocean Drive is iconically

## THIRTEEN THINGS NOT TO MISS

**7am on Ocean Drive, South Beach** See why the photographers loved South Beach: early morning light that's crystal-white. It's one of the few times you'll be able to enjoy Ocean Drive in relative solitude. See p.36.

*Cafecito* at *David's Café*, South Beach Thimblefuls of Cuban coffee keep Miami going, and there's nowhere better for a quick shot than at *David's* on the beach. See p.129.

**Deering Estate, South Miami** A peaceful counterpoint to the flashy opulence of its sibling estate at Vizcaya; visit for some rare peace and nature only a short drive from the city. See p.104.

**Holocaust Memorial, South Beach** The heavy concentration of Holocaust survivors in South Florida makes this monument topical and still troubling: a masterfully sobering memorial. See p.45.

**Ice cream at *Lakay Bakery*, Little Haiti** Try one of the creamy Caribbean flavors, while French and Creole are spoken around you. See p.135.

**The Living Room Building, the Design District** A new landmark for the city: both an irresistible photo opportunity and a surreal visual farce. See p.97.

Miami. The rest of **Miami Beach** – both central and north – is often ignored, condemned for its forest of monolithic condo buildings. That's a shame, as the area is home to notable Miami Modern architecture such as the *Fontainebleau* and *Eden Roc* hotels, as well as some of the best beaches in the city, especially further north in Sunny Isles Beach and Haulover Park.

Across Biscayne Bay from Miami Beach, **downtown** prominently displays the Latin heart of the city, bustling with Spanish-speaking businesses and small Cuban lunch

**Miami Art Museum, downtown** An outstanding modern collection showcasing top-tier conceptual art that's curated intelligently but accessibly. See p.23.

*Pelican Hotel*, **South Beach** A campy delight of a hotel, owned by jeanswear company Diesel, where each room follows a different kitschy theme. See p.120.

*Rascal House*, **Sunny Isles Beach** A diner that's changed little since the northern beach's 1950s heyday – and that includes much of the staff. See p.146.

**Stiltsville, Key Biscayne** This is precious modern Miami history – a waterbound village of seven ramshackle huts standing in the mud flats off Key Biscayne. See p.93.

**Venetian Pool, Coral Gables** Coral Gables' civic amenities don't come better than this: a quarry turned lagoon that's both loungeworthy and historic. See p.73.

**Villa Vizcaya, Coconut Grove** Opulent, excessive and unmissable, Vizcaya is Miami's early wealth made manifest in one crazy, baroque palace. See p.86.

*Yambo*, **Little Havana** Step into Central America at *Yambo*, where the food is superb and the vibe authentic. See p.149.

counters; most major sights can be found along its central artery, Flagler Street. To the north of downtown stand two neighborhoods poised to explode: concerted effort by developers has pumped the **Design District** full of show-rooms, housewares stores, and witty modern architecture; meanwhile, **Little Haiti**, with its deep history and vibrant immigrant culture, makes few tourist concessions – and for that reason alone is attracting increasing numbers of travel-ers. Southwest from downtown, just across the river, lies **Little Havana**, a residential neighborhood of sherbert-colored houses that became the first home of Cuban refugees as they arrived in America. It's still the immigrant heart of the city, though with an increasingly diverse Latin population. Southeast from here, the Rickenbacker Causeway leads out from downtown to **Key Biscayne**, a tony island on the bay whose smart central village is sand-wiched between Miami's two best parks.

On the city's southern extreme stands **Coconut Grove**, the earliest settlement in the area and an artsier, more bohemian place than much of Miami. It's not the counter-culture hotbed it once was, but it is home to two of the city's most intriguing sights – the Barnacle and Villa Vizcaya. West from here, the city of **Coral Gables** – which technically isn't Miami at all – is a Spanish-inspired confec-tion of Mediterranean Revival mansions and grand civic amenities. The brainchild of one man, George Merrick, it's an eccentric exercise in ego and enthusiasm – not to men-tion home to many second-generation Cuban-Americans.

To the south, as the suburb of **South Miami** blends with the outskirts of neighboring **Homestead,** there are several major gardens and animal parks amid the vast stretches of farmland. Here you'll also find the beginning of the road that snakes down past the **Everglades**, leading to the laid-back islands collectively known as the **Florida Keys**, capped by the old town of Key West. North of Miami, an easy day-trip is **Fort Lauderdale**, a once hard-partying town that's now peaceful and gleaming.

-------------------------------------------------

Miami has two area codes: the original ⊤305 has been joined by ⊤786. If dialing from one code to another, you'll need to dial the full number even for local calls. Note, too, that although the Keys share the same code, calling Key West from Miami is charged as a long distance call.

-------------------------------------------------

## Climate and when to visit

Miami's weather is tropically warm throughout the year: its tender winters have brought snowbirds down from the Northeast for more than a hundred years. High season is

| | F° | | C° | | RAINFALL | |
|---|---|---|---|---|---|---|
| | AVERAGE DAILY | | AVERAGE DAILY | | AVERAGE MONTHLY | |
| | MAX | MIN | MAX | MIN | IN | MM |
| Jan | 75 | 59 | 24 | 15 | 2.0 | 51 |
| Feb | 76 | 60 | 24 | 15 | 2.1 | 53 |
| March | 79 | 64 | 26 | 18 | 2.4 | 61 |
| April | 82 | 68 | 28 | 19 | 2.8 | 72 |
| May | 85 | 72 | 30 | 23 | 6.2 | 158 |
| June | 88 | 75 | 31 | 24 | 9.3 | 237 |
| July | 89 | 76 | 32 | 25 | 5.7 | 145 |
| Aug | 89 | 77 | 32 | 25 | 7.6 | 192 |
| Sept | 88 | 76 | 31 | 24 | 7.6 | 194 |
| Oct | 84 | 72 | 30 | 23 | 5.6 | 143 |
| Nov | 80 | 67 | 27 | 17 | 2.7 | 67 |
| Dec | 77 | 61 | 24 | 15 | 1.8 | 46 |

January through March, when the weather hovers around 80°F (27°C) and rainfall and humidity are low; it's also when crowd-pulling events like the Winter Music Conference and the Miami Film Festival are held.

June through August is often unbearably hot, plus stiflingly humid, and hotel rates are not surprisingly rock-bottom. The **hurricane season** is traditionally May through October, with the occasional flurry in November. Don't fret, though: warning systems are now sophisticated enough that even should a heavy storm roll in while you're there, you'll be alerted in ample time. The best times to visit may well be the shoulder seasons – April, May, October and November; the weather's good, if not flawless, and the hotel bargains still plentiful.

# BASICS

---

# Arrival

**M**ost visitors will arrive in Miami via one of the two major regional **airports**, though it's also well-connected by Greyhound **buses** and Amtrak **trains**. Major **US interstates** shuttle drivers directly into downtown – and a great view of the Miami skyline can be seen from the approaching elevated highways.

## BY AIR

**Miami International Airport** (**MIA**) (℡305/876-7000, ⓦwww.miami-airport.com) is only six miles west of downtown and well-connected to the rest of the city. Be aware, though, that there's limited signage at the airport itself, and that the parking garages are especially hard to find. **Fort Lauderdale Hollywood International Airport** (**FLL**) (℡954/359-6100, ⓦwww.fll.net) is where many of the budget flights to the area land – it's a perfectly viable alternative that's roughly 45 minutes drive from the Miami city center.

---

Miami is serviced by most of the major US airlines – for contact information, see p.223, "Directory."

---

Once on the ground, fares from the airport by **taxi** are fixed by zone – a one-way trip to South Beach, for example, is \$24 plus tip. A smart alternative for solo travelers is the **SuperShuttle** minivan, which will deliver you to any address in Miami for \$9–15 (☎ 305/871-2000, Ⓦ www .supershuttle.com) – if you want to book a trip back to the airport, call 24 hours in advance. There are also **public bus** connections from the airport to the main transit hubs: #7 goes downtown, a trip of 30 minutes or so (\$1.25, exact fare required; every 40min Mon–Fri 5.30am–8.30pm, Sat & Sun 7am–7pm), or the "J" Metrobus that trundles out to the beaches (\$1.25 plus a 25-cent surcharge to South Beach; every 30 minutes daily 5.30am–11.30pm). Don't worry if you arrive late at night: there's an **Airport Owl shuttle** that runs on an infrequent but reliable route looping through South Beach, downtown and back to the airport (\$1.25; hourly, 11.50pm–5.50am).

## BY CAR

Driving from the **north**, you're likely to approach Miami on I-95, the freeway that runs down the entire length of Florida's east coast and deposits you in downtown Miami. From here, the MacArthur and Julia Tuttle causeways both lead to the beaches.

For car rental firms and contact
information, see p.223, "Directory."

If you're coming up from the Keys, Highway 1 leads north through Coconut Grove and Coral Gables to downtown and beyond. However, it's a slower suburban route, with plenty of stoplights – you'd do better turning off onto the Palmetto Expressway, which skirts the western edge of Miami before turning east through its northern portion, or taking Florida's Turnpike from Hwy-1 and then the Don Shula Expressway (which connects to the Palmetto Expressway).

ARRIVAL

4

## PARKING

Parking is no problem in most areas – Coral Gables has plenty of spaces, as does downtown. The two shopping centers (see p.80) in Coconut Grove have ample facilities, and everywhere there's streetside parking (25¢ for 15 minutes) for the nimble and patient.

The beaches are a somewhat different story, though don't be put off by doomsayers who liken finding parking on South Beach to winning the lottery. Avoid the jams on Ocean Drive whatever the time; if you're looking for roadside metered parking, your best shot is away from the beach around Alton Rd, or along the lower edges of Washington Ave. There are three municipal lots in South Beach which normally have ample space, costing $1/hour: their overnight parking rates vary – 7th St and Collins Ave is $14/night, 13th St and Collins Ave is $6-8/night, and 17th St and Washington Ave will set you back $8/night. Few of the old Art Deco hotels have their own lots, so they offer pricey valet parking – though this often entails paying someone else to drive your car to one of the municipal lots; you'll save plenty by doing it yourself.

Coming into the city from the **west**, you're likely to be driving Highway 41, or the Tamiami Trail – follow this until it becomes SW 8th Street, which slices its way into the center of the city.

### BY BUS

There are five **Greyhound** stations in Miami: the Miami West station is a short cab ride from the airport, while the other major terminal is downtown at 100 W 6th St (☎305/374-6160 or 24-hour information line 1-800/229-9424, ⓦwww.greyhound.com). Greyhound connects

Miami directly with Key West, West Palm Beach and Fort Myers, with ongoing service across the country.

## BY RAIL

------------------------------------------------

Miami is on the **Amtrak** Silver Service route, linking South Florida with New York City via Washington DC and the Carolinas. The main station, at 8303 NW 37th Ave, is seven miles northwest of downtown (℡1-800/USA-RAIL, ⒲www.amtrak.com). The best way to connect with the rest of the city, especially downtown, Coconut Grove or Coral Gables is to hop on Metrobus #L, which connects with the Metrorail (see p.10) eight blocks away.

# City transit
# and tours

One of the pleasures of South Beach is its compact layout – if you plan to stay exclusively in this area, there's no need for a car: **walking** everywhere is easy, and there's always the **Electrowave Shuttle** or taxis if your feet need a rest. Otherwise, plenty of locals **rollerblade** around, although be aware that many stores won't let customers inside wearing skates. Elsewhere, Coconut Grove is compact enough to handle on foot, but you'll enjoy most other areas better with access to a car. On Key Biscayne, **biking** is a pleasant alternative, though in general the city roads are not especially bike-friendly.

Away from the beaches, Miami's **street ordering system** at first seems rather confusing, but quickly becomes manageable. The city's grid is centered on the junction of Flagler Street and Miami Avenue: from that point, the four quarters tagged NE, NW, SW and SE fan out. To find a street once you know its quarter, use the PARC mnemonic: Places, Avenues, Roads and Courts run north–south, while everything else runs east–west.

In a maddeningly typical display of separation, **Coral**

## ROAD NAMES AND NUMBERS

Numerous major thoroughfares in the city have nicknames alongside their official designations; the following should provide some quick reference.

Collins Avenue is Hwy-A1A

Dolphin Expressway is Route 839

Don Shula Expressway is Route 874

Florida's Turnpike (Homestead Extension) is Route 821

John F. Kennedy Causeway is Route 934

Julia Tuttle Causeway is I-195

LeJeune Road in Coral Gables is also SW 42nd Avenue

MacArthur Causeway is I-395

Palmetto Expressway is Route 826 (which is known as 163rd Street on its way to the beach)

South Dixie Highway is Hwy-1, south of the city

Tamiami Trail is Hwy-41 (and becomes SW 8th Street, also known as Calle Ocho)

**Gables** ignored this system. Instead, the area was artistically streetscaped as per the City Beautiful tradition, its spaghetti-loop suburban roads and dead ends perhaps its most European feature.

### BUSES

Both buses and local trains are run by **Metro-Dade Transit** (☎ 305/770-3131, ⓦ www.co.miami-dade.fl.us /transit). Maps for all Metro-Dade services can be picked up at Government Center Station, 101 NW 1st St, which is the main bus terminal; alternatively, there are route maps inside each bus.

**Buses** in Miami are surprisingly pleasant; they're clean

and chillingly air-conditioned, and the bus network criss-crosses the city 24 hours a day. Fares require $1.25 in exact change, including dollar bills; there's a 25-cent surcharge for a transfer slip that can be used to connect with another bus or service in the Metro-Dade network, like Metrorail (see overleaf). Travel by bus is not a speedy option, though, so allow plenty of time; it's a good choice if you're staying downtown or at the beaches, but connecting from Coconut Grove or Key Biscayne to anywhere else by bus is a painfully long process.

A jaunty alternative in South Beach is the **Electrowave Shuttle**, with one route that cruises up and down Washington Avenue and Lincoln Road and another that circles Collins Avenue at the northern end of South Beach. These multicolored minibuses come in all shapes and sizes and cost 25¢ per ride. They're a good option on steamy days in July for a 5-minute cooldown, or for getting around quickly at night without a car (Mon–Wed 8am–2am, Thurs–Sat 8am–4am, Sun and holidays 10am–2am).

## USEFUL BUS ROUTES

There's little logic to the lettering and numbering of bus routes: most, but not all, lettered buses include some part of the beaches in their track. Useful routes from Government Center are as follows:

South Beach – #C, #K
(along Washington Ave),
#S (along Alton Road)

Miami Beach – #K, #S

Coral Gables – #24

Miami International Airport
– #7

Key Biscayne – #B

Little Havana – #8

Coconut Grove – #48

Little Haiti and the Design
District – #3 (along
Biscayne Blvd)

## METRORAIL

**Metrorail** trains, also run by Metro-Dade transit (see p.8), amble along a single line connecting the northern and southern suburbs, hugging Hwy-1 through Coconut Grove and Coral Gables (5am–midnight). Some useful stops are Government Center (for downtown), Vizcaya (2 minutes walk to the mansion, see p.86) and Coconut Grove. Douglas Road and University are the designated Coral Gables stops, but neither is particularly convenient – better to hop on a bus from downtown that will deposit you at the heart of the Miracle Mile. Single-journey fares on the Metrorail are $1.25.

The **Metromover** system is an automated monorail that ribbons round the downtown central business district (daily 5.30am–midnight, later during major events at American Airlines Arena; 25¢; ⓣ305/770-3131). It's reliable, fast and clean, if a little limited – take it for a good view of the city and to get your bearings when you arrive.

## TAXIS

**Taxis** are abundant on the streets, though not especially cheap – try Central Cab (ⓣ305/532-5555) or Metro Taxi (ⓣ305/888-8888). Rates are $1.50 for the first quarter mile, and 25¢ for each additional eighth of a mile; in case of complaints, call ⓣ305/375-2460.

## SIGHTSEEING TOURS

The **Miami Design Preservation League**, at 1001 Ocean Drive (ⓣ305/672-2014, ⓦwww.mdpl.org), runs unmissable tours of the South Beach Art Deco District. They're a lively, informative introduction to the area's architecture, led by knowledgeable local enthusiasts (Thurs

6.30pm, Sat 10.30am; $15). The MDPL also offers a self-guided audio walking tour of the district (daily 10am–4pm; 1hr–1hr 15min; $5).

Another well-known option is the **Historical Museum of South Florida**'s walking tours, led by Dr. Paul George (no tours July & Aug; $15 and up; ☎ 305/375-1621, ⓦ www.historical-museum.org). Passionate about the city's history, Dr. George leads trips that include cycle tours around Little Havana and excursions to Key Biscayne by boat. Alternatively, to see the less touristed parts of the city, **David Brown**'s an ideal guide: he specializes in Miami's black neighborhoods, including Little Haiti and Liberty City. Contact him for prices or to arrange a personalized tour (☎ 305/663-4455 or ⓔ db3227@aol.com).

The non-profit **Dade Heritage Trust** (190 SE 12th Terrace; $35; ☎ 305/358-9572, ⓦ www.dadeheritagetrust .org) runs bus tours of the city, with varied themes including Women's Miami and Miami's Ghosts; if you're interested in the history of the CBD, the **Downtown Miami Partnership** runs tours of the business district (call ☎ 305/379-7070 for information and schedules, ⓦ www .downtownmiami.net) – it also produces a handy self-guided walking tour of Historic Downtown that's available from most tourist offices.

# Information and websites

There's no good information stand at the airport and, unfortunately, the downtown office of the **Greater Miami Convention and Visitors Bureau**, 701 Brickell Ave (Mon–Fri 8.30am–6pm; ☏ 305/539-3000, ⓦ www.tropicoolmiami.com), isn't geared to providing walk-in support for tourists. A better option is the **Miami Beach Chamber of Commerce**, at 1920 Meridian Ave (Mon–Fri 9am–5pm, Sat & Sun 10am–4pm; ☏ 305/672-1270, ⓦ www.miamibeachchamber.com). The most interesting spot to pick up information is undoubtedly at the **Miami Design Preservation League Welcome Center**, 1001 Ocean Drive (Mon–Fri 10am–5pm; ☏ 305/672-2014, ⓦ www.mdpl.org), which has details on walking tours and events, a great line of retro gifts and friendly staff keen to help with any questions.

Most areas of the city also have their own local information depot: some of the most helpful are the **Coconut Grove Chamber of Commerce**, 2820 McFarlane Rd (Mon–Fri 9am–5pm; ☏ 305/444-7270, ⓦ www.coconut-grove.com), the **Key Biscayne Chamber of Commerce**,

## MIAMI ON THE INTERNET

The following websites are all good sources of up-to-date information:

Ⓦ www.digitalcity.com/southflorida Often more comprehensive than Citysearch, if a little more bland and less opinionated. Good for its regular highlights of local events, as well as restaurant listings.

Ⓦ www.miami.com The online home of the *Miami Herald*, this is a comprehensive local site – unsurprisingly, strong on news and politics. It's rather let down by a messy search feature, though, and the funkier information is all drawn from *Street Miami* and its site (see below).

Ⓦ miami.citysearch.com The local chapter of the national listings website is sparky and plugged in – great for up-to-date information on the latest hot restaurants or club openings. The search facility's patchy, though.

Ⓦ miami.metroguide.com The best listings resource for Miami on the web, divided into channels: retail, event, dining, night, hotel. It doesn't provide editorial reviews, but is thorough and reliable for phone numbers and addresses.

Ⓦ www.oceandrive.com The best place to check on anything relating to South Beach – its club and bar listings are especially fresh, although the site's design is rather clunky.

328 Crandon Blvd, suite 217 (Mon–Fri 9am–5pm; ☎305/361-5207, Ⓦ www.keybiscaynechamber.org), and the **Sunny Isles Beach Resort Association Visitor Information Center**, 17070 Collins Ave, suite 266B (Mon–Fri 9am–2pm; ☎305/947-5826, Ⓦ www.sunnyislesfla.com).

# The media

There's now only one local **newspaper** in Miami, the *Miami Herald* (35¢ weekdays, $1 Sunday), which also publishes a daily Spanish language edition, *El Nuevo Herald*, that has unique content from its own editorial team. The best day to buy is Friday, when the *Herald*'s comprehensive week-long entertainment supplement is bundled free with the main paper. There's also the statewide *Florida Sun-Sentinel*, which is gaining ground on the complacent *Herald*, but lacks in-depth local news. For exhaustive detail on the area in which you're staying, pick up one of the weekly local rags – there's the *Islander News* on Key Biscayne and the *Coral Gables Gazette* for starters.

That said, the best news sources for visitors are the **freesheets**: the established, anti-establishment *New Times* (Ⓦ www.newtimesmiami.com) and its snarky, upstart rival, *Street Miami* (Ⓦ www.streetmiami.com). For the lowdown on the South Beach scene, buy a copy of the glossy magazine *Ocean Drive*, jammed with ads for the latest clubs and photographs of local celebrities. Finally, there's *TWN*, a weekly gay and lesbian freesheet (see p.181, "Gay and lesbian Miami").

On another note, Spanish speakers are in for a treat – aside from *El Nuevo Herald*, most newsstands in the city carry Spanish-language editions of big name **magazines** like *Glamour* and *Harper's Bazaar*: they even have different covers from their mainstream counterparts.

# THE GUIDE

# Downtown Miami

**W**ith its profusion of gleaming office buildings towering over smaller Cuban-owned businesses, **downtown Miami** (also known as the Central Business District, or CBD) simultaneously shows the city at its most American and its most Latin. From a distance, the sparkling high-rises make Miami look much like any other modern American metropolis; it's only when you're standing below those skyscrapers, surrounded by jostling crowds and noisy traffic, that the feel of a Latin American capital takes over. If it all feels a bit overwhelming, don't be discouraged: downtown is actually one of Miami's most compact districts, and holds two of the area's best museums, while providing the clearest sense of the everyday influence Cuba has on the city, from office workers lighting at tiny streetside cafés for a midmorning *cafecito*, or Cuban coffee, to the bilingual signage in almost every store.

Geographically, the Miami River divides downtown in half: on the south bank, big business and big buildings line **Brickell Avenue**, known as "Millionaire's Row" in the early twentieth century. The surrounding area, bounded by I-95 to the west, Coconut Grove to the south and Biscayne Bay to the east, has been christened **Brickell** by developers and is a prime candidate for gentrification, slowly becoming peppered with coffee shops and yuppie housing.

North of the river, things get a bit more active; **Flagler Street** functions as the city's central artery, joining **Bayfront Park** with the **Metro-Dade Cultural Center** to the west. It's a commercial bazaar that hums with jewelers, fabric stores and cheap electronics outlets. There are few name brand shops here: this is a place of diners and discounters, stores in low-slung buildings playing loud music and spilling their wares out onto the sidewalk. At the same time, Flagler Street also offers up a successful showcase of the architecture on which modern Miami was built, beginning with the **Alfred I. DuPont Building**.

Further north, past the iconic, if derivative, **Freedom Tower**, lie **Overtown** and **Liberty City**, two of Miami's historically black neighborhoods. Both are areas that the strenuous tourist gloss applied by the city in the late 1990s has yet to reach, and can still be somewhat dicey. However, they are vibrant neighborhoods, with a fierce sense of history, and are worth a visit during the day or on a tour.

The CBD is definitely a place to visit during the day – at weekends and in the evening, restaurants are shut since there's little residential space amid the office buildings. However, public transportation is thorough and an elevated monorail, the **Metromover** (see p.10), circles downtown's main loop, making it a handy way to orient yourself.

---

The area covered by this chapter is shown in detail on color map 2, at the back of the book.

---

# FLAGLER STREET AND AROUND

The heart of downtown Miami is **Flagler Street**, choked with cheap fabric stores, electronics shops and, for some reason, dozens of discount shoe outlets. Although at lunchtime the area's throbbing with life, by 6pm it's deserted:

unlike many other American city centers, Miami has yet to undergo residential revitalization, and there are still few apartment complexes or converted lofts downtown.

Along the street are a few architectural highlights, as well as the central force of Miami's cultural output, the **Metro-Dade Cultural Center**, full of grand intentions as a public space though falling a little flat. Noted architect Philip Johnson designed the complex, echoing the Mediterranean Revival style found elsewhere in the city: the result is a series of anodyne ranch buildings around a communal piazza that remains eternally empty thanks to the punishing Miami sun. Still, the Center does boast two of downtown's top attractions, the **Historical Museum of South Florida** and the **Miami Art Museum**.

## The Alfred I. DuPont Building and the Gusman Center for the Performing Arts

**Map 3, 6E**.

Two notable buildings stand along the eastern portion of Flagler Street. Near SE 2nd Avenue, the **Alfred I. DuPont Building**, at no. 169, is one of the best examples of Depression Moderne design in the city, with its simple but imposing black façade. Now home to the Florida National Bank, its interior is spectacular and ornate, especially the fanciful wrought-iron screens and bronze bas-relief elevator doors.

Opposite the DuPont Building, the **Olympia Theater at the Gusman Center for Performing Arts**, no. 174 (☎305/374-2444, ⊛www.gusmancenter.org), was built in 1926 as a vaudeville house by the Gusman family. Much like the Mathesons and their mustard gas millions (see p.89), the Gusmans profited through government contracts in World War I: theirs was to provide condoms for departing American soldiers. The building's hodgepodge of architectural styles veers towards a Spanish-Moorish theme, with turrets, towers and intricately detailed columns, and recent renovations have brought out the stunning moldings in its lobby ceiling; it's also noteworthy as the first air-conditioned building in Miami. However, the only way you'll be able to see inside the whole building (and not just the lobby) is by catching a performance (see p.178 for ticket information) – if you do, note the kitschy ceiling in the auditorium, twinkling with fake stars and the illusion of slowly moving clouds.

## Burdine's and the Coppertone sign

Further west, on the corner with Miami Avenue, the original **Burdine's** department store at no. 22 is notable for its Streamline Moderne design, all hard edges rounded off and corners curved to convey gentle movement. This edition of "Florida's department store" was founded as a dry goods shop in 1898, a mere two years after the city was incorporated.

Crossing over Miami Avenue onto West Flagler Street, look for the giant relief of the famous **Coppertone Sign** – a young girl whose pet dog is tugging down her bikini bottom. Originally located along Biscayne Boulevard, the iconic sign was transferred here when the building to which it was attached was threatened with demolition.

## Historical Museum of Southern Florida

**Map 3, C6**. Mon–Wed, Fri–Sat 10am–5pm, Thurs 10am–9pm, Sun noon–5pm. $5, $6 combined ticket with Miami Art Museum.

Facing the Metro-Dade Cultural Center piazza, the **Historical Museum**, at 101 W Flagler St (℡305/375-1492, ⊛www.historical-museum.org), is home to detailed, interactive displays covering prehistoric Florida up until the present day. Some of the exhibits are a little worn around the edges, but there's plenty to entertain kids including dress-up boxes with period clothes and pioneer toys, while for adults, there's a small but instructive map collection that shows Europeans' gradual charting of the area. Where perhaps the museum is strongest, though, is in its post-1950s display: a pair of tiny boats used by Cuban and Haitian refugees to reach Miami in the late 1970s sit next to TVs running archive news footage showing local hostility to the Mariel boatlift in 1980. In its first-floor research facility, the Historical Museum houses the archives of the now-defunct *Miami News*, the city's first daily newspaper, and walk-in visitors are welcome to scan the decades of news photography onsite.

---

Together, the Historical Museum and the Art Museum are now seeking a major new complex at the Port of Miami, which, if approved, would be shared with the Museum of Science, currently located in Coconut Grove (see p.87).

---

## Miami Art Museum

**Map 3, C6**. Tues–Fri 10am–5pm, Sat–Sun noon–5pm. $5, $6 combined ticket with Historical Museum.

Directly across the Metro-Dade Cultural Center piazza from the Historical Museum, the **Miami Art Museum**, also at 101 W Flagler St (☏305/375-1700, ⓦwww.miami-artmuseum.org), holds a remarkable collection of postwar art, setting acknowledged modern masterpieces alongside quirky, newer works. The first floor of the building offers a rotating selection, changed twice yearly, from the museum's own collection. It's accessible and intelligently curated: among notable works, look for sketches by Robert Rauschenberg and art stuntman Christo (see p.48), not to mention surrealist pioneer Marcel Duchamp's *Boîte en Valise*, which consists of witty maquettes of his previous masterworks, all in a handy carrying case. But it's the museum's conceptual art collection that is most stunning, especially the bevy of works by the late Cuban-American artist Felix Gonzalez-Torres: his organic pieces, designed to change through viewing – for example, a stark ream of embossed paper that visitors are intended to sample sheet by sheet - are remarkable. The museum often manages to hook prime traveling exhibits, too, which are mounted in its gallery space on the upper floor.

Opposite the museum looms the **Main Public Library** (Mon–Sat 9am–6pm, Thurs 9am–9pm, Sun 1–5pm; closed Sun in summer), which, besides the usual lending sections, has temporary painting and photography exhibits showcasing local literary and artistic talents – the narrow focus of which typically makes them worth checking out – as well as a massive collection of Florida-related magazines and books.

## Gesú Church

**Map 3, D6**. Mass held Mon–Fri 8.15am, 11am, 12.10pm, Sat 4pm, Sun 8.30am & 11.30am (English), 10am & 1pm (Spanish).

Just north from the Alfred I. DuPont Building, the **Gesú Church**, at 118 NE 2nd St (☎305/379-1424), is home to Miami's oldest Catholic parish. This large Mediterranean Revival building, built in 1925, sticks out amid the cramped storefronts of downtown, painted in colors of peach sherbet and lemon meringue. However, the church's foamy, baroque appliqué exterior is more noteworthy than its stout inner sanctum, framed by modern stained glass from Munich.

## US Federal Courthouse

**Map 3, D5**. Mon–Fri 8.30am–5pm.
Two blocks northwest from the Gesú Church, the unremarkable 1931 Neoclassical structure at 300 NE 1st St was
originally the city's post office, but was commandeered a
year later to serve as the **US Federal Courthouse**. The
New Courthouse next door replaced it in the late 1960s,
when the city's soaring crime rate outstripped its facilities.

Most voluntary visitors stop by for a glimpse of Denman
Fink's 25-foot mural, *Law Guides Florida's Progress* – depict-
ing Florida's evolution from swampy backwoods to modern
state – in the small courtroom on the second floor. The
WPA work is more impressive for its size rather than skill
but look for Fink's portrait of his young nephew, George
Merrick, the founder of Coral Gables, as he delivers produce.

## Bayfront Park

**Map 3, F6–G6**.
At the east end of East Flagler Street lies **Bayfront Park**, at
301 N Biscayne Blvd (ⓦwww.bayfrontparkmiami.com), a
pleasant enough urban greenspace, dotted with sculptures
and large, leafy trees. There's no specific local connection to
Isamu Noguchi's white geometric *Challenger Memorial* at the
park's southwest corner: it's simply that the park was completed in 1986, around the same time as the space shuttle
exploded mid-flight, and the designer included the monument as a late addition.

At the opposite end is the highly charged **Torch of
Friendship**, which commemorates a burning local issue.
Built in 1960, then rededicated in JFK's memory four years
later, it centers on a lighted torch, surrounded by crests of
every Latin American country save one. Cuba's emblem is
purposefully omitted, leaving a pointed blank space

between Costa Rica and the Dominican Republic, intending to add her symbol only when Cuba was free of communism. That said, the site's now rather forlorn and the city takes little interest in it; it's also missing many of the original crests, which means that Cuba's omission no longer stands out.

At its northern tip, the park leads into the **Bayside Marketplace** (Mon–Thurs 10am–10pm, Fri–Sat 10am–11pm, Sun 11am–9pm; ☎305/577-3344, ⓦwww.bayside marketplace.com), which features the usual upscale chain stores and restaurants in an open-air complex by the water, and is usually packed with tourists.

---

There's a small, unofficial tourist information booth at the entrance to the Bayside Marketplace, good for maps.

---

# SOUTH OF MIAMI RIVER

Fifteen minutes' walk south from Flagler Stret, crossing the Miami River takes you from the soul of the city to its wallet. In little more than twenty years, Miami has become second only to New York in serving as the headquarters of international banks, and the forest of mirrored buildings that cluster along **Brickell** (rhymes with pickle) **Avenue** sprouts new offshoots every year. Money was the original foundation of this area: early developers Mary and William Brickell planned a wide tree-lined avenue that could be built up with mansions for their friends. In doing so, they created the city's most desirable neighborhood, nicknamed **Millionaires' Row.** After a period of decline, the Brickell district has undergone intensive residential redevelopment in recent years, bringing a trickle of funky restaurants to the streets west of Brickell Avenue (see "Restaurants," p.137).

# Miami Circle

**Map 3, E8**.

Local developer Michael Baumann purchased the land east of Brickell Avenue at the Miami River – once the site of a 1950s apartment complex – for $8 million in the mid-1990s and planned to throw up a premium-priced high-rise. Archeologists were hired to clear the area for construction as per local ordinances and, unfortunately for Baumann, they found something – a coral rock circle, 38 feet in diameter, carbon-dated to be at least 10,000 years old and now known as the **Miami Circle**. Its age is the only indisputable thing: experts argue over the circle's original purpose, whether it was a religious, community or commercial center, or even who might have built it. While they debate, others are considering how best to display this find for the local community; no final decision's been made, and thus you can't visit yet. Don't weep for Baumann, though – he was able to strongarm the city into paying $26.7 million to purchase the land back from him, turning a tidy profit of more than $18 million without laying a single brick.

---

If you're determined to see the Miami Circle,
stay in the nearby *Sheraton* (☎305/373-6000; ④)
and ask for a room that overlooks the site.

---

# The Atlantis

**The Atlantis** apartment complex, at 2025 Brickell Ave, is the project that turned the Arquitectonica design team from wannabes to design rock stars. Like a cored apple, the building has a square hole through the middle, filled with a single palm tree, a jacuzzi and a fire engine-red spiral staircase. Built some twenty years ago, its playful is even more eye-catching now amid the earnest bombast of nearby sky-scrapers. You won't be allowed inside unless you know someone who lives there, which might be just as well: even its designers admit the interior doesn't live up to the exuberance of the exterior, and claim the building to be "architecture for 55mph" – in other words, seen to best effect from a passing car.

# NORTH OF DOWNTOWN

North of the downtown loop, sights thin out considerably and neighborhoods grow rougher: patches like Bicentennial Park are closer to the crime-hobbled Miami of the 1980s than the glossy city of today. The **Port of Miami** is still one of the busiest cruise ship docks in the world, though, and on any given day you can drive down Macarthur Causeway to the beach to see half a dozen mammoth ships queuing patiently at the dock.

One of the most arresting additions to the local skyline is the **American Airlines Arena** on the old Port of Miami site. A high profile project for local design celebrities Arquitectonica, the AA Arena is an origami building floating by the Bay, its stark, rounded walls like stowed wings. It's the site of many big-name concerts as well as home to the Miami Heat basketball team (see p.216). Directly opposite the Arena is the **Freedom Tower**, new headquarters of the Cuban-American National Foundation.

## Freedom Tower

**Map 3, E4**. Call for opening hours and prices.
Often nicknamed Miami's Ellis Island, the **Freedom Tower**, at 600 N Biscayne Blvd (℡305/592-7768, ⓦwww .canf.org), served not only as an immigration processing post but also as a community center for the more than

360,000 Cuban refugees who arrived between 1961 and 1974. It was one of three replicas of Seville's Giralda Belltower built in Miami by the same architects who designed New York's Grand Central station: the others were the *Roney Plaza* hotel in Miami Beach (since demolished), and Coral Gables' *Biltmore* hotel (see p.74). Since its construction as the headquarters of the *Miami News* in 1925, this Mediterranean Revival structure has lain more often empty than occupied thanks in part to its impractical and eccentric shape, with a high, narrow turret and little versatile office space. However, the building was purchased in 1997 by the late Cuban-American telecom billionaire Jorge Mas Canosa, and is set to open in 2003 as the headquarters of the Cuban-American National Foundation, with refugee raft simulations, Cuban art exhibits and a research center.

## Bicentennial Park

**Map 3, F3**.

Troubled from the day it opened in 1977 (the men running the food stands on opening night were mugged for the day's takings), **Bicentennial Park**, at 1075 N Biscayne Blvd, is a problematic eyesore for the city to which little attention is paid. For 25 years, its 35 acres have served as a refuge for the area's homeless and is not a place to dawdle, especially at dusk. This may change if joint plans by the **Museum of Science** and the **Miami Art Museum** – to regenerate the greenspace and move both attractions there in a specially designed center known as Museum Park Miami – progress, although that's several years away. In the meantime, you'd do better to avoid it altogether and lounge waterside in Bayfront Park further south.

**NORTH OF DOWNTOWN**

# OVERTOWN

Northwest of downtown lies one of the oldest neighborhoods in Miami: **Overtown**, which was originally known as Coloredtown. Local zoning laws forbade the sale of land to blacks except in this area, soon securely cordoned off from the rest of downtown by the railroad. Even so, a settlement developed that was larger even than the existing black neighborhood in Coconut Grove (see p.83). By the 1930s, Coloredtown was a vibrant entertainment district: NW 2nd Avenue between 6th and 10th streets was variously known as "Little Broadway," "The Strip," and even "The Great Black Way." One of the driving forces behind Little Broadway was the black promoter **Clyde Killens**, who started out as a drum accompanist for silent movies. From there, the outlandish Killens achieved pre-eminence managing hotels and nightclubs, not to mention being one of the first black Miamians to register to vote.

Although the postwar years proved tough for the local economy, Overtown's decline accelerated rapidly in the 1960s, as the construction of the I-95 Expressway devastated the area. It was nothing more than an act of urban social vandalism with 20,000 people forcibly displaced. The neighborhood never recovered and it became a poster child for Miami's crime problem in the late 1980s. Now, although it's slowly clawing its way back to economic health, the district's still a dangerous place for visitors even in the daytime: the best way to see it is on an organized tour (see p.11).

## Overtown Historic District

**Map 3, B3**.

If Coloredtown was Miami's Harlem, then its counterpart to the Apollo Theater was the **Lyric Theater**, at 819 NW 2nd Ave, the center of a two-block area now known as the

**Overtown Historic District**. The theater was built in 1913 by black entrepreneur Geder Walker, who dreamed of rivaling Europe's grand opera houses, though by the late 1940s it had been converted into a church. It was recently restored to its original opulence at a cost of more than $1.5 million and is the only standing reminder of the district's funky heyday.

Also of interest nearby is the **Greater Bethel A.M.E. Church**, at 245 NW 8th St, a Mediterranean Revival building that's home to the oldest black congregation in Miami.

## Miami City Cemetery

Just north of Overtown, at 1800 NE 2nd Ave, lies the **Miami City Cemetery**, the city's first. Founded in 1897, with separate black, white and Jewish sections, it's the final resting place for early pioneers, including Julia Tuttle. Other than that, there's little to recommend it, especially since it's in a run-down part of town – the Woodlawn Cemetery (see p.64) has richer pickings for grave hunters.

# LIBERTY CITY

Much further northwest lies **Liberty City**, with wider streets and more parkland than Overtown, but with equally dicey urban issues and again best visited during the day by car or with a tour.

The district centers on **Liberty Square**, located at NW 12th Avenue between 62nd and 67th streets. Nicknamed Pork'n'Beans by locals on account of its pinkish-orange color, this was the first public housing development in the state and began drawing blacks from Coloredtown in the early 1930s. Look for remnants between 63rd and 64th streets of the six-foot high segregation wall that was erected to keep the black and white communities separate. Look, too, for tributes to the late civil rights leader Martin Luther King: there's a particularly moving mural at NW 62nd Street and 7th Avenue.

## THE LIBERTY CITY RIOTS

May 1980 was a grueling month for race relations in Miami. First, thousands of Cuban refugees poured into the city as part of the Mariel boatlift (see p.285) and caused widespread resentment. Meanwhile, the tinder of tensions waiting for a spark in Miami's black community finally ignited. There had been sporadic protests before – notably, what officials called a "civil disturbance" in Liberty City in 1968, at the same time Richard Nixon was accepting the Republican presidential nomination at the Convention Center on the beach. But it was the Arthur McDuffie murder case that set Miami's black neighborhoods ablaze.

McDuffie was a black former Marine turned insurance salesman with no criminal record, who was stopped by four white police officers in December 1979 and beaten to death. They later claimed that he had provoked them by making an obscene gesture as he rode past on a borrowed motorbike. Tried in Tampa to avoid inflaming local passions, the four police officers were found not guilty (by an all-white jury) on the afternoon of May 17, 1980, six months to the day after McDuffie's death, and by evening the riots had started. The citywide curfew that followed lasted nearly a week: by then, disturbances had reached as far south as Homestead. Where previous riots had been primarily aimed at property, in protest at slum conditions, this was racial violence: shocking stories, notably that of a young white motorist dragged from his car and mutilated by the mob, made headlines across America. When it was over, eighteen people had died, both white and black, with more than 400 injured – not to mention that the property destroyed was valued at more than $200 million.

LIBERTY CITY

On the southwestern fringes of Liberty City, the **Black Archives History and Research Foundation of South Florida**, at 5400 NW 22nd Ave (Mon–Fri 9am–5pm; ☎305/636-2390), houses historical documents gathered from the local community. It's not, however, designed for drop-in visitors; call ahead if you want to use the facilities or go on a **tour** of Overtown and Liberty City (groups of ten or more necessary).

The only other local attraction is the **African Heritage Cultural Arts Center**, at 6161 NW 62nd St (☎305/638-6771, ⓦwww.metro-dade.com/parks), which offers Afrocentric classes in performing and fine arts along with a small gallery and theater.

# South Beach

To most visitors, the charms of the rest of Miami are eclipsed by seductive, chic **South Beach**, a colloquial designation for the area that stretches from the southernmost tip of Miami Beach north to 23rd Street. It's the area most people visualize when Miami is mentioned, and the partying and palm trees here perpetuate the image. Here, row upon row of Art Deco gems – especially along the much-photographed **Ocean Drive** – look exactly as they do on film: sleek, classic and ultra-cool.

Although the pioneer John Collins had lamely tried to launch fruit farming further up the beach near what's now 41st Street, it wasn't until he joined forces with entrepreneur Carl Fisher that South Beach germinated. When Fisher drew up his original plan, he wanted to create a winter resort, to be called "Fairyland" – a story that many gay locals recount with ironic relish. By the 1920s and 1930s, it had indeed become a prime target for America's wealthy, but after World War II, when the soldiers (including Clark Gable) who were billeted here for training had left, the smart set moved north to newer hotels in Central Miami Beach, and the district began to crumble. By the early 1980s, South Beach was a no-go area, shared by geriatric retirees and criminals, many of them undesirables left over from the Mariel Boatlift. Its hip rebirth came at the end of the decade, when German catalog photographers discovered South Beach's unique combination of spectacular early-morning light, rockbottom prices and lack of expensive shooting permits. These photographers began spending extended periods in South Beach, and soon developers noticed the area's advantages, too – not to mention the beautiful people enjoying them. One of the first groups to decamp en masse here in the late 1980s was Miami's gay community, which soon was working in parallel (if not together) with the developers to recreate the resort with its new, funky, fabulous scene.

Even if many in the local gay community have now moved on, South Beach has retained its glossy, glamorous reputation. At the heart of it all is the **Art Deco Historic District**, the preserve of old Deco buildings between Fifth and 23rd streets, and Ocean Drive and Lennox Avenue. Parts of the district, notably along Ocean Drive between 5th and 10th streets, have become worryingly Disneyfied, despite the stringent preservation orders, and this is where you'll find sidewalk cafés showcasing congealed samples of menu items and ferocious carnival-barker staff hailing passersby to take a table. But further north, it's as fun and stylish as ever: there are funky restaurants and hotels in the area around the junction of Collins Avenue and Lincoln Road, and **Lincoln Road Mall** is a great place to sashay even if you don't plan to spend. Below 5th Street, the area known as **South Pointe** is still gentrifying and a little edgy.

---

The area covered by this chapter is shown in
detail on color map 3, at the back of the book.

---

# ALONG OCEAN DRIVE

You may not see many photo shoots taking place along **Ocean Drive** at 7am anymore, but the early-morning light is still spectacular; it's easy to understand why South Beach became the fashion location of choice in the early 1990s and is well worth getting up early one morning to enjoy. One of the first hotels to cater to the fashionistas was the *Park Central* (no. 640), with its signature octagonal porthole windows. It's famous, too, as the place where the Vampire Lestat lodges when he visits Miami in Anne Rice's *Tale of the Body Thief* (1992).

The place to strut a well-toned, well-tanned body is **Lummus Park**, bordering Ocean Drive between 5th and 15th streets and named after pioneer brothers who ran competing banks in Miami's early days. Although the gleaming beach seems quintessentially Miami, the fine white sand was actually imported from the Bahamas to replace the too-coarse local variety. You can rent deckchairs and umbrellas from one of many concessions on the waterfront, and there are bathrooms and showers on the grassy boardwalk that separates the beach from Ocean Drive. Open-air concerts are often staged here and it's also the site of the throbbing Winter Party each March (see p.190, "Gay and lesbian Miami"). Notice too the quirky, ornamental lifeguard towers painted in neon colors and designed by local artists including Kenny Scharf – they're a fun addition to the seafront, if rather bedraggled now.

## Casa Casuarina

**Map 4, F5**.

The original structure at 1114 Ocean Drive was an apartment complex built in 1930 as a replica of the Alcázar de

Colón in Santo Domingo, the home built by Christopher Columbus's son in 1510 which claims to be the oldest house in the Western Hemisphere. Italian fashion designer Gianni Versace renamed the place **Casa Casuarina** when he purchased it in 1992 to create his own Miami palace – but since then people have always simply called it the **Versace Mansion**.

In a brazen act of architectural vandalism just before a preservation order could be enacted, Versace also bought the adjoining *Revere Hotel*, and promptly knocked it down to install a swimming pool. That aside, Versace was a popular, easy-going member of the South Beach community, often spotted in local bars and clubs, until his murder on the steps here in 1997. The mansion's still a ghoulish tourist attraction, but is now owned by developer Peter Loftin, who, in partnership with local hotelier Chris Blackwell, paid a cool $19 million for the place, with plans to turn it into either a deluxe hotel or an upscale club.

## Art Deco Welcome Center

**Map 4, F5**. Mon–Fri 10am–5pm.
Headquarters of the Miami Design Preservation League, the **Art Deco Welcome Center**, at 1001 Ocean Drive (℡305/672-2014, ⓦwww.mdpl.org), sits on Lummus Park in a jaunty Nautical Deco building, complete with faux smokestack, that was formerly the headquarters for the local Beach Patrol. The ambling, informative tours run by the League are unmissable (see p.10, "City transit and tours"), and there's also a small **museum** which makes a smart starting point for a comprehensive Art Deco tutorial.

The League also arranges an Art Deco Weekend each January (see p.208, "Festivals and events").

**ALONG OCEAN DRIVE**

# DECODING ART DECO

Miami became a haven for Art Deco in large part due to the wrecking power of South Florida's hurricanes. In 1926, the city was leveled by a devastating storm, and architects taken with Art Deco rebuilt whole city blocks in the newly modish style. Cheap and sleek, it was ideal for developers anxious to throw up fresh hotels as quickly as possible, although shoddy construction methods doomed some treasured buildings to demolition less than fifty years later.

By that time, in the mid-1970s, many buildings, sound or unsound, were seen as old-fashioned and scheduled to be razed for condo construction – at least they were until one woman, Barbara Baer Capitman, began her relentless campaign for their preservation. Thankfully, she succeeded, and in 1979 the 1200-building Art Deco Historic District was formally declared in South Beach.

But the Art Deco style is by no means uniform – one of its core features was how readily it absorbed local influences: a brief guide to its major forms in Miami follows below. Note that the pastel colors usually associated so strongly with Deco were a marketing gimmick Capitman & co. devised in the 1980s – originally most buildings were whitewashed, their features picked out in dark brown or navy blue.

Tropical or Miami Deco (most popular 1920s–1930s) is the base style from which all the other Deco types spring. Look for ornamental "eyebrows" above the windows, the signature mark of Miami Deco, which proved more than decorative, casting shade that kept rooms cool in the days before air conditioning (as a rule, the wider the eyebrow, the later the building). Notice too, repetitions of three – windows or columns, for example – as well as decorative reliefs and murals, whose frequent palm tree, fountain and flamingo subject matter localized the style. Even when first constructed, rooms in Deco hotels tended to be sparse and stark, and expense was focused on common areas.

**Depression Moderne** (1930s) appeared with the onset of the Great Depression, and was less ostentatious and ornamental than its predecessor. Money was spent subtly on interior spaces, like murals and ironwork. The US Post Office (1300 Washington Ave) is the best example of this style in South Beach; downtown's Alfred I. DuPont Building (169 E Flagler St; see p.21) is another outstanding example.

**Streamline Deco** (1930s–1940s) bridges the simplicity of early Deco and the goofy playfulness of Miami Modern, or MiMo. As in many MiMo designs, all elements of Streamline buildings are designed to give a feeling of movement, and the hard edges are rounded off – see the adjoining *Cardozo* (no. 1300) and *Carlyle* (no. 1250) hotels on Ocean Drive. A more extreme version of fluid movement is **Nautical Deco**, which uses fake smokestacks, porthole windows and railings to mimic grand oceangoing liners – see the *Albion Hotel* (1650 James Ave) or the Miami Design Preservation League (or MDPL) headquarters at 1001 Ocean Drive.

**Mediterranean Revival** (1920s–1930s) was a contemporary alternative for those, like Carl Fisher, who disliked the sleek modernity of Art Deco: about a third of the district's buildings are classified as Mediterranean Revival. Many at the time sniffed that this was how gangsters and movie stars – ie, those with more money than taste – liked to commission houses. Structures in this style are asymmetrical to give the impression of organic extension over time, and often have ornate ironwork and tile roofs. Two strong examples of this style are Casa Casuarina, at 1114 Ocean Drive, and the whole of Española Way.

For more on Miami's architecture and the full story of Capitman's crusade, see "Contexts: Architecture" on p.292.

DECODING ART DECO

# WASHINGTON AND COLLINS AVENUES

Named in honor of one of Miami Beach's pioneers, **Collins Avenue** (Hwy-A1A) is the main traffic artery running the length of the island and, eventually, leads north to Fort Lauderdale's beachfront. At its southernmost end, one block west of Ocean Drive, it's crammed with hotels in all price ranges, as well as South Beach's swankiest shopping strip between 5th and 7th streets.

**Washington Avenue**, a further block west from the beach, is the district's commercial heart, where supermarkets and schools stand alongside nightclubs and cheap cafés. Although the low-rise buildings seem architecturally unappealing, most have simply had their Art Deco features hidden behind false frontage, and are gradually being restored as the strip gentrifies. Even so, Washington Avenue is still as gritty as the Deco district gets, and having a stroll here is a welcome antidote to the vacation atmosphere of the other main drags. It also holds two star attractions: the **Wolfsonian-FIU** and the local **Post Office**.

## Wolfsonian-Florida International University

**Map 4, F5**. Mon–Tues & Fri–Sun 11am–6pm, Thurs 11am–9pm. $5, free Thurs 6–9pm.

The **Wolfsonian**, at 1001 Washington Ave (☎305/531-1001, ⓦwww.wolfsonian.fiu.edu), is built around one private collection: the vast acquisitions of Mickey Wolfson, heir to a local TV and movie fortune and scion of the Wolfson family. He was one of the pioneers of South Beach's renaissance, and his museum is dedicated to decorative and propaganda arts from 1885 to 1945 – fitting for a resort, like South Beach, that was built half on publicity and half on pretty buildings. Wolfson's trinkets are housed in a solid Mediterranean Revival building, with ornamental flourishes around the doors and windows, which originally served as the headquarters of Washington Storage. This was one of the companies that catered to the wealthier residents of South Beach in the 1920s, storing the contents of their holiday homes for safekeeping during hurricane season – there are several contemporary photographs in the museum's lobby. The funky steel hut on the sidewalk in front of the building is not original: it was shipped in from elsewhere in Miami, and acts as a home for temporary modern art exhibitions overseen by the museum.

The best sections here focus on the dozen or so World's Fairs held in the early twentieth century: the anachronistic company propaganda displayed in such showy pavilions has an ironic resonance. Take Heinz and its tribal Deco statuary, for example, representing the happy natives from the different countries that joyfully contributed ingredients to Heinz's 57 varieties. However, despite some outstanding individual pieces (look for work by British arts & crafts pioneers like William Morris and Charles Rennie Mackintosh in particular), the museum is confusingly laid out, and different areas muddle together as you walk around. The temporary exhibitions it hosts, though, are often high-profile and more satisfying.

## United States Post Office

**Map 4, F4**. Mon–Fri 8am–5pm, Sat 8.30am–2pm.
This main branch of Miami Beach's **Post Office**, located at 1300 Washington Ave (☎305/672-2447, ⓦwww.usps .com), is an architectural gem, and its sweepingly curved Depression Moderne exterior stands out like a smooth, squat turret against the rows of boxy Deco buildings nearby. Funded by the WPA during the Great Depression, it's worth stepping inside to see the ornately bombastic metalwork and geometric murals that fill the rotunda.

# ESPAÑOLA WAY

Sandwiched between 14th Place and 15th Street stands **Española Way**, a six-block development conceived in 1925 by entrepreneur Carl Fisher as an antidote to growing enthusiasm for Art Deco. He personally preferred the Mediterranean Revival style anyway, and this pedestrianized strip is a mustard and ochre explosion of narrow alleys and deliberately uneven buildings, originally conceived as an artists' colony. It limped along until the arrival of Cuban bandleader Desi Arnaz (later to find fame as the real- and TV-life husband of *I Love Lucy*'s Lucille Ball). He's the hero of the frequently repeated and dubiously self-promoting story that the rumba dance craze of the 1930s kicked off here on Española Way before taking the US by storm. His home venue was the *Village Tavern*, located inside what was then a swanky hotel but is now the *Clay Hostel*, at the corner of Washington Avenue (see review p.125).

The faux-decrepitude of the strip is at its most intolerable between Washington and Drexel Avenues. There's a patchy artisans' market here at weekends with rather too many homemade candles for sale, as well as small craft stores and a few artist studios.

# LINCOLN ROAD

Along the northern edge of the Historic District stands **Lincoln Road Mall**, conceived in 1959 by store designer-turned-architect Morris Lapidus: he claimed that he "designed Lincoln Road for people – a car never bought anything." To do this, he pedestrianized six blocks and installed whimsical space-age structures to provide intermittent shade for strolling shoppers. For a while, it was known as the Fifth Avenue of the South, filled with expensive stores and plush restaurants. But as South Beach declined in the 1970s, the chi-chi shops trickled away and its renaissance has been relatively recent. Now, again filled with trendy restaurants, sidewalk cafés and boutiques, it's here that South Beach struts its stuff every Sunday afternoon – rollerblading, dogwalking or window-shopping – and has arguably replaced Ocean Drive as the local heart of the area. There was much controversy over recent development on Lincoln Road's western end: an arthritic building housing the only cinema in the area was eventually bulldozed, and replaced with a gleaming new shopping complex that includes a modern, multi-screen movie house that's convenient if jarring.

The mall is bookended by two Art Deco theaters: the sleek, low-rise **Colony Theater** (no. 1040) and the pristine **Lincoln Theater** (no. 541), home to the always reliable New World Symphony (see p.178, "Performing arts and film"). The Lincoln, especially, has some remarkable Tropical Deco reliefs, featuring trippy triffid-like palm trees painted in deep shades of green.

One of the quirkier attractions on Lincoln Road is the **Art Center of South Florida**, nos. 800-810-924 (studios daily 10am–11pm, gallery space Mon–Wed 1–10pm, Thurs–Sun 1–11pm; ☎305/674-8278, ⓦwww.artcentersf .org). Founded in 1984 when real estate prices here had hit rock bottom, this collective spreads across three buildings and provides 52 studios for artists and sculptors: alongside traditional painters, you'll find plenty of edgier works in mixed media, photography and even textiles. Each artist works and exhibits onsite: feel free to wander around the studios or stop by the official gallery space (no. 800) – the work's better than its very commercial location might suggest.

LINCOLN ROAD

# NORTH OF LINCOLN ROAD

**North of Lincoln Road** you step outside the Historic District, and sights thin out as the buildings become larger, more eclectic and ramshackle. The Deco-esque hotels along upper Collins Avenue, like the *Shelborne* (no. 1801) and Ian Schrager's *Delano* (no.1685), were constructed later – and are therefore larger and more space-age – than their counterparts further south. Some of their playful architectural flourishes are precursors of the style known as Miami Modernism (MiMo) that would explode after World War II with the construction of buildings like the *Fontainebleau Hilton* hotel further north (see p.53, "Central Miami Beach and north").

Along Washington Avenue, just above 17th Street, stands the **Jackie Gleason Theater of Performing Arts** (no. 1700; ☎305/673-7300, ⊛www.gleasontheater.com), named in honor of the star of the classic TV show *The Honeymooners*, which was filmed there. It now hosts regular Broadway tryouts and commercial smashes (see p.177, "Performing arts and film"). The sexy sculpture in front of the main entrance is pop art pioneer Roy Lichtenstein's *Mermaid*.

Nearby are the massive white walls of the **Miami Beach Convention Center**, at 1901 Convention Center Drive (☎305/673-7311). This was once a premier venue for prestige exhibitions, although it's now long been bypassed by newer, warehouse-esque convention centers like those in Las Vegas. It was here that Richard Nixon received the Republican presidential nomination in August 1968, just as Miami's racial tensions finally flared into violence with the Liberty City riots (see p.32).

Further north are the cramped offices of the **Miami Beach Chamber of Commerce**, at 1920 Meridian Ave (Mon–Fri 9am–5pm, Sat & Sun 10am–4pm; ☎305/672-1270, ⊛www.miamibeachchamber.com), for maps and tours of the area – though only if you've bypassed the more pleasant Art Deco Welcome Center on Ocean Drive.

## Holocaust Memorial

**Map 4, E1**. Daily 9am–9pm; $2 donation for brochure.

Just blocks from the sidewalk cafés and jostling crowds of Lincoln Road, a visit to the **Holocaust Memorial**, at 1933-1945 Meridian Ave (☎305/538-1663, ⓦwww .holocaustmmb.org), is a contemplative, sobering experience. Atmospheric, graphic and impacting, the memorial centers on a massive cast bronze hand stretched in desperate supplication to the sky, reaching from a cluster of dozens of agonized human figures, and tattooed with a fictitious Auschwitz ID number.

To reach this central sculpture, visitors pass through curved black granite colonnades, etched with archive photographs that pull no punches in their depiction of concentration camp horrors. The memorial begins with a sculpture of a mother protecting her two fearful children, and an uplifting quote from *The Diary of Anne Frank*. The dark walls around the central sculpture, filled with names of those killed in the Holocaust, strike a sad counternote, as does the final sculpture: the original mother and children, now dead, accompanied by more words of Anne Frank's: "... ideals, dreams and cherished hopes rise within us only to meet the horrible truths and be shattered."

## Bass Museum of Art

**Map 4, F1**. Tues–Wed, Fri–Sat 10am–5pm, Thurs 10am–9pm, Sun 11am–5pm; $6.

The only fine art museum on Miami Beach, the **Bass Museum**, at 2121 Park Ave (☎305/673-7530, ⓦwww .bassmuseum.org), is housed in a stark, temple-like 1930s

Art Deco building designed by Russell Pancoast, the architect son-in-law of John Collins. What began as the local public library became a museum to house the private collection of local bigwigs John and Johanna Bass, which was donated to the city in 1963. There are some fine pieces – the sixteenth-century Flemish tapestry *The Tournament* is one of the museum's gems – and a notable drawing collection featuring Honorés Daumier and Toulouse-Lautrec. However, many of the big names in the collection, such as Rubens, Jordaens and Botticelli, are represented by minor works. The museum is undergoing a massive renovation overseen by the Japanese architect Arata Isozaki that will triple its exhibition space and unite it with the Miami City Ballet and local library to form the **Miami Beach Cultural Park**. When that will happen is anyone's guess: it's already well behind schedule and officials have learned the hard way to be tight-lipped about reopenings.

## SOUTH POINTE

South of 5th Street, at the tip of the island, the area of **South Pointe** is pimpled with high-rises you won't see elsewhere in South Beach, due to sluggish preservation orders that, until recently, allowed developers to bulldoze buildings at will. The first of these high-rises, South Pointe Towers, will soon be joined by several more, approved before new zoning laws came into effect. South of Fifth (or "SoFi" as local realtors have taken to calling it) was originally the city's Jewish ghetto, since Fifth Street marked the northernmost point where Jews could buy housing. By the late 1980s, though, it had been taken over by crack houses and criminals, spurred by the arrival of undesirables in the wake of the Mariel boatlift. For this reason, gentrification has proceeded more slowly here than elsewhere in South

Beach, and it's a still a little more raw than the manicured streets further north. There are many unpleasant examples of late 1980s neo-Deco garishness – angular concrete buildings in turquoise, ochre and raspberry, conjuring an image of Art Deco with shoulder pads.

------------------------------------------------

**The beach at 3rd Street is the most family-oriented in this area, while the best waves for surfing are down at the eastern tip of the island in South Pointe Park.**

------------------------------------------------

Here, at the end of Washington Avenue, there's a pleasant waterfront greenspace with wide lawns and good facilities that's a sleepy place to pass the afternoon. The park looks out over **Government Cut**, a waterway first dredged by Henry Flagler in the nineteenth century to create easy access to the growing Port of Miami. In so doing, he amputated the southernmost tip of South Beach to create exclusive **Fisher Island** (see p.49). The waterway has been substantially deepened since then, and is now the main route by which Miami's endless parade of cruise ships reaches the main harbor.

## Sanford L. Ziff Jewish Museum of Florida

**Map 4, E7**. Tues–Sun 10am–5pm; $5.
Housed in a deconsecrated Art Deco synagogue located at 301 Washington Ave, the **Sanford L. Ziff Jewish Museum of Florida** (☎305/672-5044, ⓦwww.jewishmuseum.com) commemorates Jews in Florida from the late 1600s until today. Finished in 1936, the building is one of architect Henry Hohauser's earliest local projects, and has been lovingly restored at a cost of more than $2 million, including the eye-catching Moorish copper dome.

Although records show that there were Jews in the

**SOUTH POINTE**

Sunshine State from the earliest times of European settlement, it was only after World War II that the local Jewish population exploded. At one point, South Beach was even home to the second largest community of Holocaust survivors in the country; today, some fifteen percent of South Florida's population is Jewish, also among the highest concentrations in the country.

---

**Ask one of the many docents at the Jewish Museum to take you around on an informal tour – they're extremely knowledgeable and friendly.**

---

Along with temporary shows, the building houses a permanent exhibition that's compact, but so crammed with information that it's almost overwhelming in its thoroughness. Though the early documents and photographs are interesting enough, the museum's at its strongest when exposing how recently anti-Semitism continued unchecked in South Beach, as with hotel signs from the 1950s which guaranteed guests "Always a view, never a Jew." One of the most awkwardly telling documents is a brief letter from 1929 that was written by the mayor of St Louis to Carl Fisher: in it, he asks Fisher if he would get "his best friend of Earth, Mr. William Lewin," courtesy in his golf club. The mayor goes on to write that he would be "everlastingly grateful," as he knows that "on account of [Lewin's] nationality" it could be a problem.

# THE ISLANDS

Miami Beach's islands made headlines for two weeks in 1983, when the art stuntmaster Christo wrapped eleven of them in 200-foot-wide bright pink plastic skirts – a project he called *Surrounded Islands*. That's little reason to go visit now, and most of them are fairly inaccessible in any case.

## Venetian Islands

Threaded together by the Venetian Causeway, the **Venetians** include five neat artificial islands – Rivo Alto, DiLido, San Marino, San Marco and Biscayne – as well as the raggedy but natural Belle Isle. There's little to see on any of them other than upscale residences, but a sauntering drive along this causeway is a pleasant detour, plus it's a great place for jogging.

## Flagler Memorial Island

The **Flagler Memorial Monument** sits on its own specially constructed island, just south of the Venetian cluster. Built in 1920, it was commissioned by Carl Fisher in memory of the father of Miami, railroad magnate Henry Flagler: four giant statues stand looking out over the water, their backs to an enormous obelisk. Unfortunately, the monument's in a poor state now thanks to pollution, neglect and vandalism, and the fact that it's impossible to visit without a private boat means it won't be dolled up for tourism anytime soon.

## Palm, Hibiscus, Star and Fisher islands

While **Palm** and **Hibiscus islands** were dredged expressly for luxury housing in the early twentieth century, **Star Island** was initially designed to house the Miami Beach Yacht Club: it was only later converted to residential use in the 1920s. These islands are certainly prime real estate now, crammed with swanky residences. All the islands are public and accessible from MacArthur Causeway – just tell the gatekeeper that you're sightseeing and he should let you through, although the high fences and thick hedges around most of the homes means there's little to see.

THE ISLANDS

**Fisher Island**, just across Government Cut, has always been the poshest of all the islands: Carl Fisher sold it to William Vanderbilt and his wife Rosamund in the 1920s, and they built a spectacular winter estate here. It's now an exclusive resort, virtually inaccessible to anyone other than hotel guests and full-time residents of the new condo developments – and even then, only by boat.

## Parrot Jungle

**Map 1, F5**. Daily 10am–6pm; $21.95.

The oddly delightful **Parrot Jungle** recently moved to a new facility on one of the offshore islands; head to 1111 Parrot Jungle Trail on Watson Island (ⓉT305/666-7834, Ⓦwww.parrotjungle.com) to see parrots both very loud and very tame. Bring plenty of quarters if you want to feed them, as there are seed vending machines throughout. There are also exhibits on primates and reptiles, although they're less compelling than the squawking, gaudy birds: don't miss the tame flock of candy-colored flamingos, eerily identical to their plastic, ornamental counterparts.

# Central Miami Beach and north

**A**rt Deco and all-night parties give way to Modernism and massive tower blocks as South Beach settles out into **central Miami Beach**. Although most visitors to Miami Beach rarely stray up Collins Avenue past 23rd Street, there's plenty to see here, even if the sights are more scattered than in South Beach. Between 22nd and 44th streets you'll find the city's densest crop of buildings in the **Miami Modern** style, while further north there's the swanky shops of **Bal Harbour**, housed in a distinctly un-chic concrete center. Beyond the shops are unremarkable **Surfside** and the nude beaches at **Haulover Park**, as well as the most sumptuous sands on the island at package-holiday destination **Sunny Isles Beach**. Continuing on, Collins Avenue (Hwy-A1A) passes through Golden Beach, the northernmost community of Miami Beach, before eventually reaching Fort Lauderdale (see p.229). Alternately, a detour inland on the Sunny Isles Causeway at 163rd Street will deposit you in the confusingly named mainland district of **North Miami Beach**.

---

The area covered by this chapter is shown in detail
on color map 4, at the back of the book.

---

# CENTRAL MIAMI BEACH

**Central Miami Beach** had its heyday in the 1950s, when it was popular with Rat Pack celebrities like Frank Sinatra and Sammy Davis Jr, who came here to perform or vacation. However, by the 1980s, the smart set had moved on, leaving housing here to be split between two groups: wealthy Latin expats looking for pied-à-terres as second homes and seniors wanting to spend their last years soaking up the sun. Inevitably, this diminished the area's vibrancy, and it's only now that Central Miami Beach is starting to warm up again as a holiday destination.

It's in this underappreciated area that the **Miami Modern** (**MiMo**) style is at its fiercely whimsical best, in such places as the *Fontainebleau Hilton* and *Eden Roc* hotels. The value of these and other buildings has been recognized with the creation of the **John S. Collins Oceanfront Historic District** between 22nd and 44th streets, bestowing the same protection (if not prestige) on landmarks here as in South Beach's Art Deco Historic District. North from here, above 44th Street, Collins Avenue continues on through what's known as **Condo Canyon**, an endless row of residential skyscrapers, brightly colored but architecturally bland, eventually crossing 63rd Street, the unofficial northern boundary of Central Miami Beach.

---

For more information on the Miami Modern
style, see "Contexts: Architecture" on p.288.

---

West of Collins Avenue across Indian Creek are the mansions of Miami Beach's old money families, on and around **Pine Tree Drive** – one of the first areas to be tamed when Europeans settled on the beach. In fact, Pine Tree Drive is named for the windbreak of Australian pines that one of those settlers, John Collins, planted here upon his arrival.

## Forty-first Street

**Map 4, D4–G4.**

It was on the site of what's now **41st Street** that Collins established his first plantation, growing potatoes, avocadoes and bananas. Today, the drag is the heart of Miami Beach's Jewish community – tagged, ironically enough, Arthur Godfrey Road in honor of the 1940s radio personality, a notorious anti-Semite (a hotel he co-owned in Bal Harbour had a sign informing guests: "No dogs or Jews allowed"). Forty-first Street is dotted with kosher restaurants and neighborhood stores, busiest on a Saturday when the local orthodox community gathers for temple. Stop by *Arnie & Richie's Deli* for a true taste of the local flavor (see review p.131).

Forty-first Street is the site of *Jimmy'z*, one of the ritziest supperclubs on the beach – see p.167 for a review.

## Fontainebleau Hilton

**Map 4, G3.**

The **Fontainebleau Hilton**, at 4441 Collins Ave (☎305/ 538-2000, ⓦwww.hilton.com), is one of the masterpieces of Miami Modernism, a giant white space station perched on the beach. Designed by store dresser-turned-architect Morris Lapidus in 1954 (who called his style "the architecture of joy"), the central chateau building was loathed by critics at the time for its swoopingly curved wings and out-landish decoration.

However, the hotel quickly became grand central for glamour, regularly hosting big stars like Judy Garland, Frank Sinatra and Elvis, and attracting movies like the James Bond picture *Goldfinger* to film there. There's little of interest inside the building, which has fallen victim to a schizo-phrenic décor that retains some of Lapidus's touches (his trademark bowties embedded in the terrazzo floor of one lobby and enormous Belgian glass chandeliers overhead, for example) but overpowers them with gilt chairs and corpo-rate carpeting. Regardless, it's a breathtaking building from a distance.

Sadly, the gaudy but well-known *trompe l'oeil* mural added in the 1980s by Richard Haas to one of the satellite buildings is scheduled to disappear when the structure's demolished to make way for a condo tower, although no final date has been set for its razing.

The nearby **Eden Roc** hotel, 4525 Collins Ave (☎305/531-0000 or 1-800/327-8337, ⓦwww.edenrocresort.com), is another curvy Lapidus confection, crowned with a giant green sign. Unfortunately, its rooms retain none of their signature MiMo features, but the sleek modernist lobby has been snappily restored to its original design, and its sunken sofas are a slinky throwback to the times of Sammy Davis Jr.

## Indian Creek

**Map 4, F1–F5**.

In mid-beach, Collins Avenue skirts along the edge of a wide, peaceful waterway known as **Indian Creek**. The boats grow larger as you travel further north, like ocean-bound answers to the luxury condos that overlook them.

It was on one of these moored houseboats that Andrew Cunanan, the serial killer who murdered **Gianni Versace** in 1997 (see p.37), was found dead from a supposedly self-inflicted gunshot wound. To avoid ghoulish profiteering, the boat itself was seized by the city for demolition – although not before the owner's onsite manager was able to offer impromptu crime-scene souvenirs for sale to passers-by.

Despite this bloody incident, the canal is a soothingly calm place; the shady benches dotted regularly along the grassy path make for a glorious, lazy stroll by the water.

## NORTH BEACH

By the end of the 1980s, the area between 63rd Street and 87th Terrace – proud but homely **North Beach** – began absorbing those who'd been economically or socially expelled from the newly cool South Beach. They brought with them social problems of their own as crime rates rose and the infrastructure of this working-class community frayed. Ten years later, the neighborhood's picking up again, thanks to aggressive investment in businesses and buildings, and there are some good restaurants around the area's heart at **71st Street**, as well as pleasant oceanfront parks.

West along 71st Street leads to the posh houses on **Normandy Isle**, where the streets are named, in another of Miami's tributes to old-world Europe, after French towns: Calais and Biarritz drives, for example. Brochures optimistically tout **Ocean Terrace**, a two-block slice of fine MiMo buildings between 73rd and 75th streets, as the next Ocean Drive: even if that's unlikely, there's a growing café scene here that makes for a pleasant evening by the water.

## SURFSIDE AND BAL HARBOUR

Moving north along Collins Avenue (or Hwy-A1A), the next major settlement, **Surfside**, is a self-contained, unremarkable beachside community, and is best skipped over in favor of the tony **Bal Harbour**, just past it, whose most telling feature is its name, anglicized to underscore pretensions to culture, history and wealth. It's ironic, then, that Miami Beach's most self-consciously ritzy area should have such humble beginnings. Originally a soldiers' training camp in World War II, the town was incorporated in 1946 when many of those soldiers who remembered Miami fondly came back to stay.

Most visitors today, though, come to Bal Harbour for one thing: the **Bal Harbour Shops**, at 9700 Collins Ave (☎305/886-0311, ⓦwww.balharbourshops.com). This bi-level, open-air mall positively drips with designer names: Fendi, Prada and Gucci all have their Miami outposts here, although the exclusivity is becoming diluted with the arrival of everyday stores like The Gap. It may be a fun place to window-shop, but don't expect any bargains – even the cafés are premium-priced.

# HAULOVER PARK AND SUNNY ISLES BEACH

Moving on north from Bal Harbour brings you to the nude beaches at **Haulover Park**, which are in actuality far more salubrious than their racy reputation might suggest. The golden coastline here stretches for several sand-packed miles before delivering you to the mouth of package-holiday hell – although, admittedly, with great sand – in **Sunny Isles Beach**.

## Haulover Park

**Map 1, G3.** Parking $4/day.
Famous for being Miami's one nude beach, **Haulover Park**, at 10800 Collins Ave (☎305/944-3040), is far more than that: the glorious, wide sands make the journey up from the Deco district worth the trip, and there are good

## THE BAREFOOT MAILMEN

Florida was the last state east of the Mississippi to join the US, gaining full statehood in 1845. For this reason, its civic amenities were often primitive until a widespread railway network was established in the 1920s. The postal service was especially underdeveloped; mail traveled between settlements in South Florida on a circuitous route that took a letter to New York and back again before delivering it.

This frustrating and impractical service ended in 1885 when the **Barefoot Mailman service** was established. For seven years, mail traveled between scattered coastal settlements the only way it could: on foot. Eleven mailmen walked the beach, intermittently utilizing small boats, for the 136-mile, six-day journey from Palm Beach to Miami and back. Overnights were spent at the houses of refuge run for shipwrecked sailors in Orange Grove and Fort Lauderdale; individual travelers who wanted to walk with the postmen for safety could pay to join the trip. Remarkably, only one man, James Hamilton, died on duty, drowning when he tried to swim across an inlet after his boat was stolen in 1887. The barefoot mail route ended when a new country road was built connecting Palm Beach with Lemon City, then the largest settlement in the Miami area, and a stagecoach service began.

facilities – showers, picnic tables and bathrooms – along the boardwalk that runs parallel to the oceanfront. Look here, too, for the small **plaque** commemorating the route of the Barefoot Mailmen (see box above).

For information on nearby tennis courts, see "Sports, fitness and ocean activites," p.220.

The "clothing optional" section to the north is clearly marked by warning signs on the footpath, although you

HAULOVER PARK AND SUNNY ISLES BEACH

don't have to strip off to sunbathe even there: either way, there's a volleyball court for sporty nudists, and an unofficial gay section at the northernmost end.

## Sunny Isles Beach

**Map 1, G1**.

**Sunny Isles**, a blatant Las Vegas rip-off, was founded in 1952 expressly as a holiday resort. Dozens of trendy motels quickly sprung up here along the ample beach; two were even named *Sahara* and *Suez* in Vegas's honor. However, the resort rapidly lost its luster and spent much of the rest of the century languishing as an undesirable package-holiday destination clogged with bargain-minded sunseekers.

The still-sumptuous beaches here do provide some saving grace: while elsewhere in southern Florida resorts have been bedeviled by coastal erosion, Sunny Isles' heavy investment in renourishment – basically, Rogaine for beaches, where dredged sand is dumped onto thinning shoreline – has paid off. Unfortunately, there is a downside to this oceanfloor harvesting: shifting the massive sands has altered tideflow here, and created dangerous new riptides that can catch swimmers off-guard.

---

If you're craving great diner food, head to *Rascal House*
in Sunny Isles Beach – see review on p.146.

---

# NORTH MIAMI BEACH

Continuing north through Golden Beach on the A1A throws you back into the Miami of the early 1980s, the houses stocked with old ladies enjoying the warm weather. Eventually, via the nondescript resort town of Hollywood, Collins Avenue will bring you to Fort Lauderdale (see p.229), although it's a roundabout route and you're better off using faster, interior roads like I-95.

The remaining local sights require a detour west on the Sunny Isles Causeway, across the 163rd Street bridge, to the mainland area confusingly known as **North Miami Beach** – not the safest neighborhood, so keep your wits about you if you plan to wander around. Here you'll find one of the city's oddest sights, William Randolph Hearst's Ancient Spanish Monastery.

## Ancient Spanish Monastery

**Map 1, F2**. Mon–Sat 10am–5pm, Sun 1.30–5pm.

Oddly anachronistic among the gas stations and strip malls, the **Ancient Spanish Monastery**, at 16711 West Dixie Hwy (℡305/770-3131, Ⓦwww.spanishmonastery.com), is an unremarkable medieval building from Spain whose checkered history is far more interesting than the surprisingly diminutive structure itself.

The monastery's drawn-out relocation began in 1925 when magpie-like newspaper magnate William Randolph Hearst purchased the place while visiting Europe, and then had it dismantled and shipped to America, planning to incorporate the building into his Hearst Castle in California – itself stitched together from other such souvenirs he'd snapped up.

However, upon arrival in New York, the disassembled monastery was quarantined by customs due to an outbreak of foot-and-mouth disease in Spain, and never made it to the West Coast, as Hearst's financial troubles set in soon after. It was sold at auction and gathered dust in a Brooklyn warehouse for almost thirty years before being purchased as a tourist attraction in the early 1950s and reassembled by its new owners.

Today, the monastery is a working Episcopal church with

a tiny chapel that was formerly the monks' refectory, while the cloisters themselves are small and rather frayed around the edges. Getting there is difficult without a car; however, if you're determined, buses #3 from downtown and #H, #E and #V from the beaches drop off at the corner of 163rd Street and West Dixie Highway. Call ahead to check whether it's open, especially at weekends, as hours can be erratic.

NORTH MIAMI BEACH

# Little Havana

**L**ittle Havana, a quiet district of sherbet-colored, low-rise buildings and dilapidated houses, is where the vibrant Cuban streak that colors Miami is seen most vividly. Wandering the streets, it's not unusual to see statues of Cuba's patron saint, the Virgin Mary, in residential gardens, and rare to find a newspaper box on the street that sells the English-language *Miami Herald* rather than *El Nuevo Herald*. Along Calle Ocho (aka SW 8th Street), the neighborhood's main drag, tiny stores and restaurants with hand-painted signs stand elbow to elbow. If the weather's right it's easy to forget you're not in Latin America: salesmen will come into restaurants to peddle videos or CDs while you eat, and the neighborhood *McDonald's* even serves *café cubano* alongside its Big Macs and apple pies.

Little Havana hasn't always been the predominantly Latin enclave it is today: until the early 1960s, it was a largely working-class Jewish neighborhood known as Riverside, built as the city's first real estate subdivision in the early twentieth century. After Castro took power in Cuba in 1959, financially unsettled Cuban refugees were drawn here by the low rents, and soon set about creating a replica of their homeland in America. They were unofficially fettered, though, by the Miami city council, which attempted to deny business licenses anywhere north of 8th Street to those who didn't speak English (which is why Little Havana sprang up in southwest Miami). However, this economic obstacle was soon sidestepped, and these upwardly mobile refugees gained an economic foothold in their adopted city – so much so, in fact, that Little Havana is increasingly a misnomer, as the successful Cuban community decamps to wealthier neighborhoods, especially Coral Gables.

That said, this is still a heavily Latin residential area, and sights proper are few and far between: most visitors come to eat authentic Cuban food like *vaca frita* (fried beef), buy a hand-rolled cigar made from tobacco grown from Cuban seeds, or just browse the shops. Take time, though, to walk around the back streets – at least in daylight hours – for this is where you'll see the real signs of a transplanted ethnic community: there may be a man selling fruit from his van on a quiet corner or crude posters haranguing passers-by about the latest political injustice in local government. The city council is also trying to energize the area through a program called **Cultural Fridays**: on the last Friday of each month, Calle Ocho between 10th and 15th avenues is transformed into a venue for music and street stalls, in an attempt to turn the neighborhood into more of a destination.

---

**The area covered by this chapter is shown in detail on color map 5, at the back of the book.**

---

# CUBAN MEMORIAL BOULEVARD

**Map 5, D5**.

The **Cuban Memorial Boulevard**, SW 13th Avenue between Calle Ocho and SW 12th Street – close to the houses of many former political prisoners and Brigade 2506 members – is home to several monuments, often draped in Cuban flags. The **Eternal Torch in Honor of the 2506th**

**Brigade**, at the corner of SW 13th Avenue and Calle Ocho, memorializes one of the fiercest incidents in Cuban exile politics. Named after the ID number of one of the Brigade's fallen members, it features the Brigade's crest, commemorating the incident that put JFK second only to Castro on many Cuban-Americans' hit list. In April 1961, a ragtag band of US-trained Cuban exiles landed at the Bay of Pigs in an abortive attempt to overthrow Castro's regime. They were all either captured or killed – 117 men died fighting or drowned when their ship sank, while 1180 were taken prisoner. Depending on personal political affiliations, locals will tell you that the reason the invasion failed was either the soldiers' lack of preparation or JFK's lack of interest in Cuba – he withheld air support that may have changed the battle's outcome. Each year on April 17, a dwindling number of veterans gather here in their fatigues to reaffirm pledges of patriotism in exile to their Cuban homeland.

A block or so south stand a cluster of other monuments: there's a simple stone column commemorating Jose Martí and a moody bronze bust of Antonio Maceo, both heroes of Cuba's War of Independence with Spain. Notice the doleful statue of the Virgin Mary, Cuba's patron saint, as well as the **Island of Cuba Memorial** featuring a large bronze map.

---

Looming over the loose group of monuments on Cuban Memorial Boulevard is a massive kapok tree, holy to the Afro-Cuban religion of *santeria* (see p.101): you'll frequently see offerings left at its base.

---

# MÁXIMO GÓMEZ PARK

**Map 5, C5**.

West along Calle Ocho from the Brigade 2506 memorial, **Máximo Gómez Park**, at the corner of SW 14th Avenue, is officially named after a hero of the Cuban War of Independence. However, this gated concrete hideaway is nicknamed "Domino Park" – old Cuban men really do gather here to play dominoes and spend the day arguing about politics. In fact, access to the park's open-air tables is (quite illegally) restricted to men over 55. Bear in mind that these oldtimers are camera-fierce rather than camera-shy, and don't take kindly to snapshots by enthusiastic visitors. The fence and key cards that guard its entrance aren't geared to prevent tourist intrusion, though – they were installed after a spate of shootings in the 1980s. You shouldn't have any problem stopping by during the day, though, as the gates will normally be open.

# WOODLAWN CEMETERY

**Map 1, D5**. Daily sunrise–dusk.

Even further west, at 3260 SW 8th St, lies the enormous, serene **Woodlawn Cemetery** (☎305/221-8282), crowded with mausolea and statuary and filled with the manicured graves of many prominent local figures. The father of Coral Gables, **George Merrick**, is buried here, but not in the Merrick plot: his wife Eunice Peacock had him moved into her own family's area two decades after he died. It's also the final home for several expat Cuban bigwigs, including two deposed presidents: **General Gerardo Machado**, unseated in 1933, and **Carlos Prío Socarras**, one of the prime movers behind his downfall, who was himself driven from office (and the country) in 1952. The cemetery's also the site of a black marble wall in tribute to the "Unknown Cuban Freedom Fighter," one of the many killed during the abortive Bay of Pigs invasion.

# UNIDOS EN CASA ELIÁN

Sun 10am–6pm; free.

Northwest from the heart of Little Havana is the house where **Elián González** stayed (at 2319 NW 2nd St) during his controversial time in Miami. Elián was a flashpoint in recent Miami politics: after his mother was killed trying to reach America with her son, he was forcibly returned to his father in Cuba by the federal government, despite enormous local protest. This house has been turned into an oddly discomforting museum in his honor: display cases house Elián's playthings, alongside dozens of photo collages and mawkish poems written in tribute by local residents. Frankly, the only reason to come here is in an attempt to understand how raw and vivid a wound the Elián controversy carved into Miami's Cuban community – as this house shows, it's far deeper than an outsider might suspect.

# ORANGE BOWL

**Map 5, C2.**

Unless you're taking in a concert or a game (see p.217), there's little reason to visit the vast **Orange Bowl**, due north from Máximo Gómez Park at 1501 NW 3rd St. Home to the University of Miami's perennially successful college football team, the Hurricanes, the Orange Bowl is also known locally as the place where JFK accepted the Brigade 2506 flag after the Bay of Pigs debacle and promised to return it in "free Havana." Older Cuban exiles grimly joke that he was referring to a well-known bar in Miami, rather than the city itself.

# Coral Gables

T he city of **Coral Gables** is a curate's egg of urban planning, separated from Miami proper by more than just politics. It has a distinct local council and residential regulations, and seems to regard itself as an upper class cousin to Miami, sandwiched as it is between gritty Little Havana and oddball Coconut Grove. Its twelve square miles of broad boulevards and leafy streets are lined by elaborate Spanish- and Italian-style architecture; you'll also find civic amenities like fountains and even a swimming pool dotted throughout the area. Designed by founder George Merrick to inspire civic pride in its residents, some say the plan for this European-style city has worked a little too well: this is the snootiest part of Miami, and its architectural beauty is somewhat blighted by a suburban smugness you won't find elsewhere.

That said, it's a fascinating place to visit, largely because all the landmarks that sprouted during its development still stand. The **Merrick House**, George Merrick's charming family home, remains, as do projects like the majestic **City Hall** and the **Miracle Mile** downtown. The grandiose **Biltmore Hotel** has reopened for business and the delightful **Venetian Pool** is an unmissable Miami sight. The **International Villages** and **Entrances** are spectacular follies, born jointly of Merrick's grand vision and sales savvy, adding further variety to the city's European-style architecture. Indeed, even the street layout is European, with winding roads that amble through a haphazard grid of residential streets and tiny, ground-level white rocks that act as street signs – remember to bring a map to navigate, especially if you're driving.

For a detailed look at the area covered in this chapter, see color map 6, at the back of the book.

## Some history

Whereas Miami's other early property developers built cheap and fast in search of a quick buck, the creator of Coral Gables, a local named **George Merrick**, fired by the **City Beautiful Movement** (see "Contexts: Architecture," p.290), was equal parts entrepreneur *and* aesthete. Drawing direct inspiration from Mediterranean Europe, Merrick quickly appointed his uncle, artist **Denman Fink**, as Coral Gables' creative director, and recruited **Phineas Paist**, one of the architectural masterminds behind Villa Vizcaya (see p.86, "Coconut Grove"), to plan the plazas, fountains and artfully aged stucco-fronted buildings.

Merrick envisioned a Floridian Venice, declaring from the outset that no two houses could be the same, and that all designs had to be approved by the official city architect. The layout and buildings quickly took shape, according to Merrick's vision, often working around potential disasters: he transformed an abandoned quarry into the Venetian Pool and disguised the construction ditches that ringed the infant Coral Gables into a network of canals (see below).

As the city took shape, Merrick focused on his own flair for selling, combining snappy sloganeering ("Where Your Castles in Spain are Made Real") with publicity stunts like a Spanish-themed land auction in 1921, or the ninety coral pink buses he bought to ferry in prospective residents from across Florida. This relentless hard sell worked: in less than five years, the city had brought in more than $150 million.

Coral Gables' heyday was short-lived, though: soon after the *Biltmore Hotel* first opened, Miami was devastated by a major hurricane in 1926 and its tourism lifeblood was cut off. Ironically, the carefully built, ornamental city of Coral Gables was the district least damaged by the winds. But the Great Depression set in before the local economy could recover, and Merrick's money soon had disappeared. He retreated to the Florida Keys to run a resort before returning to serve as postmaster of the city of Miami until his death in 1942.

However, Merrick's vision lives on, as local residents have collectively embraced his grand design, enacting stringent ordinances on everything from appropriate color schemes to the times during which unsightly trucks may be parked outside a private house. And in addition, Coral Gables has recently undergone a transformation which has yet to manifest fully: affluent, second-generation **Cuban-Americans** have begun to move into the area, and some say that Coral Gables, not Little Havana, is the new center of Miami's Cuban community. Still, there's little commercial evidence of Cuban presence here – this is one place in Miami where it's hard to find a quick *cafecito*.

# THE ENTRANCES

Merrick was an entrepreneurial showman, and his plan to ring Coral Gables with eight impressive **entrance gates** was another theatrical flourish. He had originally planned on eight entrances to frame the main access roads, but only four were completed before funds ran out. Three of these, all along a two-and-a-half-mile stretch of SW 8th Street, are well worth seeking out.

The million-dollar **Douglas Entrance** (Map 6, G1; junction with Douglas Road), was the most ambitious, consisting of a gateway and tower with two expansive wings of shops, offices and artists' studios. During the Sixties it was almost bulldozed to make room for a supermarket, but survived to become a well-scrubbed business area, still upholding Merrick's Mediterranean themes. Further west, the sixty-foot-high vine-covered **Granada Entrance** (Map 6, C1; junction with Granada Boulevard) is based on the entrance to the city of Granada in Spain – a massive Renaissance gateway erected by Carlos V in the sixteenth century. The **Country Club Prado Entrance** (Map 6, A1; junction with Country Club Prado) is an elaborate recreated Italian garden, bordered by freestanding stucco and brick pillars topped by ornamental urns and gas lamps. The fourth entrance, **Commercial** (also known as the Alhambra), is at the corner of the Alhambra Circle and Douglas Road (Map 6, G3) but doesn't come close to matching the others in flair or style.

---

The best way into Coral Gables from points east is along SW 24th Street, Coral Way, which turns into the Miracle Mile between Douglas Road (SW 37th Avenue) and LeJeune Road (SW 42nd Avenue).

---

# THE MIRACLE MILE AND AROUND

The five-block expanse of the **Miracle Mile**, conceived by Merrick as the centerpiece of his business district, has seen better days: it's filled with small, no-name shops – including plenty of cobwebby ladies' boutiques – but is virtually devoid of customers. Thankfully, though, the strip is slowly recharging its retail batteries with an aggressive redevelopment plan that aims to lure casual cafés and stores back to the main street. The local government has also loosened liquor laws, allowing bars to remain open until 2am rather than midnight in the hope of re-energizing downtown Coral Gables nightlife. In large part, it's working; the area's at its liveliest and least hollow on weekday evenings when staff from many of the big-name businesses which have offices locally stop by for drinks or dinner after work. Architecturally, this strip is filled with Mediterranean Revival buildings of only passing interest, save for the odd standout.

## Omni Colonnade Hotel

**Map 6, G4**.

Halfway west along the Miracle Mile, the **Omni Colonnade Hotel** can be found at 180 Aragorn Ave (just north of the Mile), at the corner of Ponce DeLeon Blvd (☎305/441-2600). The Colonnade building initially was to house Merrick's local real estate sales office – but was completed only months before the 1926 hurricane that wiped him out, and he never moved his offices from across the road. It served as a sometime movie soundstage in the 1930s and 1940s until Los Angeles decisively eclipsed Miami as the home of America's infant film industry; during the war, it became an army training facility. Now it's an upscale hotel and one of the more architecturally impressive buildings on the Miracle Mile – be sure to take note of its ornate center fountain, as well as the stylistic spiral and peak flourishes on the structure itself.

## The Actors' Playhouse at the Miracle Theater

**Map 6, F4**.

Originally built in the 1940s as Coral Gables' main cinema, the **Actors' Playhouse**, at 280 Miracle Mile (☎305/444-

9293, ⓦwww.actorsplayhouse.org), was converted to a theater in the mid-1990s to provide a home for an acting company displaced by Hurricane Andrew. The classic theater has been sensitively restored, and stylish accents like intricately etched glass in the lobby and a gleaming, metallic ticket booth embellish the otherwise rather plain Art Deco building. In addition to hosting traveling productions, the Playhouse's two small auditoria also feature readings by local writers and performances by the resident children's theater company.

For more information on The Actors' Playhouse, see "Performing arts and film," p.175.

## Coral Gables City Hall

**Map 6, F4**. Mon–Fri 8am–5pm.
At the western end of the Miracle Mile, **Coral Gables City Hall**, at 405 Biltmore Way (ⓣ305/460-5217, ⓦwww.citybeautiful.net), was planned as the heart of the city. This coral rock building, designed by the prolific Phineas Paist, is set at the busiest intersection in downtown Coral Gables – a pity, since the noise and traffic diminish its impressive façade: fronted with twelve stately columns as well as a replica of the city's seal, it's topped off by a multi-tiered, Spanish-inspired clock tower and plenty of ornamental moldings. Inside, you'll see sales posters from Coral Gables' heyday, as well as newspaper clippings that illustrate how frenzied the Florida land boom of the 1920s truly was. There's also a blandly decorative **mural** of the *Four Seasons*, painted by the ubiquitous Denman Fink, in the belltower.

For detailed information on the dozens of local landmarks, stop by the Historic Preservation office on the second floor of the Coral Gables City Hall (Mon–Fri 8am–5pm).

THE MIRACLE MILE AND AROUND

# CORAL WAY AND DESOTO BOULEVARD

The forced rebirth of downtown Coral Gables is most glaring as the Miracle Mile turns back into **Coral Way** immediately west of LeJeune Road (or SW 42nd Street). Here, Mediterranean Revival high-rises proliferate, nurtured by tax credits offered those who construct in a locally appropriate style. It's an oddly soulless strip, and there's little to detain a casual visitor. The most pleasant detour is a wander round the residential streets south of Coral Way, canopied with enormous banyan trees. Stop by Fink's **DeSoto Fountain** near the Venetian Pool: it's an imposing centerpiece at the junction of Granada and DeSoto boulevards and another example of Merrick's determination to provide aesthetic as well as civic amenities, in accordance with City Beautiful precepts (see "Contexts: Architecture," p.290). Most streets here are named for Spanish provinces and towns – the few which aren't (Bird Road and Douglas Road, for example) honor notable early locals.

If you do stick on Coral Way (moving west), you'll come across three interesting houses after crossing Toledo Street. **Merrick House**, the first, was George's family home and is now a museum (see below). Further west stands **Poinciana Place** at no. 937, one of the earliest structures in the city, built close to Merrick's home when he married Eunice Peacock in 1916: its Mediterranean Revival style would serve as a template for later construction. Finally, there's the grand **Doc Dammers House** at no. 1141, named for the smooth-talking auctioneer who lived there and became Coral Gables' first mayor.

## Coral Gables Merrick House

**Map 6, C4**. Wed 1–4pm, Sun 1–4pm; $2.

Designed by George's eccentric and artistic mother Althea,

the **Coral Gables Merrick House**, at 907 Coral Way (℡305/460-5361), has been ably restored into a compact showpiece of Floridian shotgun design, its central ventilating hallway and wraparound veranda ideal for muggy South Florida summers. The simple wooden structure at the rear of the building was home to the Merricks when they arrived here in 1889 from New England to run a 160-acre fruit and vegetable farm. The venture was such a success that the shack was later augmented by a grander house of coral rock and termite-resistant local pine: it was christened Coral Gables, passing its name on to the city that later grew up around the family farm. The place now showcases artwork by Denman Fink, as well as various Merrick memorabilia, along with an informative video that gives an overview of Coral Gables history (see p.67). Upstairs, look for the chest Merrick received from King Alonso XIII of Spain, who decorated him in 1927 for creating a Spanish-inspired city in North America.

## Venetian Pool

**Map 6, C4**. June–Aug Mon–Fri 11am–7.30pm; Sept–Oct & Apr–May Tues–Fri 11am–5.30pm; Nov–Mar Tues–Fri 10am–4.30pm; year-round Sat–Sun 10am–4.30pm; Apr–Oct non-resident adults (age 13 & up) $8.50, non-resident children (ages 3–12) $4.50; Nov–Mar adult non-residents $5.50, non-resident children $2.50.

South of the Coral Gables Merrick House, along DeSoto Boulevard, you'll find the magical **Venetian Pool**, at no. 2701 (℡305/460-5356, ⓦwww.venetianpool.com). As local coral rock was plundered to build the original homes in Coral Gables, an unsightly quarry developed in the heart of the area, which Merrick, along with uncle and artist Denman Fink, ingeniously transformed into this, one of Miami's most appealing attractions.

Intended as another civic project for the benefit of local

residents, it's a delightful place to spend an afternoon. Surrounded by shaded porticos, wrought-iron railings, palm-studded paths and Venetian-style bridges, the deep-blue water winds its way through coral rock caves and spills over two waterfalls – there's even a landlocked beach for sunbathers. Locker rooms are spotless, as are the tiled colonnades that display photographs of the pool in its hey-day when watersport celebrities like Johnny Weismuller and Esther Williams performed here.

---

Curiously, the head lifeguard at the Venetian Pool lives onsite, in the ornate turret above the ticket hall.

---

## Coral Gables Congregational Church

**Map 6, B5**.

Just southwest from the Venetian Pool, the **Coral Gables Congregational Church**, at 3010 DeSoto Blvd (☎305/448-7421, ⓦwww.coralgablescongregational.org), is another of Merrick's lofty civic projects, designed as a replica of a church in Costa Rica: it's a bright, ornate Spanish Revival flurry whose belfry echoes the imposing tower of the *Biltmore* across the street. The interior is dark and vaguely ominous, with much elaborately-wrought ironwork and fine acoustics, especially notable during the regular jazz and classical concerts held here (see p.176, "Performing arts and film").

## The Biltmore Hotel

**Map 6, B5**.

Merrick's crowning achievement – aesthetically if not financially – was no doubt the **Biltmore Hotel**, at 1200 Anastasia Ave (☎305/445-1926 or 1-800/727-1926,

ⓦwww.biltmorehotel.com), which wraps its broad wings around the southern end of DeSoto Boulevard. The third in a trio of Miami towers inspired by the Giralda bell tower in Seville, Spain, the *Biltmore* looms majestically over Coral Gables. Its architecture is Mediterranean Revival with a strong Moorish influence shown in its ornate surface decorations: in fact, the hotel looks like a movie set, with 25-foot-high frescoed walls, vaulted ceilings and immense fireplaces. When it was built, it was the last word in elegance, especially notable for an enormous chevron-shaped pool, and it attracted celebrity guests like Judy Garland and Bing Crosby (not to mention Al Capone, who hosted splashy parties on the 13th floor in what's still unofficially known as the "Capone Suite").

Surprisingly, given its grand scale, the hotel took less than a year to construct: from March 1925, workers lived in a tent city nearby and worked 24 hours a day to meet the opening date of January 15, 1926. Since then, the *Biltmore* has weathered rough seas: the hotel was sold to new owners during the Depression, became a military hospital for burn victims after World War II, and then, following the hospital's closure, an illicit hangout for local teenagers. Eventually, it was renovated at a cost of $55 million, a project that included partially filling in the pool, as it was too deep for modern safety regulations. The *Biltmore* reopened as a hotel in 1993 but the new owners promptly went bust and it closed again for two years before current management took over.

If you can't afford to stay here (for a review, see p.123), at least step in to marvel at the space. It's easy enough to wander round without a guide: otherwise, there are **free tours** every Sunday at 1.30, 2.30 and 3.30pm – though these are mostly disappointing. For a sprightlier take on its history, stop by each Thursday evening when a local historian recounts the grisly stories of ghosts and murders at the *Biltmore* – meet at the main lobby by the fireplace at 7pm.

The neighboring **Biltmore Country Club**, also open to the public, is as stately as it sounds. You can poke your head inside for a closer look at its painstakingly renovated Beaux Arts features, but most people turn up to knock a ball along the lush fairways of the **Biltmore Golf Course**, which, in the glory days of the hotel, hosted the highest-paying golf tournament in the world.

---

For listings of where to play golf in the Miami area, see Chapter 19, "Sports, fitness and ocean activities."

---

## THE INTERNATIONAL VILLAGES

Even before the great hurricane of 1926, the market for housing in Merrick's new city had begun to soften. To revive interest, he cooked up a gimmick that's now one of the area's signature features: the International Villages. Fourteen were planned, each representing a different style and each overseen by different architects. Unfortunately, time and money meant that only seven were built, six of which are now National Historic Landmarks and are representative of some of the priciest real estate the city has to offer.

The eight buildings of the Chinese Village (Map 6, E9; bounded by Sansavino Ave, Castania Ave, Menendez Ave, Maggiore St and Riviera Drive) are arguably the most dazzling, notable for their brightly colored roofs and ornately carved balconies. Equally interesting is the French Normandy Village (Map 6, F6; 400 block of Viscaya Ave at LeJeune Rd), which looks thoroughly Elizabethan, thanks to its thick, chocolate-brown beams. It has weathered surprisingly well, too, given that it was once owned by the University of Miami and housed five fraternities.

CORAL WAY AND DESOTO BOULEVARD

# SOUTH CORAL GABLES

The southern reaches of Coral Gables are primarily residential, aside from the campus of the **University of Miami**, built on land donated by Merrick (with the theory that a world-class city would need a world-class university). The school almost went bankrupt in its early years, but is now a thriving institution, known especially for the successful Hurricanes football team (see p.217, "Sports, fitness and ocean activities").

Merrick's late additions to the city plan, architectural stunts known as the **International Villages**, are mostly in

Close by, the Dutch South African Village is less eye-catching (Map 6, F6; 6600–6700 block of LeJeune Rd). Look for the gabled and dormered roofs inspired by the houses that were built by wealthy Boer settlers in South Africa, as well as connecting windows that make the two-storied houses look like bungalows. In contrast, there are the simple white houses of the Florida Pioneer Village (Map 6, B8; 4300–4600 block of Santa Maria St), which feature pillars and verandas in homage to the homes built by early settlers.

Eighteenth-century-style townhouses make up the French City Village (1000 block of Hardee Rd); you'll know them by the four-foot-high walls that surround the buildings. Its rural companion, the French Country Village (500 block of Hardee Rd and around) includes buildings designed to echo French farmhouses, with steeply pitched, crossed-gabled roofs.

Finally, the Italian Village (Map 6, D7; bounded by San Antonio Ave, San Esteban Ave, Monserrate St and Segovia St) is a larger, looser collection of homes in Italian country and Venetian styles, and as a result stand out less from their Mediterranean Revival neighbors.

SOUTH CORAL GABLES

this area (see box pp.76–77), and it's here you'll find the **canals** which sparked Coral Gables' claim to be the Venice of America. In fact, much like the Venetian Pool, they're simply dolled-up byproducts of construction: having hewn chunks of coral rock from the ground to build houses, Merrick simply filled the holes with water and called them canals, employing real gondoliers every night to authenticate his claim.

## Lowe Art Museum

**Map 6, C9**. Tue–Wed, Fri–Sat 10am–5pm, Thurs noon–7pm, Sun noon–5pm; $5, free first Tues each month.

From its beginnings in 1950 as Miami's first professional exhibition space in a few rooms on campus, the **Lowe Art Museum**, at 1301 Stanford Drive (℡305/284-3535, ⓦwww.lowemuseum.org), has grown through acquisitions and renovations to be one of the largest museums in Florida. Its collection is large and diverse, featuring nineteenth-century, contemporary, Native American and Renaissance art, even a sizeable amount of Cuban ephemera, thanks to a donation from the controversial Cuban Museum of the Americas in Little Havana, which closed its doors in 1999. Unfortunately, though, that diversity is its downfall: the Renaissance collection is sprawling and nondescript, while the Impressionist works are primarily small, early canvases by Sisley and Monet. Works that do stand out include the eerily lifelike *Football Player* by local sculptor Duane Hanson, and some paintings by pop innovator Roy Lichtenstein.

# Coconut Grove

The latent pioneer spirit of South Florida surfaces in **Coconut Grove**, an area known for being both tolerant and, at times, ornery. It's always seemed uneasy about being a part of Miami, which annexed it in the late nineteenth century. Eccentrics and artists have made their homes here for more than a century (the local Hare Krishna temple is just off Virginia Street), and older locals will usually treat outsiders with respectful suspicion. In recent years, the area has gentrified somewhat, blighted by bland shopping centers and towering bay-view apartments, but it has somehow managed to remain a refreshingly off-kilter, resoundingly real place.

From its beginning, the Coconut Grove community has been diverse: having sprung up after the Civil War around the tropical plantation of a Confederate doctor, the area was originally home to migrant Bahamian laborers and liberal-minded Anglo settlers, as well as characters like wacky philosoper-environmentalist Ralph Middleton Munroe (who built the house at the Barnacle State Historical Site – see p.81). Facilities in the town were highly developed by 1896, with a library, churches, a yacht club and the first school in Dade county. Up until then, a chunk of dense hardwood hammock had kept the new city of Miami at bay, but city growth and Henry Flagler's railroad merged the two and Coconut Grove was soon annexed. The populace – abetted by their early independence, as well as the many liberal-minded artists and leftists who migrated here thanks to tolerant attitudes – has tried to secede several times since then, though to no avail.

Separatist attitude aside, Coconut Grove is still part of Miami proper – in fact, the **Miami City Hall** moved here to the Dinner Key Marina on Biscayne Bay in the 1950s. Geographically, the southwestern portion of the area is leafy and residential, with chunks of thick hammock and enormous canopies of greenery on most streets, while pedestrian-friendly **central Coconut Grove** holds two well-known shopping centers, the open-air **CocoWalk** and posh **Streets of Mayfair**. East from here, there's the once countercultural, now well-tended **Peacock Park**, as well as sublime historical site **The Barnacle**. Moving north up Bayshore Drive past City Hall, Biscayne Bay is lined with greenspace before arriving at **Villa Vizcaya**, the spectacularly overwrought mansion built by millionaire James Deering.

--------------------------------------------------

The area covered in this chapter can be seen in detail on color map 7, at the back of the book.

--------------------------------------------------

# CENTRAL COCONUT GROVE AND AROUND

The Grove's central district is compact and walkable, with shops and restaurants fanning out northwest from the intersection of Main Highway and Grand Avenue. **CocoWalk**, a hacienda-inspired outdoor mall, was a revitalizing force for the neighborhood when it was built in the early 1990s, while the more imposing **Streets of Mayfair** shopping center just across Virginia Street was less successful: although it has a good range of stores (including one of the few large bookstores within reach of downtown; see p.192, "Shopping"), it's oddly monolithic and unappealing, with its zigzagging walkways and copper sculptures. Better to head south, and grab a coffee at one of the many sidewalk cafés lining Main Highway. While there, you might also want to take a look around the south Grove – or, as it's known colloquially (if unfortunately) – "**Black Coconut Grove**." Centered on **Charles Avenue**, this somewhat depressed area throws the wealth surrounding it into sharp relief.

## Peacock Park

**Map 7, C7**.

Surrounding The Barnacle is **Peacock Park**, the epicenter of Coconut Grove counterculture in the 1960s thanks to the hippies who camped out here. The park has now been spruced up and is the best of several local greenspaces, with a few public tennis courts and some peculiar abstract sculptures sprinkled throughout. It's especially pleasant for the superb **views** of the Bay it affords – and if rollerblading along the catwalk of Ocean Drive in South Beach is a little intimidating, come here and practice first.

------

Peacock Park is where most of Coconut Grove's festivals take place – see "Festivals and events," p.207, for details.

------

## The Barnacle State Historical Site

**Map 7, C7**. Fri–Mon 9am–4pm; tours depart at 10 & 11.30am, 1 & 2.30pm on the porch; $1.

Set back from the road behind tropical hardwood hammock lies one of the city's most intriguing sights: Ralph Middleton Munroe's pagoda-pioneer house, **The**

**Barnacle**, at 3485 Main Hwy (☎305/448-9445). Built in 1891, the self-consciously simple structure is informed by nautical innovations, reflecting Munroe's professional passion as a naval architect, his eco-concerns, and his philosophical devotion to the Transcendentalist Movement. Munroe built the house completely above ground to prevent flooding and improve airflow – helping to alleviate some of the discomfort of Miami's humidity – and in 1908, raised it further, adding a floor under the original one. There's also a recessed verandah that enables windows to be open during rainstorms and skylights which allow air to be drawn through the structure.

The only way to see inside the house is on a guided tour: inside, you'll see many original furnishings alongside some of Munroe's intriguing photos of pre-settled Coconut Grove. The grounds are also a pleasant place to dawdle: once a month, magical fundraisers are held here, featuring live classical music played from the verandah while the audience lolls on the waterfront lawn – call for details of the next concert.

## Coconut Grove Playhouse

**Map 7, B6**.

The blue-and-white Mediterranean Revival building at 3500 Main Hwy started out as a movie theater in 1926, costing a then-staggering $400,000 to build. It became the **Coconut Grove Playhouse** (☎305/442-4000, ⓦwww .cgplayhouse.com) in the mid 1950s when an entrepreneur bought the abandoned building hoping to bring Broadway to Coconut Grove. He certainly invested heavily in its refurbishment – there were lavish onsite apartments for the stars with gold plumbing fixtures in some bathrooms – and at least initially, he succeeded, luring performers like Tallulah Bankhead and Chico Marx. The theater's greatest claim to fame, though, is that Samuel Beckett's *Waiting for Godot* had its US premiere here in 1956. Now, the interior's less compelling than the ornate exterior, and there's no reason to go inside other than to take in a performance.

For Coconut Grove Playhouse ticket information,
see "Performing arts and film," p.175.

## Charles Avenue

**Map 7, A7**.

In the nineteenth century, there was a small Bahamian village called Kebo on the site that Coconut Grove now occupies, and many black immigrants settled here during Miami's construction boom, notably along what's become **Charles Avenue**. It's remained a largely black, working-class neighborhood and is noticeably less chichi than surrounding areas.

There aren't many specific sights, other than a few so-called "**shotgun**" **houses** on the 3200 block of Grand Avenue, built around long, narrow hallways: cheaply made at the time from local hardwoods, they're now cherished for the same reason. Notice how the **cemetery**, at no. 3650, is tiled with gravestones: due to the combination of hard coral rock and a close-to-the-surface water table, coffins here could not be sunk deep into the ground, and so the dead were buried in unusually shallow graves.

## Plymouth Congregational Church

**Map 7, A7**.

In the heart of South Coconut Grove, the small neighborhood church of **Plymouth Congregational**, at 3400 Devon Rd (☎305/444-6521, ⓦwww.plymouthmiami.com),

CENTRAL COCONUT GROVE AND AROUND

sports a delightfully weathered façade of coral rock and cast-iron door taken from an old building in the Basque region of Spain. In a former incarnation as the Union Congregational Church, this was where George Merrick's (see p.67, "Coral Gables") father came down from Duxbury, Massachusetts to work as a minister.

# BAYSHORE DRIVE AND AROUND

From Peacock Park, **Bayshore Drive** heads northeast, skirting Biscayne Bay and running by most of the sights in the area. Southwest off of Bayshore Drive, along Pan American Drive, you'll find the **Miami City Hall**, as well as the Marina, a mooring for lines of ultra-pricey yachts.

Continuing north you'll come across the area known as **Silver Bluff** between the 1600–2100 blocks. This limestone ridge is where the earliest Coconut Grove settlers made their homes, on one of the highest and safest points in the flat and flood-prone city. These settlers were later joined by the well-heeled notables of 1910s Miami, and today the area remains a preserve of the wealthy, with the early mansions replaced by equally expensive modern counterparts.

Finally, further up the Drive you'll come to the last sights of Cococut Grove, just below Little Havana: the magical **Villa Vizcaya**, the interactive **Museum of Science** and the **Space Transit Planetarium**, and the modernist church of **La Ermita de la Caridad del Cobre** – a shrine to Our Lady of Charity.

## Miami City Hall and around

**Map 7, D6**.

The cheerful **Miami City Hall**, at 3400 Pan American Drive (☎305/250-5300), provides a rare dash of Deco in

Coconut Grove. A flared white building flecked with blue reliefs, the structure was built in 1934 as a terminal for Pan American Airlines' seaplane service to Latin America, but was quickly adapted to house soldiers during World War II. It then became an unlikely site for City Hall, bought for an astonishing $1 million in the 1950s with much local grumbling about wasting public money. The grand globe that once graced its lobby is now in the Museum of Science (see p.87), and there's no public access to the building's interior; a small plaque in front reminds visitors that this is where the veterans of the Bay of Pigs stepped ashore after their release from Cuba in 1962.

Just south from here, near the end of Bayshore Drive, Dinner Key can be found, named after a popular early twentieth century picnic spot, while nearby is the former

## THE LIZARD KING TAKES MIAMI

Coconut Grove's famed eccentricity and tolerance made it a natural refuge for hippies in the 1960s – that is, until their mass arrival stirred up the locals, who grumbled about the dozens of stoned teenagers wandering around Peacock Park.

The crackdown on local counterculture began in March 1969, during the infamous Doors concert at the Dinner Key Auditorium, at which Jim Morrison was said to have exposed himself to the crowd. As the story goes, Morrison appeared at the auditorium very late and very drunk, and taunted the more-than-capacity crowd before (allegedly) baring his crotch.

At his trial eighteen months later, Morrison pleaded not guilty and was cleared of the felony charge of lewd and lascivious behavior. However, the doomed rock singer did receive hard labor sentences totaling 240 days for exposure and profanity, which were still under appeal when he died in Paris in July of 1971.

Dinner Key Auditorium, where Jim Morrison was charged with indecent exposure after allegedly dropping his leather trousers onstage in 1969 (see box above) – it's now called the **Coconut Grove Exhibition Center**.

## Villa Vizcaya

**Map 7, I2**. Daily 9.30am–4.30pm, grounds open until 5.30pm; $10, free tours every 40 minutes.

In 1914, farm-machinery mogul James Deering spent $22 million in two years to build his monumental folly, **Villa Vizcaya**, at 3251 S Miami Ave (☏305/250-9133, ⓦwww .vizcayamuseum.org). Every day Deering filled each room of his recreated sixteenth-century Italian villa with fresh flowers, and never let good taste get in the way of acquisition. He and his decorator-in-chief Paul Chalfin spent several summers in Europe cherry-picking dozens of classical, Renaissance and Rococo antiques, all geared to convincing Vizcaya's visitors that the structure was at least 400 years old. Taken individually, the rooms are appealing, but in a single house this orgy of styles is an architectural sugar rush.

---

Deering employed one thousand workers to build Villa Vizcaya: at the time, ten percent of Miami's population.

---

Still, Vizcaya is an unmissable sight: note the spectacular ceiling in the East Hall, the earliest of all in the house, and the master clock in the Butler's Pantry, to which all other clocks at Vizcaya were linked to keep them in sync. Notwithstanding its Spanish name, the house is also another example of Miami's obsession with Venice, notably the waterfront terrazzo and stone barge. The grounds are undeniably beautiful, from the orange jasmine maze garden to the mythological statues lining the walkways. Making the place even more surreal, the walkways are often clogged with teenage girls, enveloped in gloriously over-the-top meringue dresses; they're being officially photographed for their *quince*, the Cuban version of a Sweet Sixteen.

## Museum of Science and Space Transit Planetarium

**Map 7, I1**. Daily 10am–6pm; $10.

Dedicated to making science simple, the **Museum of Science** at 3280 S Miami Ave (☎305/646-4200, ⓦwww.miamisci.org) is great for kids – but less so for adults – with interactive, engaging exhibits, and a rolling program of exhibits and live demonstrations from in-house educators. In its main hall stands the Pan Am Globe which was once the centerpiece of the airline's terminal in Coconut Grove: the museum acquired it in 1960 and, in a fit of political correctness ten years later, repainted it to show geographical features rather than political boundaries.

The **Space Transit Planetarium** features the standard domed auditorium, but its presentations are better than average. There's a **wildlife refuge** attached, which houses the usual injured birds and snakes, although the Seaquarium's a better choice if you want to learn about animal rescue (see p.91, "Key Biscayne and Virginia Key"). Note that the museum is aggressively pushing a move to downtown, into a specially constructed complex shared with the Miami Art Museum.

## La Ermita de la Caridad del Cobre

**Map 7, H2**.

Looking rather like an angular meringue half-dipped in dark chocolate, the modernist church **La Ermita de la Caridad del Cobre** stands near Mercy Hospital at 3609 S Miami Ave, close to the southeastern border of Little

Havana. Named for Cuba's patron saint, the Virgin of Charity, and known affectionately as "La Ermita," the church is the spiritual center of Cuba-in-exile. Built on 10¢ donations from newly arrived immigrants, it was consecrated in 1973 and significantly renovated (this time through $1 donations) twenty-five years later. Iconic and symbolic, every element of the building resonates with the island country: the six concrete columns forming the mantel represent the six traditional provinces that existed before Castro, while beneath the altar, there's Cuban soil, sand and rock, salvaged from a wrecked refugee boat. Finally, an emotive, if patchy, mural behind the altar traces the history of Cuban immigration, and the conical-shaped church is angled to allow worshippers to look out across the bay in the direction of Cuba.

# Key Biscayne and Virginia Key

The island of **Key Biscayne**, with its luxury apartments and enormous mansions, is one of the most desirable addresses in Miami. It's not unusual to see white-uniformed nannies wheeling their charges between condo complexes, and the overall impression is of a secluded and wealthy community that's barely ruffled by its proximity to the city. Most people, though, are drawn here by the **beaches** and **parks**, which are some of the lushest around the city.

So named because the island was thought to be part of the Florida Keys (it isn't), Key Biscayne was settled at the same time as Miami Beach, though as a farming community rather than as a resort. However, when wide-scale agricultural development quickly proved impractical, the island fell largely into the hands of the Matheson family, who had made millions from the chemical industry, providing blue jean dye to Levi's and mustard gas to the US government during World War I. And, once this first wealthy family had made the island their secluded home, Key Biscayne soon became known as an unshowy place where the wealthy could live undisturbed: even President Nixon spent his winters here. Recently, its reputation for seclusion and safety has also attracted rich expats from Latin America, and it's estimated that two thirds of the island's population is now Hispanic.

Unless you have access to a boat, **getting to Key Biscayne** will require taking the soaring Rickenbacker Causeway from downtown ($1 toll for vehicles), which stops off at **Virginia Key** along the way. Since the island was never intended as a resort, services for visitors are still patchy: public transport is almost non-existent – you can take bus #B from downtown (service ends at 7pm), or better still, rent a bike (see p.218, "Sports, fitness and ocean activities). There's also little nightlife other than a couple of local bars, but the beaches and parks are arguably the best in the city. Note too how few tall trees and palms there are on the island – Key Biscayne was the point farthest north to be touched by Hurricane Andrew's devastating force.

# VIRGINIA KEY

Non-residential **Virginia Key** is an unavoidable, if scenic, obstacle on the way to Key Biscayne. The quiet island houses several marine research facilities, as well as the **Miami Seaquarium**. Besides this attraction, there's not much more to do here other than stretch out on fine **Virginia Key Beach** (daily 8am–sunset; $2), signposted from the main road and notable as the location of the first black-designated beach in the city during the time of segregation.

---

If you want to dodge the nominal entrance fee to Virginia Key Beach, tell the guard you're going to *Jimbo's* (see review, p.161) and it will be waived.

---

## Miami Seaquarium

**Map 1, F6**. Daily 9.30am–6pm; adults $23; children age 3–9 $18.

The theme park-style **Miami Seaquarium** is one of the city's major family attractions. It offers the usual performing spectacles, such as those starring Lolita the acrobatic killer whale and a trio of dolphins, who perform tricks to a thumping track of cheesy dance music, as well as education on marine life for interested visitors. Feeding sessions throughout the day are ringmastered by one of the park's rangers, who'll provide detailed background on the animal species in question. The crocodile feeding sessions are especially fun; to see the reptiles at their hungriest and most ferocious, be sure to visit on a hot day, as the sun stimulates their appetites.

The Seaquarium's also one of the foremost marine life rehab centers in the area: especially interesting are the turtles, often rescued from Biscayne Bay after eating plastic bags they've mistaken for jellyfish, and the some half-dozen manatees, a docile yet fiercely intelligent species now under constant threat of injury (and eventual extinction) by modern speedboats.

# KEY BISCAYNE

**Key Biscayne** is roughly divided into three sections, starting with sprawling **Crandon Park**, which, along with a glorious state park at the south end, complete with a weathered lighthouse, sandwiches the small Village of Key Biscayne.

To find out more about the (mostly vanished) historical sites around the island, stop by the **Chamber of Commerce** at 87 W McIntyre (Mon–Fri 9am–5pm; ⓣ305/361-5207, ⓦwww.keybiscaynechamber.org), which can provide an informative map. Other than that, there's little to do in the center of town and most visitors head straight for one of the nearby beaches.

## Crandon Park Beach

**Map 1, F6**. Daily 8am–sunset; $4 per car.

As part of living in one of the best natural settings in Miami, the people of Key Biscayne have access to the finest landscaped beaches in the city – **Crandon Park Beach**, a mile along the main drag, Crandon Boulevard. The three-mile stretch is popular with families, and it's easy to understand why: the golden beach is wide and glorious, and the ocean sandbar reduces waves and eliminates riptide, making swimming safe and easy. However, be advised that on weekends the park is filled by the sounds of boisterous kids and hisses of sizzling barbecues – if it's peace and quiet you're after, you'd do better to head down to the less popular southern coast of the island.

## Bill Baggs Cape Florida State Recreation Area

**Map 1, F7**. Daily 8am–sunset; $4 per car.

The luscious **Bill Baggs Cape Florida State Recreation Area**, named after the late Florida newspaper editor who campaigned for its creation, was leveled by Hurricane Andrew in 1992 – the many exotic plants that were here, such as the shallow-rooted Australian pine, could not withstand the 220mph winds. Ten years on, it's slowly returning to normal through a rigid replanting program, which aims to reintroduce tougher, indigenous species, using as its guide a historical list of vegetation that could be found here in the nineteenth century.

Stretching the park's length, a wide **boardwalk** divides the picnic shelters from the soft, sandy beach. Along the

## STILTSVILLE

A few hundred yards off the southern tip of Key Biscayne, Stiltsville is an undeniable oddity. At the settlement's height, there were 27 houses standing on stilts above the ocean mud-flats: now, only seven remain, their number winnowed down by successive hurricanes. The buildings themselves are nonde-script, except for a jagged wooden ribcage like a row of arrows pointing to the sky.

Stiltsville's origins are murky: some claim that shacks first appeared in the bay as early as the 1920s for Prohibition-era parties, while others maintain that the settlement was erected by local fishermen as a tax dodge in the 1940s. Eventually, it became a regular party venue – one notable institution was the short-lived *Bikini Club*, a bar opened in the early 1960s where any girl in a bikini got a free drink. Either way, it's now techni-cally part of Biscayne National Park (see p.109, "South of the city"), and is caught up in byzantine federal government regu-lations, denied official historic status since none of the original buildings remain and those that still stand are less than fifty years old. Local preservationists have established a Save Our Stiltsville campaign online at ⓦwww.stiltsville.org, but at time of writing, the elevated shantytown's survival is by no means assured.

boardwalk, the concession next to the *Lighthouse Café* has rentals for bikes, rollerblades, ocean kayaks and windsurf boards, as well as deckchairs and umbrellas; you can also bring your tackle and try your luck on one of the eight fishing platforms. The **beach** itself is dotted by natural "umbrellas" of young palm trees – planted after Hurricane Andrew ripped out their predecessors.

At the southernmost tip lies the restored **Cape Florida Lighthouse**, an 1845 replica of one built twenty years pre-viously which was destroyed in the first Seminole War. It's only with the ranger-led **tour** (daily 10am & 1pm; free) that you can climb the 118 steps and visit the lighthouse keeper's original quarters, but the journey to the top is worth it for the clear **views** of Key Biscayne island and South Beach to the north, and the last few huts of **Stiltsville** (see box above) to the south.

# Little Haiti and the Design District

On Miami's run-down north side lie two chunks of the city that have only recently appeared on visitor itineraries: the trendy, avant-garde **Design District** and the vibrant immigrant community of **Little Haiti**. Sights are few and far between in both areas, but a walk around each reveals even more coolness and color in perennially multifaceted Miami.

The Design District has a funky, if somewhat artificial, vibe, and the sales blurb that insists on calling it the next South Beach may be right, at least to some extent: the stores here are swanky and stylish, and developers have made an effort to erect buildings of modern architectural interest. Unlike South Beach, there's relatively little nightlife, or streetlife, really, although that's bound to change as restaurants move in, encouraged by the still comparatively low rent.

On the other hand, Little Haiti is a robust neighborhood that grew up in the last twenty years thanks to the arrival of thousands of Haitian refugees. Though there are few sights here, it's refreshingly authentic and a great place to try cheap, tasty Caribbean food. Economically, though, it's struggling: unlike local Cuban-Americans, Miami's Haitian community has yet to make significant inroads in politics or business – although the city of North Miami Beach did recently elect the first Haitian-American mayor in the country.

The area covered by this chapter is shown in
detail on color map 8, at the back of the book.

# THE DESIGN DISTRICT

The **Design District**, bounded by 36th Street and 41st Street between Miami Avenue and Biscayne Boulevard, was originally a pineapple plantation owned by Theodore Moore, known as the "Pineapple King of Florida." On a whim, Moore opened a furniture showroom in 1921 on NE 40th Street, and had soon created what became known as **Decorators' Row**. During Miami's Art Deco building boom of the 1920s and 1930s, this was the center of the city's design scene, filled with wholesale interiors stores selling furniture and flooring. By the early 1990s, though, the district was derelict, crime-ridden and filled with factories, with only a handful of interiors shops still holding out alongside the *Piccadilly Garden* restaurant (see review, p.153). That's when developer Craig Robins, one of the masterminds behind the gentrification of South Beach, moved in and began buying buildings, spearheading the regeneration process with aggressive plans including an emphasis on public art and sculpture.

He's succeeded: almost overnight, the Design District's main drag along **40th Street** has been reborn as a temple to the *Wallpaper*★ lifestyle of conspicuous but elegant consumption, and the district is now dotted with funky, high-priced houseware boutiques alongside marquee names like Knoll and Holly Hunt. The showrooms are all open to the public, so feel free to browse – although prices are steep enough that browsing's likely all you'll be able to do.

---

The Design District is liveliest during business hours Monday through Saturday, or on Gallery Walk night (dates vary, so check Ⓦ www.designmiami.com for schedule).

---

## The Living Room Building

**Map 8, C9**.
The **Living Room Building**, a neighborhood mascot of sorts for the district, can be found at 4000 Miami Ave, at the junction with 40th Street. A whimsical landmark, with a sense of campy fun that's rare in Miami, the low-rise office building's signature feature is an entranceway that has been turned inside out and decorated with 40-foot walls, a giant concrete couch and oversized lamps, all painted in fruity pinks and oranges. Topping it off, there's even a "painting" on the wall – or, rather, a gloriously simple hole through which the sky and shifting clouds can be seen. Sadly, at time of writing, the building had not yet found a tenant, and so is unopen to the public.

## The Melin Building

**Map 8, D9**.
The headquarters of Robins' real estate firm is located inside the enormous **Melin Building**, at 3930 NE 2nd Ave, where the thing to see is the sculptural oddity in the atrium. It's a giant hybrid shoe-gondola, designed to fit the Statue of Liberty's foot, and created by Antoni Miralda for the Venice Biennale art show in the early 1990s. Truly

bizarre, the high-heeled sculpture has a black lacquer body flecked with foamy silver appliqué shapes, and a slatted, reinforced interior like that of a boat.

---

A pleasant café owned by Miralda, the *Meeting Point* overlooks his sculpture.

---

## The Rubell Collection

Open Thurs–Sat, call for hours.

Just south of the Design District proper, the **Rubell Collection** is housed in a cavernous lemon-yellow warehouse – once used by the DEA to store evidence – at 95 NW 29th St (☎305/573-6090). Owned by the Rubell family, who also run the *Albion* and *Beach House* hotels in Miami Beach (see reviews, p.115 and p.121), it's a superb display space for one of the best modern art collections in the country. Here, the family displays just a fraction of their vast acquisitions, having spent the last thirty years snapping up an eclectic mix of oddities and masterpieces by American and international artists. There's work by photographer Cindy Sherman, including one of her earliest photographs, plus punk modernist Jeff Koons, the late Jean-Michel Basquiat and graffiti master Keith Haring, whom the Rubells championed early on in his career. Alongside the big names sit many lesser-known but equally interesting pieces by tomorrow's superstars – don't miss the filigree paper collages by British artist David Thorpe.

---

The Rubell Collection is scheduled to move to an even larger site in North Miami sometime in 2003; call to check the current location before heading over.

---

THE DESIGN DISTRICT

# LITTLE HAITI

Impervious to the needs of outsiders, **Little Haiti** is a residential neighborhood rarely visited by casual tourists. Unlike in Little Havana, though, here – the area bounded on the east and west by Biscayne Boulevard and I-95, from 40th Street to 85th Street – you'll find an undiluted immigrant neighborhood, whose residents live, shop and work within its confines. Streetside signage is in both English and Kreyol, and you'll also hear French spoken in some stores. To get some of the local flavor it's best to wander along the central drag of **NE 2nd Avenue**, and simply enjoy the Caribbean colors, music and smells. Do be mindful, though: the area is relatively safe, but it's still a good idea to stick to both the main streets and the daytime.

## NE 2nd Avenue

**Map 8, D2–D8**.

With buildings painted in ripe, fruity colors of raspberry and lime, and daubed with hand-written signage, not to mention music blaring out of the odd record store, **NE 2nd Avenue** has a distinct Caribbean feel to it. Adding to the effect is the brightly colored ironwork of the **Caribbean Marketplace**, at no. 5927, designed as an urban renewal project to showcase Caribbean crafts while drawing tourist dollars to the area. Unfortunately, the bank foreclosed on the venture due to bad management, and the Marketplace is now in commercial limbo.

----

You can't miss the enormous Union Jack
painted on local landmark *Churchill's Hideaway*;
for a review of this bar/club, see p.161.

----

Don't be surprised to see chickens wandering round among the pigeons at the unnamed park three blocks north at 62nd Street, which marks one of the hubs of the neighborhood. Next to the park stands the simple, modernist **Notre Dame Church**, which acted as a processing center for the stream of Haitian immigrants who arrived in Miami in the late 1970s. The church is still at the heart of the neighborhood, attached to the Pierre Toussaint Center, which provides everything from medical care to job listings for local residents.

## The Dupuis Building

**Map 8, D5**.

Near the park on the corner of 62nd Street and NE 2nd Avenue, one of the oldest houses in Miami, the **Dupuis Building**, sits in what was once the heart of Lemon City. This white porticoed structure, built in 1902, first housed Lemon City's doctor and pharmacy. Later it was turned into the local post office before finally being abandoned several decades ago. Now derelict, it's still a rare remaining sign of how early European settlement took place here.

## Fifty-fourth Street

**Map 8, C6–D6**.

The heart of Miami's *voudou* and *santeria* culture is **54th Street**, especially along the blocks immediately west of NE 2nd Avenue, where it's lined with several *botanicas*, where believers can purchase ritual potions, candles and statuettes. Almost all will permit a casual visitor to browse their merchandise, although the (mostly female) owners are notoriously tight-lipped with strangers. It goes without saying that photographing the racks of gaudy statuary and glass jars packed with herbs is both rude and foolish.

## SANTERIA

A secretive Caribbean religion with an oral tradition, santeria was one of the many spiritual hybrids created by colonial rule. Slaves, brought from their homes in Africa to the New World, were forcibly baptized and converted to Christianity – although this conversion proved to be largely cosmetic. To preserve their own religions, the gods, or *orishas*, in the African pantheon were "translated" into Christian saints, so that they could be worshipped without fear of reprisal. Even the name *santeria* began as slang, when colonial Spaniards noticed how greatly their African slaves venerated the saints rather than Christ.

Much like the gods of Ancient Greece, *orishas* have flaws and favorites: each is identified with a given color, food and number, and all require animal sacrifices and human praise for nourishment. Altars in *santeria* temples will often be covered with offerings of cigarettes or designer perfume – the *orishas* are apparently all too human in their vulnerability to flattery and expensive gifts. Religious services, conducted in secret by a priest or priestess, involve channeling the gods through dances and hypnotic trance.

Estimated numbers of those practicing *santeria* worldwide vary wildly, from 60,000 up to 5,000,000; regardless, it has a hidden but powerful role in local Miami society, as many people are at least part-time believers. Wandering round the city, you'll see signs of *santeria* activity if you look hard enough – streetside offerings, usually nailed to holy kapok trees, are common in Little Havana and Little Haiti.

SANTERIA

# South of the city

Few visitors venture into the polished suburbs that sprawl out to the **south of Miami**, but it's here you'll sense a distinctly Floridian feel to life, a slower pace that's dominated by the land, as opposed to the breathless, international vibe of urban Miami. Parks and gardens abound, as well as some of the city's most idiosyncratic attractions, scattered nearby meandering Old Cutler Road and **Highway 1** – or the South Dixie Highway, as it's also known – as it carves its way down to agricultural **Homestead** and, finally, Florida City and the Keys.

Touring this area is **impractical without a car**, for while there is fragmented local bus service in each town, little public transport joins the centers. It's better to rent a car (for rental companies, see "Directory," p.223) and shuttle between the attractions – you can easily take in most of what the region has to offer in two days or so – and then, if you're so inclined, head down to the Keys. Also, note that along Highway 1 it's best to **stick to the main route**, as the latticework of roads that quilts the surrounding area is poorly signposted and easy to get lost within.

## SOUTH TO HOMESTEAD

As Coral Gables and Coconut Grove give way to **South**

**Miami**, the architecture grows more modern but the suburban houses stay just as big. Around **Old Cutler Road**, a pleasing drive from Coconut Grove through a thick belt of woodland, you'll find a series of worthy sights, beginning with the **Fairchild Tropical Garden**, with its showy collection of exotic plants; nearby, the **Charles Deering Estate** offers a dignified taste of pioneer wealth.

Further west, just a short detour over the Florida's Turnpike, the **Miami Metrozoo** is an enormous, sophisticated facility that's home to hundreds of "wild" animals. South from here, off either the Turnpike or Highway 1, **186th Street** is lined with garden centers and greenhouses selling pricey tropical plants, while one block further down there's the vast, 30-acre **Fruit and Spice Park**. Finally, the last sight before arriving at farming-centric Homestead is **Monkey Jungle**, where the visitors are in cages and the monkeys roam free.

## Fairchild Tropical Garden

**Map 1, D7**. Daily 9.30am–4.30pm; tram tours every hour until 3pm; adults $8, children 3–12 $4, children under 3 free; 1st Wed of month is Contribution Day – visitors set own admission fee.

On the far southern fringe of Coconut Grove, in Matheson Hammock Park, lies the **Fairchild Tropical Garden**, at 10901 Old Cutler Rd (☏305/667-1651, ⓦwww .fairchildgarden.org). Founded on the site of a former mango plantation, the Garden was built to be a living encyclopedia of exotic plants for locals, and resident scientists still scour the world for unusual or endangered species to add to the collection.

The easiest way to take in the 83-acre garden is on one of the 45-minute **tram tours**. The tour winds through the Garden's different habitats, including a fine collection of rare plants from the Bahamas and the Tropical Rainforest area, specially watered by an ingenious tree irrigation system. That said, it's the Windows to the Tropics hothouse that's perhaps the biggest draw, filled with beautiful bromeliads, orchids and other sensitive plants. It also houses the Garden's most famous resident, "Mr Stinky," a six-foot-high Sumatran *amorphophallus titanum* that made headlines in 1998 thanks to the rare blooming of its giant flower that's been described as smelling like "rotting elephant corpse."

## The Deering Estate

**Map 1, C8**. Daily 10am–5pm, last admission 4pm; estate tours daily 10.30am, 12.45pm, 3pm, house tours daily 11.45am, 2pm, 4.15pm; adults $6, children under 17 $4.

Even though Charles Deering's half-brother James was the mastermind behind Villa Vizcaya (see p.86), the rustic **Deering Estate**, at 16701 SW 72nd Ave (☏305/235-1668, ⊛www.deeringestate.com), could not be more different from Vizcaya's opulent excess. While James wanted fountains and formal gardens, Charles set about creating an estate that would preserve the area's natural vegetation. He bought the moribund town of **Cutler**, bypassed by Flagler's railroad, and tore it down, sparing only one building, Richmond Cottage, which he modernized and electrified, and then built an adjoining house to hold his multi-million-dollar art collection; both were done in the Mediterranean Revival style, with a strong Moorish influence: the façade was built from oolitic limestone that erodes well and produces an illusion of age.

Unfortunately, there's little to see inside either structure, as Deering donated his art collection to the Art Institute of Chicago after the hurricane of 1926 and his daughters sold off much of the furniture once their mother died. However, the estate is a tranquil bolthole from the ritz of the rest of Miami, ideal for an afternoon spent reading a book by the ocean on its sweeping front lawns. Free **ranger-guided trips** into the woodland hammock on four-wheel-drive golf carts are fascinating, taking in avocado groves, local plants and a 1500-year-old Tequesta burial mound where human remains dating back 10,000 years have been found.

---

Chicken Key, just offshore from the Deering Estate, is so named because it was used as a poultry pen by Native Americans; the Deering Estate runs daily canoe tours out to the Key for $20 – call for details.

---

## Miami Metrozoo

Daily 9.30am–5.30pm, last admission 4pm; adults $8.95, children 3–12 $4.75, children under 3 free; tram tour $2.

Just west of Florida's Turnpike, the **Miami Metrozoo**, at 12400 SW 152nd St (☎305/251-0401, ⍉www.miamimetrozoo.com), is a vast compound where dozens of species are grouped according to their native continent: there are familiar animals, like giraffes and ostriches, alongside less commonplace creatures such as the llama-like guanaco and the anoa, which resembles a small buffalo. It's well designed, too, with humane, open enclosures – more moat-and-hill than fence-and-cage – and the frequent plaques employed to detail each species' survival status is a great educational opportunity for kids.

It's best to arrive early, as most of the animals are liveliest before the baking midday sun takes hold; visitors, though, can hop onto the air-conditioned monorail that runs through the park if the heat becomes unbearable. Attraction-wise, there's a rolling schedule of feeding demonstrations, which offers a chance to talk with the animals' knowledgeable keepers; the zoo's famous group of white Bengal tigers (only one of which is actually white) is fed at 11am.

## Fruit and Spice Park

Daily 10am–5pm; free tours at 11am, 2pm, 2.30pm; $3.50.

As the name suggests, the **Fruit and Spice Park**, at 24801 SW 187th St (☎305/247-5727, ⓦhttp://co.miami-dade .fl.us/parks/fruitandspice.htm), houses exotic fruit and spice plants – 30 acres of them in all. The different fruits and plants are grouped together by species or theme – for example, there's an oddball banana plantation that showcases fifty different varieties, as well as a poisonous plant patch, carefully screened off from visitors. There's even a citrus quarantine to keep their specimens safe in response to the devastation wrought locally by blight. Disappointingly, though, there are no maps available for those who'd rather walk through the grounds unaccompanied, and labeling of plants is also spotty, so the park's a must-see for avid garden-ers and plant fanciers only.

## Monkey Jungle

Daily 9.30–5pm, last admission 4pm; adults $15.95, children 3–9 $9.95, children under 3 free, senior citizens (65+) $12.95.

An amateur primate behaviorist first set up this park at 14805 SW 216th St to observe monkeys in the wild; when funding got tight, he began charging admission, and **Monkey Jungle** was born (☎305/235-1611, ⓦwww.mon-keyjungle.com). Now there are thirty species living here – supposedly with the twist that the monkeys roam free, while humans visit in caged walkways. It's a diverting, if not especially informative, biopark: in fact, plenty of the mon-keys *are* in cages, and signage is infrequent. Bring quarters to feed the animals: in a clever touch, dishes dangle from chains over the walkways, which the monkeys have learned to reel in like fishermen once a passing human has stocked a platter with seeds.

# HOMESTEAD AND AROUND

Decimated when the nearby airforce base closed down, **Homestead** has now been hit hard by citrus blight, and the area's definitely seen better times (see box below). One positive by-product of its agricultural economy, though, is a thriving "**pick your own**" business, where for a nominal cost per pound you can pick produce to take home – look out for the roadside signs. In addition, the town is filled

## HURRICANE ANDREW VS. HOMESTEAD

Homestead hit the headlines around a decade ago for all the wrong reasons: it was here that Hurricane Andrew hit with full force on August 24, 1992. Although a comparatively compact storm, its winds reached speeds of more than 200mph – at least, that's the estimated force, as the official windspeed gauge broke at 164mph.

The three towns of Homestead, Florida City and Naranja were puréed, and Homestead Air Force Base was also wrecked – it later closed, with a devastating effect on the local community. Once the storm passed on, it had left 60,000 houses destroyed, 200,000 people homeless and damage that would cost an estimated $20 billion to repair – one of the greatest natural disasters in modern American history.

Since then, the physical scars have healed – buildings have been reconstructed in the towns and farmland has been replanted. However, the economic wound is still bleeding, with Homestead and the surrounding area still struggling to thrive, providing a gritty glimpse of Florida life.

HOMESTEAD AND AROUND

with itinerant fruitpickers, lending it a sort of bordertown transience: to take a look around – though there's not much to see – follow Krome Avenue south to reach the center of town.

The last two places of interest before Hwy-1 curves down to the Keys are the twin delights of the eerie, magical **Coral Castle** and the mostly-underwater **Biscayne National Park**, a must-visit for any snorkel or dive enthusiast.

Note that if you're headed to the Keys after visiting sights in the area, a good place to stop overnight is in Florida City, just further south along Hwy-1, where things are perkier than in Homestead: in a smart move, the town's refashioned itself into a sort of **gateway to the Keys** for holidaymakers, thereby lessening its reliance on fruit farming, and bolstering the local economy.

## Coral Castle

Daily 7am–9pm; adults $9.75, children 7–12 $5, children 6 and under free, senior citizens (62+) $6.50.

The **Coral Castle**, a memorable – if tacky – stop-off at 28655 South Dixie Highway (℡305/248-6345, ⓦwww .coralcastle.com), is as unique and odd as the story behind it. Ed Leedskalnin, a 5-foot-tall, 100-pound immigrant, allegedly built it as a tribute to the 16-year-old fiancee who jilted him in his home country of Latvia. Leaving heartbroken, he traveled the world, working as a stonemason, logger and rancher, and eventually found himself in Florida. Buying land near Homestead, he quarried coral rock from his land and, singlehandedly, used this rock to build a simple house as well as an ornamental garden decorated with crescent moons and heart-shaped tables.

No one knows how this tiny man moved such massive blocks of stone: he worked at night, and never revealed his methodology to anyone before dying in 1951. Engineers have consistently scoffed at his feats, before trying and failing to replicate them – scientists are still baffled by the nine-ton gate, for example, which can be moved with a hefty push from a single finger.

The esoteric iconography of the Coral Castle is pegged to Leedskalnin's fascination with astronomy, astrology and ancient Egypt. He used divining rods to check the area's alignment with ley lines, or supposed linear configurations of ancient sites, and surprisingly, electromagnetic testing has confirmed their presence – there's a cluster that's especially thick around the Moon Pond. This has made the Coral Castle an important site for local New Agers, and there have even been several Wiccan "baptisms" on the site.

## Biscayne National Park

Water portion open 24 hours a day, Convoy Point daily (except Christmas) 8am–5.30pm, Visitor Center 8.30am–5pm.

Unique among national parks since 95 percent of it is underwater, **Biscayne National Park**, at 9700 SW 328th St (℡305/230-7275, ⊛www.nps.gov/bisc), is well worth the 20-minute detour. Technically, the Florida Keys begin here with the tiny Boca Chita Key, and the **reef** in this park is the same **coral formation** that draws enthusiastic snorkelers and divers to the John Pennekamp State Park (see p.252) off Key Largo. Ironically, it's better preserved and more spectacular here than at the well-known dive sites further down the coast: stop by the excellent **visitor center** at Convoy Point for detailed information.

There's only one company running **trips to the reefs** (℡305/230-1100, ✉dive970@aol.com), while options for seeing the park include a three-hour **glass-bottomed boat tour** (daily, departs 10am; $20), a **snorkel trip** (Mon–Fri 10am & 1.30pm, Sat–Sun 1.30pm; $30) or a

HOMESTEAD AND AROUND

**sunset cruise** (Fri–Sun in season, check for times; $13). Overnight **camping** is permitted on Elliott Key and Boca Chita Key, although facilities are basic, so bring everything you'll need (Nov–May; round-trip boat ride $25).

# LISTINGS

LISTINGS

# Accommodation

**M**iami has plenty of **accommodation** to suit travelers of every budget, from chic boutiques to homey hotels, as well as a smattering of hostels. Starting prices for hotels hover around $100, and will rocket in high season (January–March) or when major conventions are in town. A smart alternative is to come in May or December – rates will be much lower, and, although the weather can be variable, it should be beachworthy most days. Also, if you're hoping to see Miami without renting a car, it makes most sense to stay downtown or on South Beach, as connections by bus are most regular to these areas.

Unsurprisingly, a huge percentage of the hotels and guest houses are clustered together on **South Beach**, most of them lining two streets, **Ocean Drive** and **Collins Avenue**. All the chic boutique hotels are here, as well as the funkier chain outposts. There's also the added thrill of staying in one of the many photo-ready Deco masterpieces – but do remember that Deco hotels were built in a different era, and rooms can be tiny.

Heading north, the enormous 1950s hotels in **Central Miami Beach**, like the *Fontainebleau* and the *Eden Roc*, make fun, kitschy places to stay for any would-be Rat Packer. There's a smaller selection of pleasant places in **Coconut Grove** and **Coral Gables**, though no incredibly

## ACCOMMODATION PRICE CODES

Accommodation prices quoted below are according to the cost of the least expensive double room in low season. High season runs from January to March, with shoulders in December and April to May. July and August is when rooms are cheapest – though don't be afraid to bargain out of season. Remember that an additional 10 percent or so in hotel taxes will be added on to your bill.

- ❶ up to $40
- ❷ $40–60
- ❸ $60–80
- ❹ $80–100
- ❺ $100–130
- ❻ $130–170
- ❼ $170–225
- ❽ $225–300
- ❾ more than $300

compelling reason to stay in either neighborhood. Otherwise, **downtown** is crowded with sub-par or over-priced chain hotels while **Little Havana**, **Little Haiti** and the **Design District** are not yet geared to providing visitor accommodation. If you're planning on spending a few days in Miami before heading down to the Keys, it's worth considering one of the guesthouses around **Homestead** or **Florida City** – although be aware that the trip to South Beach is quite a hike.

# HOTELS AND GUESTHOUSES

## DOWNTOWN

------------------------

### Best Western Marina Park

**Map 2, F5**. 340 Biscayne Blvd
☏ 305/371-4400 or 1-800/528-1234, ⓦ www.bestwestern.com/marinaparkhotel.
Conveniently located near all the major attractions and public transport, this is an above-average option – especially given the rather

ratty other chain outposts downtown – with clean, large rooms close to the waterfront. ❸

## Intercontinental

**Map 2, G7**. 100 Chopin Plaza ⓣ 305/577-1000, ⓦ www.intercontinental.com. The pick of downtown's chain hotels, this *Intercontinental* high-rise features spectacular views of Biscayne Bay and the Port of Miami. The rooms themselves are stylishly furnished, with good amenities for business travelers like power outlets built into the desktops. ❻

## SOUTH BEACH

## Albion

**Map 3, F2**. 1650 James Ave ⓣ 1-877/RUBELLS or 305/913-1000, ⓦ www.rubellhotels.com. A sensitive conversion of a classic Nautical Deco building, this is one of the best hotels in the city, thanks to its affable, unflappable staff, gorgeously simple rooms and a whimsical, elevated pool

that has portholes cut into its sides. ❻

--------------------

**For a review of the *Albion*'s hotel bar, *The Fallabella*, see p.163.**

--------------------

## Aqua

**Map 3, F3**. 1530 Collins Ave ⓣ 305/538-4361, ⓦ www.aquamiami.com. This recent motel conversion has preserved little other than the original *Sea Deck* sign out front. The superb, spartan-chic rooms have raw concrete floors with tart tangerine and bright blue accents – IKEA-inspired, funky and stylish. All rooms look over a tranquil courtyard, and there's a private sundeck, too. ❹

## Hotel Astor

**Map 3, E5**. 956 Washington Ave ⓣ 1-800/270-4981 or 305/531-8081. Famous for its Sunday gospel brunch (see review p.140), the *Astor* is distinguished from other boutique hotels by its staff – easy-going and helpful, they're renowned on the strip, and regulars rave that they're *the* reason to stay at the *Astor*. As for the rooms, they're standardly stylish with all the modern conveniences. ❺

## Best Western South Beach

**Map 3, E5**. 1020 Washington Ave Ⓣ 305/532-1930, Ⓦ www.bestwestern.com. A cluster of four hotels (the *Kenmore*, *Taft*, *Bel Aire* and *Park Washington*) owned and operated by Best Western. The rooms have been renovated to remove all character, but amenities have been added; ask for a junior suite in the *Taft* building, as those rooms have kitchenettes at no additional cost. ❹

## Brigham Gardens Guesthouse

**Map 3, F4**. 1411 Collins Ave Ⓣ 305/531-1331, Ⓦ www.brighamgardens.com. The *Guesthouse* is actually a cluster of buildings crowding round a shady courtyard, and is one of the best low-cost options in the area, with friendly management and an onsite laundry. Quirky,

individual rooms have an eccentric, Caribbean feel thanks to delightfully mismatched furniture; fully equipped kitchenettes in the studio rooms are worth the extra expense. Hotel room ❸, off-season studio ❹

## Delano

**Map 3, G2**. 1685 Collins Ave Ⓣ 305/672-2000, Ⓦ www.ianschragerhotels.com. Schrager-owned and Starck-designed, this celebrity hangout is still hot, but cooling. The all-white rooms have Starck's signature witty touches – witness the single green apple left for you on its own sconce "to keep the doctor away." There's snob value in staying here and the bar is still a scene, but the staff can be snotty and the service touch-and-go. ❼

- - - - - - - - - - - - - - - - -
For a review of the *Rose Bar*, in the *Delano* hotel, see p.162.
- - - - - - - - - - - - - - - - -

## Doubletree Surfcomber

**Map 3, G2**. 1717 Collins Ave Ⓣ 305/532-7715 or 1-800/222-

TREE, Ⓦ www.doubletree.com.
A fashion and media favorite,
this unassuming hotel has
direct beach access, a full-sized
pool and spacious, airy rooms.
Camera crews often use its
terrace to film TV shows, and
– a good vote of confidence –
it's one of the places that
locals will lodge their relatives
when they visit. ⑥

## Essex House

**Map 3, F5**. 1001 Collins Ave
Ⓣ 305/534-2700 or 1-800/553-
7739, Ⓦ www.coralcollection
.com.
The *Essex House* has bland,
corporate-style rooms which
are luxurious but could be
anywhere. The building,
though, is a gem, with a
superbly restored Egyptian
Deco lobby – plus, the
management is friendly. ⑤

## Fairwind Hotel

**Map 3, F5**. 1000 Collins Ave
Ⓣ 305/531-0050,
Ⓦ www.fairwindhotel.com.
A good mid-range option,
the *Fairwind* offers basic,
brightly colored rooms that
are clean and convenient –
but watch out for the noisy

bar/restaurant in the hotel's
courtyard; ask for a quiet
room when you book. This
hotel was known as the
*Fairmont* for more than fifty
years, before a lawsuit from
the well-known chain forced
the owners to alter their
signage in the late 1990s. ③

## Henry Hotel

**Map 3, E7**. 536 Washington
Ave Ⓣ 305/672-2511 or
1-800/253-5346,
Ⓦ www.henryhotelsonsobe.com.
The *Henry Hotel* offers
reasonably priced, basic
rooms with the look of a
high-end 1970s motel, with
in-window AC, linoleum
floors and free continental
breakfast. It's also right by the
beach, and management is
flexible on rates depending
on the season. ③

## Hideaway Suites

**Map 3, F6**. 751 Collins Ave
Ⓣ 305/538-5955 or 1-888/881-
5955, Ⓔ reserve@hideawaysuites
.com.
Arguably the best budget deal
on the beach, each suite in
this tiny 10-room hotel has a
fully-equipped, modern

kitchen, bright, simply decorated sleeping areas, sparkling bathrooms and, best of all, its own washer and dryer. Book well ahead in high season. **④**

## The Hotel

**Map 3, F6**. 801 Collins Ave ⓣ 305/531-2222, ⓦ www .thehotelofsouthbeach.com. Designer Todd Oldham oversaw every element in this jewel-like hotel's renovation, using zesty colors on everything from the lobby to the bathrobes. The luxurious rooms are like a millionaire's tropical hideaway, their stylish look only part of a thoughtful aesthetic of smart improvements – for example, the shower control is not under the shower head, so you won't have to scald yourself every time you turn on the water. Expensive, but a treat. **⑧**

## Kent Hotel

**Map 3, F5**. 1131 Collins Ave ⓣ 305/604-5068 or 1-800/OUTPOST, ⓦ www.thekenthotel.com. Famed 1960s fashion designer

Barbara Hulanicki has created a crazy, lavender-and-lucite trip in this renovated Deco hotel. There's lots of brushed steel in the rooms, which are comfortable, if a little dark thanks to their smallish windows. The Lucite Suite, where all furniture is made from transparent plastic, is extraordinary, while the small onsite garden, crowded with tropical plants, is a pleasant, shady place to spend an afternoon. **⑤**

## Lily Guesthouse

**Map 3, F6**. 835 Collins Ave ⓣ 305/535-9900, ⓦ www.southbeachgroup.com. Owned by the same people as the *Shelley* (see opposite) the *Lily* has bigger rooms but more basic furniture, and can be noisy, as several of the suites are on the roadside ground floor. The rooms all have fridges and CD players, though, and it's still well-situated for a night out. **④**

## The Loft Hotel

**Map 3, F5**. 952 Collins Ave ⓣ 305/534-2244, ⓦ www.thelofthotel.com.

A sleek low-rise building converted from apartments, the *Loft* has a chic, rather LA feel with modern, wrought-iron furniture and an airy garden. Its rooms all have kitchenettes and it manages to be both stylish and affordable. ❹

### The Marlin

**Map 3, F4**. 1200 Collins Ave
Ⓣ 305/604-5063 or
1-800/OUTPOST,
Ⓦ www.themarlinhotel.com.
The rooms here are decked out like a fading rockstar's bedroom (in fact, Aerosmith's Steven Tyler often stays here): they combine enormous beds with hi-tech gadgets, faux African linens and plenty of brushed steel. Not the hotspot it once was, but if your idea of South Beach is expensive, flashy trash, the *Marlin's* your place. Offseason studio ❼

- - - - - - - - - - - - - - - - - - - -
For a review of the *Marlin Bar*, see p.163.
- - - - - - - - - - - - - - - - - - - -

### Hotel Nash

**Map 3, F5**. 1120 Collins Ave

Ⓣ 305/674-7800,
Ⓦ www.hotelnash.com.
Recently renovated, the *Hotel Nash* is understated and elegant, its deluxe rooms fitted out in Calvin Klein–style luxury, awash with shades of taupe, mushroom and white. The South Beach outpost of the over-hyped restaurant, *Mark's*, is just off its lobby, too. ❻

### Nassau Suite Hotel

**Map 3, F4**. 1414 Collins Ave
Ⓣ 305/532-0043 or 1-866/859-4177, Ⓦ www.nassausuite.com.
There's a definite Bahamian feel to this hotel's large rooms, thanks to the airy decor washed in blues and whites. Not a hotspot, but an elegant bolthole amid the frenzy of the beach. ❻

### The Park Central

**Map 3, F6**. 640 Ocean Drive
Ⓣ 1-800/727-5236,
Ⓦ www.theparkcentral.com.
The *Park Central* was one of the first hotels to be reborn during the South Beach renaissance of the early 1990s. Now the rooms, with crisp white linens and pale green

walls, have a colonial safari feel – the black-and-white photographs throughout add to the effect. There's also a sky-high roof deck for sunbathing and sightseeing. ⑤

## Pelican Hotel

**Map 3, F6**. 826 Ocean Drive ⓣ305/673-3373, ⓦwww.pelicanhotel.com. Owned by the Italian jeanswear company Diesel, the *Pelican* injects a welcome touch of campy humor into the earnest coolness of South Beach. Each room is themed, with either refurbished flea market finds or specially constructed furniture: try the "Deco(cktail)" room for a touch of Twenties glamour, or the "Best Little Whorehouse" room, with deep red wallpaper and plenty of lush black lace. ⑥

## Shelborne

**Map 3, G2**. 1801 Collins Ave ⓣ305/531-1271 or 1-800/327-8757, ⓦwww.shelbourne.com. Site of the early Miss Universe pageants, the *Shelborne* offers all the usual amenities and is well located at the northern end of the beach, right on the ocean. The rooms are unremarkable, but have small kitchenettes. ⑥

## Hotel Shelley

**Map 3, F5**. 844 Collins Ave ⓣ305/531-3341 or 1-800/414-0612, ⓦwww.shelleyhotel.com. A budget boutique hotel, the *Shelley* is spartan but stylish, with the usual all-white rooms. There are some great comp add-ons, like a free open bar every night from 6 to 10pm and free Crunch gym passes, but there's no elevator, so don't stay here unless you travel light. Rates are often reduced on negotiation; it's owned by the same group as the nearby *Whitelaw* and *Chelsea*. ⑤

## Townhouse

**Map 3, G1**. 150 20th St ⓣ305/534-3800 or 1-877/534-3800, ⓦwww.townhousehotel.com. Many boutique hotels promise much but deliver little – *Townhouse* is an exception. Stark, white (of course) rooms are well thought-out and comfortable;

the staff is attentive but laid-back, and there's an indulgent roofdeck filled with crimson waterbeds for sybaritic sunbathing. ❹

## Villa Paradiso

**Map 3, F4**. 1415 Collins Ave
ⓣ 305/532-0616,
ⓔ villap@gate.net.
A sister hotel to the *Loft* (see p.118), *Villa Paradiso* is more basic and retro than its sibling – think *Miami Vice* décor and leather futons. However, the place is clean, the rooms are large, and all have their own kitchenettes – plus there's even an onsite coin laundry. Good discounts for longer stays. ❸

## Whitelaw Hotel

**Map 3, F6**. 808 Collins Ave
ⓣ 305/398-7000 or 1-888/554-3123, ⓦ www.southbeachgroup .com/whitelaw.shtml.
The *Whitelaw* has stylish, slightly self-conscious rooms complete with CD players and some good add-ons are offered, too, such as free airport pick-up and an open bar in the hotel every night. ❺

## Winterhaven

**Map 3, F4**. 1400 Ocean Drive
ⓣ 305/531-5571 or 1-800/395-2322.
The *Winterhaven* is one of the best values on the beachfront, and the rooms here are standard and comfortable enough. The real draw, though, is the lobby, restored to an identical replica of its original design – notice especially the antique etched mirrors and terrazzo floor. ❹

## CENTRAL MIAMI BEACH AND NORTH

------------------------

## Beach House Bal Harbour

**Map 1, G3**. 9449 Collins Ave
ⓣ 1-877/RUBELLS,
ⓦ www.rubellhotels.com.
This chic and cheeky hotel feels more like a Hamptons summer share in Long Island than a Miami cabana. Sweet, whimsical touches abound (like a cookie jar at check-in), and the rooms themselves are big, bright and comfy. ❻

## Eden Roc

**Map 4, G3**. 4525 Collins Ave

SOUTH BEACH • CENTRAL MIAMI BEACH AND NORTH

ⓣ 305/531-0000 or 1-800/327-8337, ⓦ www.edenrocresort.com.

Now owned and operated by hotel giant Marriott, the *Eden Roc* has fully renovated rooms with standard, rather garish decor. Its greatest draw is its lobby, which alone of all the Miami Modern hotels has retained a feel of sleek Fifties glamour, with huge sofas and curvy stonework – though it's a pity about the snooty staff. ⓺

### Fontainebleau

**Map 4, G3**. 4441 Collins Ave
ⓣ 305/538-2000,
ⓦ www.fontainebleau.hilton.com.
Once the ground zero of cool in the 1950s (see p.53, "Central Miami Beach and north") this hotel hosted Lucille Ball, Sinatra and Elvis, among others. Now, it's been haphazardly renovated – the multiple lobbies still show scattered Miami Modern touches, but the large rooms have been completely overhauled: they're comfortable, corporate and lack any quirky touches. This is a favorite place for families, since it stands in enormous

grounds, and there's a children's play area and pool designed around a large fiberglass octopus. ⓻

### Roney Palace

**Map 4, E8**. 2399 Collins Ave
ⓣ 305/604-1000,
ⓦ www.roney-palace.com.
Part condo building, part hotel, the *Roney Palace* has one major plus: its rooms are arguably the largest on the beach, with kitchens, living rooms and walk-in closets; many also have ocean-facing balconies. It's a little out of the way, but a smart choice for four or more people. ⓼

## LITTLE HAVANA

### Miami River Inn

**Map 5, G3**. 118 SW South River Drive ⓣ 305/325-0045 or 1-800/HOTEL-89,
ⓦ www.miamiriverinn.com.
The charming, offbeat *Miami River Inn*, a cluster of old buildings set around a secluded courtyard and small pool, is more like a B&B than a hotel – rooms are furnished in a floral country style, with

antique beds and dressers, and there's a self-service homemade breakfast every morning. As it's somewhat off the beaten path, though, you really need a car to stay here. ❸

## CORAL GABLES

### Biltmore

**Map 6, B5**. 1200 Anastasia Ave ℗ 305/445-1926 or 1-800/727-1926,

ⓦ www.biltmorehotel.com. Miami's first grand hotel has been thoroughly restored – rooms are luxurious but unremarkable, though the giant chevron-shaped pool and onsite golf course are major pluses. ❼

---

For a more in-depth account of the *Biltmore*, see p.74, "Coral Gables."

---

### Gables Inn

**Map 6, E5**. 730 S Dixie Hwy ℗ 305/661-7999, ⓔ thegablesinn@aol.com. Coral Gables' version of a budget hotel, the *Gables Inn* is Mediterranean Revival in

style, with arched walkways painted a deep ochre, and *Biltmore*-lite rooms: plenty of bottle-green and dark wood, but this time with a linoleum floor. One of the few cheaper options in the area, it's located directly on Hwy-1 (or the South Dixie Hwy), so it can be noisy. ❸

### Hotel St Michel

**Map 6, G3**. 162 Alcazar Ave ℗ 305/444-1666 or 1-800/848-HOTEL,

ⓦ www.hotelplacestmichel.com. Country-style rooms in a small, charming hotel minutes from the center of Coral Gables. There are gold fixtures, mixed antiques and overstuffed sofas in each room – even the elevator is vintage, complete with a sliding grill and hand operation. ❺

## COCONUT GROVE

### Doubletree Coconut Grove

**Map 7, C6**. 2649 S Bayshore Drive ℗ 305/858-2500 or 1-800/222-TREE,

Ⓦ www.doubletree.com.
Formerly the *Coconut Grove Hotel*, this place has undergone a grandiose renovation, all dark wood and deep carpets. The rooms are large and nondescript: many look out over the bay, while some have balconies and small kitchenettes. ❹

## Hampton Inn

**Map 7, C3**. 2800 SW 28th Terrace Ⓣ 305/448-2800, Ⓦ www.hamptoninns-florida.com.
Basic but bright accommodation geared to the budget business traveler. Free local calls, onsite coin laundry and complimentary continental breakfast make this a good base for exploring away from the beach. ❹

## KEY BISCAYNE

## Sonesta Beach Resort

**Map 1, F7**. 350 Ocean Drive Ⓣ 305/361-2021, Ⓦ www .sonesta.com/keybiscayne.
The Miami outpost of this family luxury chain has its own private beach and

convenient facilities, but it's a little careworn at the edges – make sure to ask for a renovated room, which will be brighter and have more modern furniture. ❼

## Silver Sands Beach Resort

**Map 1, F7**. 301 Ocean Drive Ⓣ 305/361-5441.
There's little to recommend this bland motel, other than the fact that it's on the inexpensive side as far as Key Biscayne goes. It also huddles right on the beach – the pricier oceanfront rooms allow you to step right out of your door onto the sand. ❻

## SOUTH OF THE CITY

## Grove Inn Country Guesthouse

22540 SW Krome Ave Ⓣ 305/247-6572 or 1-877/247-6572, Ⓦ www.groveinn.com.
On an old fruit farm, the *Grove Inn* makes for a comfortable South Miami base, with friendly, knowledgeable owners and an informal atmosphere. ❸

## Greenstone Motel

304 N Krome Ave ☎305/247-8334, Ⓦwww
.thegreenstonemotel.com.
Smack in the middle of
downtown Homestead, this
motel is a quirky oddity.
Linking with the local
ArtSouth complex next door
that aims to bring the arts to
the masses, it has recruited
local creative types to
customize the bedrooms. If
those styles put you off, there
are also plain rooms available
with full motel amenities. ❷

## Redland Hotel

5 S Flagler Ave ☎305/246-1904,
Ⓦwww.redlandhotel.com.
An historic inn, where every
unit is named after a pioneer
family, in the center of old
Homestead. The decor's
comfy, country florals with all
mod cons, and there's a
welcoming bar in the hotel. ❹

# HOSTELS

### Banana Bungalow

**Map 4, E8**. 2360 Collins Ave,
central Miami Beach ☎1-800-7HOSTEL or 305/538-1951,
Ⓦwww.bananabungalow.com.
The Miami Beach branch of
this hostel mini–chain has
terrific facilities – a huge
pool, happy hours in the
evening at the bar, onsite
Internet access and a friendly
vibe. Dorms and private
rooms are all decorated in a
tropical jungle theme, and
there are good rates for
weekly stays in the dorms.

Dorm ❶, private room ❸

For a review of the
*Banana Bar*, see p.162.

### Clay Hotel and Hostel

**Map 3, F4**. 1438 Washington
Ave, South Beach ☎305/534-2988, Ⓦwww.clayhotel.com.
The *Clay* is located in a
landmark building on the
corner of Española Way and
has both private and dorm
rooms at budget rates. It's a
great place to meet other

**HOSTELS**

travelers, and has a fully equipped kitchen, but unfortunately, some rooms are cleaner than others: ask to see one before you commit. Dorm ❶, private room ❷

### Ninth Street Hostel
**Map 3, F6**. 236 9th St, South Beach ☎305/534-0268, ⓦ www.sobehostel.com.
A great location just blocks from the beach is the biggest selling point of this hostel: the dorm rooms are run-down and rather lovelorn,

but reasonably clean. Hostel ❶, room ❷

### The Tropics Hotel & Hostel
**Map 3, F3**. 1550 Collins Ave, South Beach ☎305/531-0361, ⓦ www.tropicshotel.com.
The private rooms are cheap but unappealing though that's no matter, as the real reason to stay here is the hostel accommodation: it's sparse yet clean, and each room sleeps four with a private bath. Hostel ❶, room ❷

# Cafés, snacks and light meals

F rom a quick Cuban coffee to a filling Jewish knish, Miami has plenty on offer in the way of **cafés**, **snacks** and **light meals**. Two unmissable local specialties are the Cuban sandwich, made with pickles, cheese, smoked ham and roast pork – all crammed into a fluffy roll that's toasted in a press – and the toxically sweet *cafecito*, a thimble-sized jolt of caffeine and sugar that's addictively energizing.

In addition, there are New York-style **pizza** joints, vintage **diners**, homestyle **bakeries**, and a range of cheap, filling **breakfast** spots – plus plenty of sidewalk cafés good for nursing a coffee while watching the crowds go by. Below we've listed some of the best options; all are fairly inexpensive. For listings of places more appropriate for a sit-down dinner, see "Restaurants" beginning on p.137.

## DOWNTOWN

**Garcia's Seafood Grille**
**Map 5, G2**. 398 NW North River Drive ☎ 305/375-0765. Join the customs guys at this lunch-only riverside fish café – it's bustling and efficient, serving tasty fresh fish at

reasonable prices, with a small lunch counter in the front and racks of waterfront picnic tables out back. The dolphin sandwich is delicious – and don't worry, it's actually mahi mahi.

### Karlo Bakery

**Map 1, E5**. 1242 Coral Way
☎ 305/858-1080.
A new bakery, unfortunately located on the corner of a major intersection; still, the European-style food is delicious, especially the buttery soft croissants and frothy *café au lait*. Super desserts, too, just right for an indulgent picnic.

### La Paris

**Map 2, C7**. 251 SE 2nd St
☎ 305/371-5181.
Packed with office workers at lunchtime, *La Paris* is one of the better Cuban diners, serving basic dishes at rock bottom prices (sandwiches $4, entrees $5). The place is absolutely without frills and there's limited counter seating, but the food is hearty and appetizing.

### Las Palmas

**Map 2, C6**. 209 SE 1st St
☎ 305/373-1333.
A typical Cuban lunch counter, serving sandwiches and deep-fried treats at breakfast and lunchtime; while there are plenty of similar cafés around downtown, this one is clean and the staff friendly.

### Top Hat Deli

**Map 2, C6**. 150 W Flagler St
☎ 305/381-6337.
Well-priced for the neighborhood, this café offers filling sandwiches for around $7 and has plentiful outdoor seating overlooking the Metro-Dade Cultural Center. Service can be slow and rather fraught, but it's a convenient stop-off when sightseeing.

## SOUTH BEACH

### A La Folie Café

**Map 3, E3**. 516 Española Way
☎ 305/538-4484.
Run by French expats, this trendily dilapidated café serves authentic, tasty crepes

and salads from $6 and is well-stocked with browsable European magazines. It's a refreshing respite from the tourist traps and conga music elsewhere on Española Way, and you're likely to sit beside locals rather than other visitors.

## Balans Lincoln Road

**Map 3, D2**. 1022 Lincoln Rd ⓣ305/534-9191, ⓦwww.balans .co.uk/miami.html.
An outpost of a small British chain of gay restaurants, *Balans* serves its stylish brunches to visitors and locals alike – don't expect warm service, but it's a great place to see and be seen on Lincoln Road. Good weekday breakfast specials, and don't miss the chunky, crunchy Balans potatoes.

## Cheeseburger Baby

**Map 3, F3**. 1505 Washington Ave ⓣ305/531-7300.
A groovy burger joint with psychedelic graphics, retro fittings and 24-hour delivery. The food holds no surprises, but the burgers and fries are tasty.

## David's Café

**Map 3, F5**. 1058 Collins Ave ⓣ305/534-8736.
Original outpost of an authentic Cuban restaurant, where suited Cuban businessmen sit alongside brassy teenagers. Try the great, filling Cuban sandwiches along with a delicious coffee, or head to the Meridian Ave branch – *David's Café II*, at no. 1654 (ⓣ305/672-8707) – for swanky dining room seating.

## Front Porch Café

**Map 3, F4**. 1418 Ocean Drive ⓣ305/531-8300.
Despite its over-tourited location, this really is where the locals go for breakfast. Portions are supersized: gigantic omelettes, wholemeal pancakes as big as frisbees, and doorstop sandwiches are all well-priced. Come here early with a newspaper and check out the morning crowd.

## Gino's

**Map 3, E6**. 731 Washington Ave ⓣ305/673-2837.
Open 24 hours a day, *Gino's*

serves true New York-style pizza to shift workers and clubbers alike: each slice comes with a free, buttery garlic knot.

### Joffrey's Coffee Company
**Map 3, E2**. 660 Lincoln Rd
Ⓣ 305/673-6474,
Ⓦ www.joffreyscoffee.com.
A large coffee house on a busy corner of Lincoln Road, this funky local institution is a great place to kick back with a coffee and watch the preening crowds of dogwalkers sashaying down the main drag on Sunday afternoon. Stick with the drinks, as the pastries are rather cardboardy.

### La Sandwicherie
**Map 3, F4**. 229 W 14th St
Ⓣ 305/532-8934.
Don't be put off by the pretentious name – open until 5am, this place serves serious sandwiches starting at around $6 from its open-air lunch counter; each giant french loaf doorstop could make two meals, crammed with fresh, crunchy greens and *charcuterie* (cold cuts).

### Lincoln Road Café
**Map 3, E2**. 941 Lincoln Rd
Ⓣ 305/538-8066.
Stop here for the hearty, cheap breakfast specials starting at $1.99 for sausage, eggs and home fries. Lunches and dinners are fine but unremarkable, with a Cuban edge, and there's sometimes live music at weekends.

### News Café
**Map 3, F6**. 800 Ocean Drive
Ⓣ 305/538-6397,
Ⓦ www.newscafe.com.
The food may be nondescript, but its location at the corner of 8th and Ocean Drive has made the *News* ground zero for the South Beach scene since the early Nineties. Enjoy the fact that its *brasserie* approach lets you sit all afternoon over a single coffee without being shooed away. Moderate.
Branch: Streets of Mayfair shopping center, 2901 Florida Ave Ⓣ 305/774-6397.

### Pizza Rustica
**Map 3, E6**. 863 Washington

Ave Ⓣ 305/673-8244.
This is a cheap beach pitstop serving huge slices of pizza for only $3.50. Un-Italian toppings like barbecue chicken combined with tangy tomato sauce make a delicious snack, and each slice is cut into six bite-size pieces while still hot from the oven.

### QueeQueg's Beach Bistro
**Map 3, E6**. 857 Washington Ave Ⓣ 305/538-1534.
This neighborhood café is a hippie hangout serving dirt-cheap burgers and sandwiches – plus it's licensed to serve wine. Laid-back and slightly tatty round the edges, with chess sets propped against the wall for anyone to use.

### Taystee Bakery
**Map 3, F4**. 1450 Washington Ave Ⓣ 305/538-4793.
Join the elderly clientele for breakfast from 6am in this supercheap neighborhood bakery, serving old-fashioned kosher breads and pastries at a couple of formica tables. A great place to eavesdrop on local gossip.

### Verandah Café
**Map 3, G2**. *Richmond Hotel*, 1757 Collins Ave Ⓣ 305/538-2331 or 1-800/327-3163, Ⓦ www.richmondhotel.com.
Ditch the crowds on Collins Avenue by heading into this secluded gem, located poolside in this mid-range hotel. Sail past reception and through the central hallway to the back of the building; cheap sandwiches can be had for around $8.

## CENTRAL MIAMI BEACH AND NORTH

---

### Arnie & Richie's Deli
**Map 4, E4**. 525 41st St Ⓣ 305/531-7691.
In the bosom of Miami Beach's Jewish neighborhood, this deli serves standbys like pastrami sandwiches, knishes and whitefish salad without fuss or fanfare – be prepared to share a table with the gaggles of local old ladies who stop in regularly.

### Laurenzo's
**Map 1, F2**. 16385 W Dixie Hwy Ⓣ 305/945-6381,

Ⓦ www.laurenzos.com.
A local institution, the diner counter inside this Italian-American supermarket serves zitti, lasagna and garlic-laced spaghetti for a cheap and filling lunch. It's hardly the funkiest restaurant around, but the pasta portions are good value if you're in the neighborhood, and it's a glimpse of old Miami.

### Miami Juice

Map 1, G2. 16120 Collins Ave
Ⓣ 305/945-0444.
A welcome healthy alternative amid the diners and fast-food joints that cluster along this stretch of Collins Avenue. It's also good for Middle Eastern specialties like falafel and hummus.

### Oasis Café

**Map 4, E4**. 976 41st St
Ⓣ 305/674-7676.
Tucked away in a strip mall, the *Oasis Café* is worth a detour for its zesty Middle Eastern food and good vegetarian options. Don't leave without trying the spicy coriander-cumin fries.

### Santa Fe News & Coffee

**Map 1, G3**. Bal Harbour Shops complex, 9700 Collins Ave
Ⓣ 305/861-0938.
An unremarkable café that's notable simply as one of the few places to grab a quiet coffee in this area, and the only eatery in the mall that isn't as premium-priced as the stores. There are magazines for sale, as well as gooey pastries and simple sandwiches.

## LITTLE HAVANA

- - - - - - - - - - - - - - - - - - - - -

### El Palacio de los Jugos

**Map 1, C5**. 5721 W Flagler St
Ⓣ 305/264-1503.
Locally renowned for its edgy seediness (it was busted as the headquarters for a major smuggling ring in 1998) this grocery store and café bustles with life. The take-out counter offers large portions of Cuban dishes, and there are cafeteria-style tables under a lean-to out back; unsurprisingly, the *batidos* (fresh juice shakes) here are excellent, too.

## Nuevo Siglo

**Map 5, D5**. 1305 Calle Ocho
ⓣ 305/854-1916.

The pick of the many local grocery store cafés, this lunch counter along the back wall of the store serves excellent *café cubano* as well as delicious pressed Cuban sandwiches with sweet pork, pickles and ham.

## Taqueria Viva Mexico

**Map 5, B5**. 1961 Calle Ocho
ⓣ 305/868-4889.

Small, bargain Mexican restaurant serving tacos at rock-bottom prices: there are plastic tablecloths, and don't expect much from the service, but the food's authentic and flavorful.

## CORAL GABLES

- - - - - - - - - - - - - - - - - - - -

## Books & Books Café

**Map 6, F3**. 265 Aragon Ave
ⓣ 305/448-9599.

A low-key oasis off the Miracle Mile, this café serves crusty French loaf sandwiches starting at $6, as well as rich, buttery pastries and sweets produced by a local bakery –

try the fresh strawberry cheesecake. There's live music every Friday from 6–8pm.

## Nena's

3791 Bird Rd ⓣ 305/446-4481.
*Nena's* is the lunchtime hub of Miami's power Cuban scene: within a derelict-looking building are two lunch counters and a couple of tables, with whiteboards on the wall describing the day's offerings – the *croqueta preparada* (Cuban sandwich) is juicy and delicious.

## Paninoteca

**Map 6, G4**. 264 Miracle Mile
ⓣ 305/443-8388.

One of the few smart choices for lunch in Coral Gables' oddly empty downtown, this café serves European-style panini with a local twist – try the Largo, which includes key lime-marinated catch of the day.
Branch: 809 Lincoln Rd
ⓣ 305/538-0058.

## Titanic Brewery

**Map 6, F8**. 5813 Ponce de Leon Blvd ⓣ 305/667-2537.
Unpretentious pub food

**LITTLE HAVANA • CORAL GABLES**

served in a friendly bar just outside Coral Gables. The hamburgers are especially good and start around $6, and there are gourmet beers on tap. In addition, the *Titanic* hosts regular performances by local bands (see p.160, "Drinking").

## COCONUT GROVE

### Bacio

**Map 7, B6**. 3462 Main Hwy ⊤305/442-4233.

Glorious sorbets and ice creams are sold at this modernist *gelateria*, staffed by Italians who give the place a laid-back, European feel. Ask for a sample before you order – the *frutti di bosco* (fruits of the forest) and *zuppa inglese* (trifle) are staff favorites. There's also a small counter for a quick *caffè*.

### Daily Bread Marketplace

2400 SW 27th St ⊤305/856-5893.

Just over Hwy-1 from Coconut Grove proper, this is a Middle Eastern grocery store and cafeteria that serves delicious,

exotic lunches in a hurry.

### Greenstreet Café

**Map 7, B6**. 3468 Main Hwy ⊤305/444-0244.

The *Greenstreet's* terrific breakfasts of fragrant fruit pancakes and hefty omelettes make this café a real scene at weekends. Also, it has a large number of outdoor tables where you can dawdle undisturbed over a coffee.

### Scotty's Landing

**Map 7, D6**. 3381 Pan American Drive ⊤305/854-2626.

Though it's hard to find, tucked away on the water near City Hall, and service can be slow, there are few better places to taste local flavor than at *Scotty's* – sit out on the water at the Marina, order a fish sandwich (around $6) and join the locals for lunch.

### Zoom

**Map 7, B6**. 3415 Main Hwy ⊤305/569-0009.

Zesty juice bar serving huge smoothies in every flavor, as well as fresh salads: an excellent place for a healthy stop, and the fruit drinks are large enough that they make a (liquid) meal on their own.

## KEY BISCAYNE
--------------------

### Donut Gallery

**Map 1, F7**. 83 Harbour Drive
Ⓣ 305/361-9985.
Open at 5.30am, this old-time diner is an untouched gem on Key Biscayne, with its red vinyl stools, faded formica tables and sweet, greasy donuts. Breakfasts start around $4.

## LITTLE HAITI AND THE DESIGN DISTRICT
--------------------

### Caribbean Café Shop

2804 NE 2nd Ave Ⓣ 305/572-9282.
With a tiny kitchen and the daily menu scribbled on a whiteboard, this Honduran hole-in-the-wall shares a storefront with the local laundry. Sit down at the counter amid the washing machines and enjoy tasty soups for less than $5.

### Lakay Bakery

**Map 8, C6**. 91 NE 54th St
Ⓣ 305/751-2912.
This tiny bakery produces outstanding homemade ice cream, using exotic and familiar fruits as flavoring – try the pineapple or the guava: two large scoops cost a paltry $1.50. There's also a small selection of flaky Haitian pastries.

## SOUTH OF THE CITY
--------------------

### Angie's Café

404 SE 1st Ave, Florida City
Ⓣ 305/245-8939.
A fun, local restaurant in Florida City that serves good, old-fashioned southern fried food – a rarity in South Florida – for breakfast and lunch.

### Main Street Café

134 N Krome Ave, Homestead
Ⓣ 305/245-7575.
Laid-back café serving homemade soups and plenty of vegetarian options, as well as gourmet coffee, beer and wine. There's live entertainment, usually folk

music, on Thursday, Friday and Saturday nights.

## Moreno's Tortilla Shop

439 West Palm Drive. No phone.

Neighborhood café primarily catering to the large number of migrant Mexican workers in the area. Worth stopping by, though, for its excellent and authentic handmade *tamales*.

## Robert Is Here

19900 SW 344th St Ⓣ300/246-1592.

Started in the mid-1950s, when his farmer father put young Robert in charge of an impromptu roadside cucumber stall, this fruitstand is now a ramshackle institution. Part farmers' market, part café, Robert and his team sell fruity milkshakes, preserves and tropical salad dressings. Close to the main entrance of Everglades National Park.

# Restaurants

**W**ith cuisine from nearly every corner of the globe, including hearty dollops of Cuban, Haitian, Italian and French, **eating** in Miami is an endless pleasure. This is the realm in which Miami's cosmopolitan, cobbled-together history produces plenty of flavor with none of the friction.

The dominant ethnic food is, of course, **Cuban** – though it's not for the weak-hearted: many of the juicy, tender, meat dishes are fried, and desserts like *tres leches* are gloriously artery-clogging. Cuban menus also often feature **Spanish** staples such as *paella* and black beans and white rice, known as *Moros e Cristianos* (literally, "Moors and Christians"). The ethnic style that's currently exploding in Miami, though, is **Haitian**: increasingly, restaurants like *Tap Tap* in South Beach are opening outside the borders of Little Haiti, and the dishes – which place emphasis on ingredients like starchy tubers and goat, much like in Jamaican cooking – are hearty and satisfying.

Recently, local chefs have taken much that's familiar from Cuban cooking (hearts of palm, avocadoes and guava) and used those same ingredients in unusual combinations, often adding light but spicy tastes like ginger or bonnet peppers. This uniquely local style, known variously as **Floribbean**, **Nuevo Cubano** or **Tropical Fusion**, also uses plenty of fresh fruit and, since the key is to keep flavor high but fat low – a popular combination in body-conscious Miami – fish and seafood are commoner than meat. Miami's cultural fusion has also nurtured numerous **pan-Asian** eateries, as well as a growing number of sushi-ceviche restaurants that bring **Latin American** and **Japanese** flavors together.

As for where to go, **South Beach** unsurprisingly holds the largest grouping of trendy restaurants. And, despite occupying heavily touristed locations, many of these establishments actually serve excellent food that lives up to the hype – though unfortunately, so do the prices. Back on the mainland, **Coral Gables** is the other chichi place to dine – restaurants there are less sceney than their counterparts in South Beach, though often more formal.

Away from these two areas, though, the pickings thin out: **Coconut Grove** has only a small cluster of restaurants at its center, and **downtown** is virtually bereft of good eateries. While in **Little Havana**, stick to Calle Ocho, as there's plenty of authentic choices on every block. Back on Miami Beach, Collins Avenue offers a few clusters of restaurants as it snakes northwards, notably around 41st Street and 71st Street. For the best **Mexican** food around, head south to **Homestead**, where several cheap, authentic canteens cater primarily to the migrant workers who staff the fruit farms each season.

The restaurant reviews below have been price-coded into five categories according to per-person meals: an **inexpensive** place will hover at less than $15, while a **moderate** restaurant should cost between $15 and $30. **Expensive** places will run between $30 and $45 per person, while the few **very expensive** establishments we've listed will cost $45 and up. Bear in mind that these quotes are based on a two-course meal, not including drinks, tip or taxes.

RESTAURANTS

# DOWNTOWN

--------------------

## Big Fish

**Map 2, D8**. 55 SW Miami Ave
ⓣ 305/373-1770. Moderate.
Known for its crab cakes, this
riverside shack offers a taste
of the Florida Keys without
leaving Miami. The
atmosphere's casual and the
design ramshackle – for
example, a bar that's built
around an enormous banyan
tree.

## Hard Rock Café

**Map 2, F5**. Bayside
Marketplace, 401 Biscayne
Blvd R-200 ⓣ 305/377-3110,
Ⓦ www.hardrock.com.
Moderate.
The local branch of the
rock'n'burger chain on the
waterside is topped with a
giant guitar – the food's
much better than you'd
expect, and it's one of the
scant few options for evening
eating downtown.

## La Loggia

**Map 2, C6**. 68 W Flagler St
ⓣ 305/373-4800,
Ⓦ www.laloggiarestaurant.

Moderate.
One of the few restaurants
that's open for dinner in
central downtown, even if it
does close early, at 9pm: a
casual Italian pasta café with
terracotta floors and plenty
of chianti bottles for
decoration. There's bar and
restaurant seating, plus a
varied wine list. Entrees start
around $10.

## Los Ranchos

**Map 2, F5**. Bayside
Marketplace, 401 Biscayne
Blvd N-100 ⓣ 305/375-0666.
Expensive.
As this chainlet of
Nicaraguan steakhouses has
grown, its food has become
less authentic, but steak
specials like *churrasco con
chimichurri* (steak with spicy
herb salsa) are tender and
delicious, while the *quattro
leches* dessert outdoes the
traditional Cuban *tres leches*.

## Rosinella

1040 S Miami Ave ⓣ 305/372-
5756. Moderate.
At this outstanding family-
run restaurant, you'll find
classic Italian comfort food at

**DOWNTOWN**

reasonable prices. Even though all the bread and pasta is made onsite, Mama Rosinella is best known for her soft, floury *gnocchi*. Another location at 525 Lincoln Rd (℡ 305/672-8777).

### Tobacco Road

**Map 2, D8**. 626 S Miami Ave ℡ 305/374-1198. Inexpensive. This bar and live music venue (see p.172, "Nightlife") also serves surprisingly hearty and fresh American diner food. The burgers are juicy, and there are regular bargain specials like lobster for $10 – just don't come here if you're in the mood for a romantic dinner.

### Tutto Pasta

1751 SW 3rd Ave ℡ 305/857-0709. Moderate. A small Italian restaurant, *Tutto* is one of the new cluster of eateries opening in southwestern downtown. There's outdoor seating and the menu features standard Italian classics – not the place for a foodie's pilgrimage, but a strong option if you're in the area.

## SOUTH BEACH

### B.E.D.

**Map 3, F5**. 929 Washington Ave ℡ 305/532-9070. Expensive. The name stands for Beverage-Entertainment-Dining, and the French food's shockingly good given the gimmicky premise: enormous white beds replace chairs, and diners recline around low tables while eating and listening to music (also good). There are two sittings every evening, at 8pm and 10.30pm – if you choose the earlier, don't expect to lounge for too long.

### Big Pink

**Map 3, E8**. 157 Collins Ave ℡ 305/532-4700. Inexpensive. This cartoonish diner, decked out in pink lucite and aluminum, is famous for its TV dinners served on vintage trays. The huge menu offers good versions of traditional burgers and salads, as well as ample desserts; the cafeteria-style tables make the varied crowd even friendlier. Open till 5am weekends with a beer *and* food happy hour on Thursday evenings.

## Bond St

**Map 3, G1**. Basement of the *Townhouse*, 150 20th St ⊤ 305/398-1806.
Moderate–expensive.

The Miami outpost of the chic New York scene eatery is smaller but otherwise identical: glamorous people, same sleek menu (the vegetarian sushi with sundried tomato and avocado is excellent) and same signature cocktail, the saketini. Expect a wait at weekend, especially on Fridays when the hotel holds its rooftop sunset parties.

## Breez

**Map 3, G3**. *Billboardlive* complex, 1500 Ocean Drive ⊤ 305/532-8999. Expensive.

Although *Breez* was choked with celebrities when it opened, the heat's cooling at this still-hot spot – a good thing as tables are easier to snag. Its menu of sushi and fish is not particularly innovative, but the food's tasty and well-prepared, and the atmosphere's funky and lively.

## Eleventh St Diner

**Map 3, F5**. 1065 Washington Ave ⊤ 305/672-2000.
Moderate.

Housed in a 1948 Art Deco-style diner car, specially shipped to South Beach from Pennsylvania, the feel here is local, diverse and friendly. Open 24 hours, it has terrific down-home food – the spinach salad is good – chatty staff and happy hour specials from 5 to 7pm and again from 10 to 12pm on Monday to Friday.

## Joe's Stone Crab

**Map 3, E8**. 11 Washington Ave ⊤ 305/673-0365. Expensive.

Synonymous with South Beach for decades, this packed, pricey restaurant serves fresh stone crabs to those who are prepared to wait up to three hours for the pleasure. Better to do as locals do and grab a portion to go from the takeout window next door.

**SOUTH BEACH**

### Kiss

**Map 3, F2**. *Albion* hotel, 301 Lincoln Rd ⊤ 305/695-4445, ⓦ www.kisssouthbeach.com. Very expensive.

Complete with (clothed) pole dancers, this steakhouse-cum-strip joint is more than just its gimmick: steaks are rich and tender, if expensive. The baroque circus décor, dark lighting and high-backed chairs keep each table intimate; there's also an equally trippy bar on the mezzanine above the dining floor (see p.157, "Drinking").

### Lario's on the Beach

**Map 3, F6**. 820 Ocean Drive ⊤ 305/532-9577. Expensive. The reason to come to Gloria Estefan's restaurant on the beach is the *mojitos*, the signature Cuban concoction of crushed mint and rum – most people concede that *Lario's* serves the best on the beach. The food, unfortunately, is so-so, dismissed by many as Cuban food for Anglos.

### Macaluso

**Map 3, C2**. 1747 Alton Rd ⊤ 305/604-1811. Moderate.

Nestled in a strip mall by the canal at the northern end of South Beach, *Macaluso* serves unpretentious, down-home Italian food that's far better than many of the chic, overpriced Italian restaurants around Lincoln Road.

### Nikki Beach

**Map 3, F8**. 1 Ocean Drive ⊤ 305/538-1231. Expensive. In the Penrods complex underneath the op-art *Pearl* (see below), *Nikki Beach* is a bar-restaurant that spills out onto the beach in a cluster of teepees where you can enjoy your cocktails. The food is standard American, heavy on light sandwiches and quirky salads, and the dining area snakes across the sand, with its own raffia roof – great fun but not the place for an intimate dinner. Sunday nights are the most popular, when DJs spin and the crowd's at its liveliest.

### Pacific Time

**Map 3, D2**. 915 Lincoln Rd ⊤ 305/534-5979. Very expensive. The first upscale restaurant to

**SOUTH BEACH**

open during Lincoln Road's renaissance, it's still a scene, but a welcoming one. Décor is shabby chic and food is a fusion of Pacific Rim countries: unusual recipes like Mongolian lamb hit more often than they miss.

### Sushi Rock Café

**Map 3, F4**. 1351 Collins Ave ⓣ 305/532-2133. Moderate. What puts the rock in this place is its clientele – wannabe and already-are rockstars – plus the loud music. The food's better than you'd expect, and it makes a funky, late-night pitstop that's open until 1am Friday–Saturday.

### Sushi Samba Dromo

**Map 3, E2**. 600 Lincoln Rd ⓣ 305/673-5337. Expensive. At *Sushi Samba Dromo*, the cuisine and space fuse Tokyo with Rio: brightly colored tiles meet black lacquered wood while the sushi chef prepares sashimi and the samba chef whips up *ceviche*. It has a great vibe, thanks more to its central location than the food: the sushi can be disappointing, but dishes

like crispy whole red snapper work better.

### Tambo

**Map 3, B2**. 1801 Purdy Ave ⓣ 305/535-2414, ⓦ www.tambobeach.com. Expensive. Tucked out of the way at South Beach's northern end, this fusion restaurant successfully combines South American and Japanese flavors: alongside fancy hand rolls, for example, you'll be served nutty breads and Peruvian dipping sauce. The atmosphere's elegant and low-key, and it's good for a light snack and a glass of wine from the extensive list.

### Tantra

**Map 3, E4**. 1445 Pennsylvania Ave ⓣ 305/672-4765, ⓦ www.tantrarestaurant.com. Expensive. Modern Indian cuisine with a Mediterranean slant served in a dense, sexy environment, where every element is designed to be sensual – there's grass on the floor, enormous embroidered cushions, plus hookahs and

SOUTH BEACH

belly dancers. It may sound gimmicky, but it works – and even if the over-the-top design puts you off, risk it for the food, which is extremely good.

### Tap Tap

**Map 3, D7**. 819 5th St
Ⓣ 305/672-2898. Moderate.
One of the few restaurants outside Little Haiti that serves authentic, tasty Haitian food, *Tap Tap* often features intriguing specials, and the drinks are cheap. Worth stopping by for the Caribbean art that's displayed on the walls or the live Haitian folk music every Thursday and Saturday.

### Toni's Sushi

**Map 3, F4**. 1208 Washington Ave Ⓣ 305/673-9368.
Moderate.
*Toni's* claims to be the oldest sushi bar on the beach, and it's especially good for vegetarians, as it has a wide selection of vegetable and noodle dishes. There's classic sushi and sashimi as well as funky new options – try the Miami Heat roll, with tuna

and peppery sesame oil. Be aware that the staff is notoriously gruff, although the bartenders in the small bar can be friendlier.

### Touch

**Map 3, D2**. 910 Lincoln Rd
Ⓣ 305/532-8003. Expensive.
Owned by the same team as *Kiss* (see p.142), *Touch* is another restaurant with a velvet rope and extra helpings of attitude. The Goth Polynesian interior is whimsical and fun, featuring real palm trees; unusually for a hip restaurant, the portions are huge and the showy modern American food delicious.

### Wish

**Map 3, F6**. *The Hotel*, 801 Collins Ave Ⓣ 305/531-2222, Ⓦ www.thehotelofsouthbeach .com. Very expensive.
Daring Floribbean food, heavy on fruit, fish and unexpected ingredients. Dinner here may not be cheap, but it's good value for a rare treat – though the cranked-up muzak can get rather overwhelming. Try the

tuna *ceviche*, and finish your meal with one of the odd, interesting desserts like herbed pineapple sorbet.

### Yuca

**Map 3, E2**. *501 Lincoln Rd* Ⓣ *305/532-9822.*
Expensive–very expensive.
Famed gourmet Cuban (or Nuevo Latino) restaurant at the beach end of Lincoln Road – ask to sit outside. From its trendy heyday, the clientele is heavy on Anglo yuppies, but the food is still remarkable – try anything with pork, or the gazpacho with cilantro oil.

## CENTRAL MIAMI BEACH AND NORTH

### Atlantic

**Map 1, G3**. *Beach House Bal Habour Hotel, 9449 Collins Ave* Ⓣ *305/695-7930.* Expensive.
Cookbook author Sheila Lukins was the "food guru" here, and she came up with a menu chock-full of satisfying, homey American basics like pot pie in an oceanfront setting reminiscent – like the

hotel – of a New England country house.

### Baraboo

**Map 1, G3**. *7300 Ocean Terrace* Ⓣ *305/867-4242.*
Expensive.
This circus-themed restaurant – named after the Wisconsin hometown of the original Ringling Brothers – is oddly trendy. Staff juggle and play with fire when they're not serving dinner (most of which leans toward Italian-inflected fish and seafood) and there are *papier mâché* clowns in the windows.

### Café Prima Pasta

**Map 1, G3**. *414 71st St* Ⓣ *305/867-0106.* Moderate.
Everyone raves about this place, and for good reason: the pasta's homemade, the tiny main room charming, and the prices reasonable – it's no surprise, then, that the wait for a table can be on the long side.

### Christine Lees

**Map 1, G1**. *17802 Collins Ave* Ⓣ *305/947-1717.* Moderate.
*Christine Lees is a local*

SOUTH BEACH • CENTRAL MIAMI BEACH AND NORTH

standby that's been serving simple Chinese food for years: the cuisine is Szechuan-Cantonese, with an emphasis on fish and seafood – people swear by the steamed shrimp. Décor is unexciting, and the place rather lacks atmosphere, but the massive portions more than make up.

### Rascal House

**Map 1, G1**. 17190 Collins Ave ⓣ305/947-4581. Moderate. Make a pilgrimage to this vintage standby, where portions of standard diner fare are huge, and breakfast is accompanied by dozens of baked treats, such as bagels, rugelach and muffins. Even better, what you don't finish you can take with you in the plastic "Waste Not" bag the waitress leaves along with your check.

## LITTLE HAVANA

### Ayestaran

706 SW 27th Ave ⓣ305/649-4982. Inexpensive–moderate. This unpretentious restaurant

serves Spanish-Cuban food in a family-style setting – the sandwiches are good and daily lunchtime specials keep prices low: try the *arroz con mariscos* (rice with prawns).

### Casa Juancho

2436 Calle Ocho ⓣ305/642-2452, ⓦwww.casajuancho.com. Expensive. Oddly reminiscent of either a Swiss chalet or Disney's idea of old Cuba, this upscale restaurant offers hearty, Spanish-inflected dishes, best for the fish. It's one of the few posh restaurants in the neighborhood, and makes for good people watching.

### El Fogon

**Map 5, A8**. 2091 Coral Way ⓣ305/856-3451. Moderate. This out-of-the-way restaurant serves massive (and authentic) Mexican dinners at minimal prices: try the house special of *cochinita pibil* (shredded marinated pork) in one of its many preparations, or order real Mexican fajitas.

### Guayacan

**Map 5, A5**. 1933 Calle Ocho

CENTRAL MIAMI BEACH AND NORTH • LITTLE HAVANA

146

☎ 305/649-2015. Inexpensive. Tasty, fresh Nicaraguan food served either at the counter or in the small, unfussy dining room to the back: it's known for its soups, with a different recipe served every day – and somehow, the unfriendly staff only seem to add to the authenticity.

### Habana Vieja
3622 Coral Way ☎ 305/448-6660.
A sprawling cream building with a tiled red roof, this restaurant's known for its *vaca frita* and *fufu de plantano*

## A BRIEF CUBAN FOOD GLOSSARY

**Aguacate** Avocado

**Ajo** Garlic

**Arepas** Cornmeal pancake

**Arroz con Pollo** Chicken and yellow rice

**Buñuelos** Cuban donuts

**Cabra or Chivo** Goat

**Camarones** Prawns

**Chorizo** Spicy, greasy sausage

**Churrasco** Marinated and grilled beef tenderloin

**Empanada** Ground beef in a tortilla, either fried or baked

**Escabeche** Pickled fish

**Langosta** Florida lobster

**Maduros** Fried sweet plantains

**Mariscos** Seafood

**Moros e Cristianos** Black beans and white rice

**Paella** Spanish dish, incorporating saffron rice with seafood or chicken

**Papa** Potato

**Queso** Cheese

**Ropa Vieja** Literally "old clothes": shredded beef, fried with vegetables

**Sesos** Brains

**Tostones** Mashed, fried plantains

**Tres Leches** Supersweet custard-like dessert, made from condensed, evaporated and fresh milk, sometimes served with sweet caramel

**Vaca frita** Beef fried with onions

LITTLE HAVANA

(mashed plantains). High-spirited and friendly, the staff make even non-Spanish speakers feel welcome.

### Sergio's Cafeteria
3252 Coral Way ⊤ 305/529-0047. Inexpensive.
Loud, noisy and fun, *Sergio's* is a Cuban diner with plenty of attitude, welcoming late-night diners and offering a wide menu at fair prices. A great place to finish up a long Friday night and chow down on one of the best Cuban sandwiches in town. Branch: 13600 SW 152nd St, South Miami ⊤ 786/242-9790.

### Versailles
3555 Calle Ocho ⊤ 305/445-7614. Moderate.
Despite a recent spruce-up, this local legend still retains it 1960s décor and mirrors, inspired by the namesake palace. Come here for the authentic Cuban food, and watch a cross-section of Miami's Cuban community come together to enjoy it with you. Traditional, delicious dishes like *ropa vieja* and *vaca frita* should be

followed with *tres leches*. Low-fat devotees will find little to eat here.

### Yambo
**Map 5, B3**. 1643 SW 1st St ⊤ 305/642-6616. Inexpensive.
This 24-hour Nicaraguan restaurant is one of Miami's treasures, with plentiful outdoor seating that's covered in mosaics and a bevy of bizarre items. Entrées are around $4 – grab them from the counter, then seat yourself – and expect to be offered videos or CDs by itinerant peddlers who thread through the crowd. There's little English spoken and the whole restaurant feels genuinely Central American.

## CORAL GABLES
- - - - - - - - - - - - - - - - - - -

### Bugatti's
**Map 6, G4**. 2504 Ponce de Leon Blvd ⊤ 305/441-2545. Moderate–expensive.
An Italian restaurant run by a German in the heart of Cuban Coral Gables, the food is surprisingly authentic – make sure to try the buffalo

mozzarella, as well as the tender *gnocchi*. The only downside is the sometimes-sniffy service.

### Caffe Abbracci

**Map 6, F3**. 318 Aragon Ave ⓣ 305/441-0700. Expensive. For a taste of local life in Coral Gables, visit this upscale Italian trattoria, which serves traditional pastas alongside more unusual combinations (try the pumpkin ravioli). There's a good wine list, too.

### Christy's

**Map 6, G4**. 3101 Ponce de Leon Blvd ⓣ 305/446-1400. Very expensive. Upscale restaurant with old-fashioned décor and a robust, steak-filled menu for carnivores only – if you dare splash out on the filet mignon, it won't disappoint. Clubby, rather formal, and very Coral Gables.

### Gables Diner

**Map 6, G3**. 2320 Galiano St ⓣ 305/567-0330, ⓦ www.gablesdiner.com. Moderate.

Fresh and unprecious compared with many of the posh eateries around the Miracle Mile, this bistro serves good meatloaf, alongside standard sandwiches and salads, for around $10.

### The Globe

**Map 6, F3**. 377 Alhambra Circle ⓣ 305/445-3555. Expensive. Yes, it's a rabid pick-up joint, but still good fun: the bar is lively at weekends, packed with a twentysomething Cuban crowd. The food is gimmicky but adventurous, drawn (as per the restaurant's name) from across the world: for an appetizer, try the Cajun egg rolls.

### Havana Harry's

**Map 6, F8**. 4612 LeJeune Rd ⓣ 305/661-2622. Inexpensive. Just like homemade, the food here comes in large, cheap portions and is authentically Cuban – try the *pollo a la plancha* (marinated grilled chicken) or the *vaca frita* (fried beef with onions). The space is tiny, though, so be prepared to wait at dinnertime.

**CORAL GABLES**

### Les Halles

**Map 6, G4**. 2415 Ponce de Leon Blvd ⓣ 305/461-1099. Moderate.

Almost too cosy, this packed French bistro serves excellent classics like *steak tartare* and *moules frites* (mussels and french fries): the décor's a little overdone in its desperate attempts to reproduce every element of a true French restaurant, but the food makes up for it.

### Miss Saigon Bistro

**Map 6, G3**. 146 Giralda Ave ⓣ 305/446-8006. Inexpensive–moderate.

It's hard to find authentic Asian food in Miami, but this family-owned Vietnamese restaurant hits the mark. The food's light and zesty – the noodles with lemongrass and chicken are particularly tasty, as are the spring rolls; what's more, the staff are welcoming and great fun.

### Normans

**Map 6, G4**. 21 Almeria Ave ⓣ 305/446-6767. Very expensive.

Superchic, top-notch restaurant, owned by chef Norman Van Aiken, one of the pioneers of New World cuisine. This is another local restaurant where fish is especially good – locals rave about the inventive paella – but expect *nouvelle cuisine*-size portions.

### Ortanique

**Map 6, F4**. 278 Miracle Mile ⓣ 305/446-7710. Expensive–very expensive.

Another chic eatery in downtown Coral Gables, *Ortanique* serves innovative, adventurous Caribbean food in a lush tropical setting, almost like a terrace garden. Deliberate as the atmosphere may be, the food's sumptuous and creative, there are always reliable fish specials, and the chocolate mango tower is a heavenly dessert.

### Restaurant St Michel

**Map 6, G3**. *Hotel St Michel*, 162 Alcazar Ave ⓣ 305/446-6572. Expensive.

Inside the B&B-like hotel (see review p.123), this rustic country restaurant is unapologetically old-fashioned, romantic and French. The food is tastiest when least fussy – stick with simple dishes to be safe, such as the delicate crepes.

## COCONUT GROVE

### Anokha

**Map 7, B6**. 3195 Commodore Plaza ℡ 786/552-1030, Ⓦ www.anokha.citysearch.com. Moderate.

Just off the main drag in Coconut Grove, this Indian restaurant is best at lunchtime, when it offers a large, tasty buffet for only $8.95 – in the evening, prices are a little higher and the menu *à la carte*.

### Baleen

**Map 7, G4**. *Grove Isle Hotel*, 4 Grove Isle Drive ℡ 305/858-8300. Very expensive.

The food at *Baleen* – like the house special, lobster "martini" served on truffled roast potatoes – is good but too expensive. The views, however, are priceless: situated on a private island just off Coconut Grove, the waterfront patio looks out over Biscayne Bay – undeniably one of the most romantic dining spots in town.

### Le Bouchon du Grove

**Map 7, B6**. 3430 Main Hwy ℡ 305/448-6060. Moderate–expensive.

Ramshackle chic with its designer dilapidated signage, *Le Bouchon* is a treasure at the heart of the Grove – funky but posh, it's a restaurant that the locals still love, serving French favorites in a brasserie atmosphere that lets you linger.

### Paulo Luigi's

**Map 7, B5**. 3224 Virginia St ℡ 305/445-9000. Moderate.

Tucked away behind the two shopping centers, this low-key Italian restaurant is old-school Coconut Grove; the atmosphere's friendly and familiar, and hearty entrees cost around $12.

### Señor Frog's

**Map 7, B5**. 3480 Main Hwy ℡ 305/448-0900. Moderate.

Don't be put off by the name:

COCONUT GROVE

the food here is terrific, tasty and affordable, with most entrees hovering around $10 for a plate piled high with Tex-Mex standbys like burritos and enchiladas. The atmosphere's a little lacking, though, due to the high ceilings and a very mainstream crowd. Branch: 616 Collins Ave ☎ 305/673-5262.

## KEY BISCAYNE

### Lighthouse Café
**Map 1, F7**. Bill Baggs Cape Florida State Park, 1200 S Crandon Blvd ☎ 305/361-8487. Inexpensive.
Tucked away in the Cape Florida State Park, this is a casual beachside café by the historic lighthouse. With plenty of outdoor seating, it's worth the trip for the tasty fresh fish and Cuban specials.

### Tango Grill
**Map 1, F7**. 328 Crandon Blvd, suite 112 ☎ 305/361-1133. Expensive.
A small Argentinian grill in one of the Key Biscayne village strip malls, *Tango Grill* serves superb *bife de chorizo* (sirloin steak) and other South American specialties to a heavily Latin crowd.

## LITTLE HAITI AND THE DESIGN DISTRICT

### 5061
**Map 8, E7**. 5061 Biscayne Blvd ☎ 305/756-5051. Moderate.
Minimalist chic restaurant-cum-deli offering upscale sandwiches in the Morningside district, with a supermarket attached: tables are covered with butcher paper and there are televisions on the walls – although the rustic industrial décor doesn't take prices any lower.

### Enriqueta's
2830 NE 2nd Ave ☎ 305/573-4681. Inexpensive.
This local diner bustles all day, serving no-frills Cuban sandwiches and massive steaks. Sit at the counter and watch the squad of old ladies

who staff the kitchen nonchalantly preparing an assembly line of pressed sandwiches.

### Lacaye Restaurant

**Map 8, D3**. 7499 NE 2nd Ave ☎305/756-5054. Inexpensive. In this low-slung coral pink building on Little Haiti's main drag, you can try Haitian specialties like fried pork or goat in a friendly environment at rock-bottom prices.

### Piccadilly Garden

**Map 8, C9**. 35 NE 40th St ☎305/573-8221. Expensive. A neighborhood institution that's weathered the up-and-down last 40 years, this dark, atmospheric ranch restaurant is renowned for its boozy brunches. Sit in the sun-dappled courtyard on wicker chairs and watch tender meat freshly barbecued in front of you.

### Soyka

**Map 8, E5**. 5580 NE 4th Court ☎305-759-3117. Expensive. Located in what developers are claiming will be the next hot area – namely, the warehouse spaces around the Design District – *Soyka* takes a Mediterranean bistro tack, serving polenta and fried calamari. However, most people come for the scene, not the cuisine – it's a massive, cavernous space, with distressed concrete walls and a generous helping of Beautiful People.

## SOUTH OF THE CITY

- - - - - - - - - - - - - - - - - - -

### Rosita's Restaurante

199 West Palm Drive, Florida City ☎305/246-3114. Inexpensive. Located off Hwy-1 at the junction for the Everglades and Biscayne National Park, *Rosita's* serves glorious Mexican food at budget prices, accompanied by spicy salsa, creamy refried beans and tangy cheese toppings. There's canteen-style seating at basic formica tables, all set to a backdrop of loud Hispanic talk radio. Well worth a detour south.

### Shorty's Bar-B-Q

9200 S Dixie Hwy, South Miami
☎ 305/670-7732. Inexpensive.
A log cabin institution, *Shorty's* is now more than fifty years old, with a perennial line outside waiting for the splendid, rich barbecue – even the crinkly fries taste smoky.

# Drinking

O ddly enough, Miami is not a hard **drinking** town. Bars, clubs and restaurants tend to blur together, and in most places you'll be able to eat dinner – or at least snack heartily – with your cocktails. There's also a thriving **hotel bar** scene, some highlights of which we've included at the end of this chapter.

As you might guess, **South Beach** is the place to head first for a night of drinking: there are plenty of options, from trendy lounges to grimy dive bars, and its compact, walkable center means you won't need to designate a driver for the evening. Weeknights here are just as good as weekends for going out, if not better: locals haughtily dismiss the so-called Causeway Crowds from across the bridges who flood the beach on Friday and Saturday nights, often clogging up smaller lounges.

Beyond South Beach, **Coral Gables** has a less trendy selection of places to drink, but is a great destination for a quality beer. On the other hand, **Coconut Grove**, which once hoped to swipe South Beach's crown in funky nightlife, has admitted defeat: bars here are less sceney, to the point of being disappointingly quiet (except at weekends). There are a couple of good drinking options over on **Key Biscayne**, while in the **Design District**, **Little Haiti** and **downtown**, just a small handful of bars draws the crowds.

It's always worth checking the alternative weeklies, *Street Miami* and the *New Times*, as they have excellent bar/club listings, highlighting the newest places as they open and the hottest parties as they're thrown.

## DOWNTOWN

### Tobacco Road
**Map 2, D8**. 626 S Miami Ave
ⓣ 305/374-1198.
This late-night dive bar lives off its reputation: it purportedly received the city's first liquor license in 1912, and the place is gloriously gritty. The bar food is standard American – burgers & fries – but the drinks list is more adventurous. There are also two stages where nightly live acts (primarily blues and

## COCKTAILS

Don't miss the chance to try one of Miami's signature cocktails. Potent and flavorful, they're often made with fresh ingredients: even if you're a confirmed cosmopolitan drinker, stray a little and sample something local, like the drinks listed below – it'll be worth it.

**Cuba Libre** A fancy name for rum, coke and a splash of lime juice.

**Mojito** A sumptuous Cuban cocktail. Mint is pounded to release its full flavor, then stirred with sugar syrup, rum, lime juice and soda water: many claim that *Lario's on the Beach* serves the best in town (see review p.142).

**Rumrunner** Another rum-based cocktail, combined with a variety of fruit flavors, often banana or blackberry: whatever the combination, expect it to be heavily alcoholic. There are plenty of bars in Key West that claim to specialize in Rumrunners.

DOWNTOWN

traditional R&B) perform – see p.172, "Nightlife."

## SOUTH BEACH

### The Abbey Brewing Company

**Map 3, D3**. 1115 16th St ⓣ 305/538-8110.

A hops-fueled antidote to the South Beach scene, *The Abbey* is as close to a neighborhood pub as the area gets. The tiny space is themed on a church – hence the wooden pew seating – and the homebrewed range of beers is superb: try the popular Oatmeal Stout or one of 12 other varieties on tap.

### Blue

**Map 3, F3**. 222 Española Way ⓣ 305/534-1009.

Opinions are divided over this tiny, lively bar: it's cool but a little clichéd, and can get clogged with grungy travelers from the nearby *Clay Hostel*. Either way, expect house music with décor – you guessed it – in different shades of blue.

### Honey

**Map 3, E6**. 645 Washington Ave ⓣ 305/604-8222.

Don't let the sexy, soft-toned décor at this South Beach newcomer fool you (although the flattering lighting will take ten years off anyone): the crowd's insatiable and it's carving out a reputation for itself as a VIP hot spot thanks to sceney weekly events. There's plenty of lounge-style seating plus a massive mahogany bar, although drinks are pricey.

### Kiss

**Map 3, F2**. *Albion* hotel, 301 Lincoln Rd ⓣ 305/695-4445, ⓦ www.kisssouthbeach.com.

Although the main restaurant downstairs (see review p.142) has a small bar area, you're better off skipping it in exchange for the circus-themed mezzanine upstairs. Here, there's ample, cushiony seating with décor in deep, rich reds slashed with yellow stripes – it has a garish sexiness that's amped up by the beautiful crowd.

SOUTH BEACH

157

## Mac's Club Deuce

**Map 3, F2**. 222 W 14th St
ⓣ 305/531-6200.
Grimy, noisy grunge bar, a remnant from pre-fabulous South Beach, which is equally fabulous in its own way. This is one of Miami's premier dive bars: drinks are cheap, plus there's a dartboard and pool table.

## Nikki Beach

**Map 3, F8**. 1 Ocean Drive
ⓣ 305/538-1231,
ⓦ www.nikkibeach.com.
A restaurant in the Penrod's complex that was formerly frat central (see review p.143), *Nikki* is a laid-back place to imbibe, its bar spilling onto the teepee-dotted private beach: take your drinks with you and watch the waves. The place is hottest on Sunday nights when well-known local DJs are booked to spin.

## Pearl

**Map 3, F8**. 1 Ocean Drive
ⓣ 305/538-1231.
Swathed in orange lights, this neo-space-age all-white eatery has a champagne bar in the center of the main room. Drinks are ultra-expensive, meaning it's really a place to go for one glass and plenty of rubbernecking before heading off elsewhere for the evening.

## Poppy

**Map 3, D2**. 927 Lincoln Rd
ⓣ 786/276-1966.
The small back bar of the restaurant *Poppy* is delightfully romantic, with walls washed in baroque, burnished golds. Open to the night sky, but canopied with tropical plants and palms, this is a gentle, chatty place to sip one of the restaurant's many good, moderately priced wines.

## Purdy's Lounge

**Map 3, B2**. 1811 Purdy Ave
ⓣ 305/531-4622.
This groovy, out-of-the-way lounge is big enough that you should be able to grab a table without too long a wait, no matter the night. The vibe's overwhelmingly local and the décor vaguely Arabian, but it's the pool tables and late license that really matter – *Purdy's* stays open till 5am every night.

## Sushi Samba Dromo

**Map 3, E2**. 600 Lincoln Rd
ⓣ 305/673-5337.

While primarily a restaurant
(see review p.143), *Sushi
Samba Dromo*'s large lounge is
one of the funkiest places in
the city to snack and drink,
and there's a nifty champagne
and sushi bar to the left of the
entrance. The waitstaff are
sweet, but don't expect
speedy service.

## Ted's Hideaway South

**Map 3, E8**. 124 2nd St
ⓣ 305/532-9869.

Twice-daily happy hours
(from noon–7pm and again
from 1am–3am) make this
local spot popular: the
atmosphere's basic and
homely, and the cheap beer
really is the only draw.

## Touch

**Map 3, D2**. 910 Lincoln Rd
ⓣ 305/532-8003.

Great fun, this *grande dame* of
the South Beach bar scene is
a restaurant as well (see
review p.145). Decorated
with palm trees in Gothic
Polynesian style, the round
bar at the front is another

great spot for people
watching – plus it's easy to
make eye contact with other
barflies. The staff is friendlier
than usual in a place this hip,
and are happy to chat on
quieter nights.

## W6 Lounge

**Map 3, E6**. 619 Washington
Ave ⓣ 305/532-4445.

Understated, thanks to its
lower South Beach location,
this artsy lounge draws direct
inspiration from New York's
SoHo. Here, though, the
drink prices and bartenders
are pleasant, making for a
stylish fallback if you don't
pass the doorman's muster at
mega-clubs like *Rumi* or
*Mynt* (see p.168 and p.167
respectively).

## Wet Willie's

**Map 3, F6**. 760 Ocean Drive
ⓣ 305/ 532-5650.

Frat boy central, this raucous
Ocean Drive bar has its own
upstairs terrace packed with
youngish tourists from
lunchtime on. The frozen
drinks are served from
washing machine-sized
mixers, and at only $5, each

SOUTH BEACH

giant helping is a bargain. The Coconut Grove outpost has a great terrace with ocean views.

Branch: Streets of Mayfair, Coconut Grove ⓣ 305/443-5060.

## CORAL GABLES

### The Globe

**Map 6, F3**. 377 Alhambra Circle ⓣ 305/445-3555.

On weekends, the bar at this popular restaurant is the place to be in Coral Gables, as it's invariably packed with a lively, twenty-something Cuban crowd. Just don't go for a quiet drink or a date – it's a raucous pick-up joint by the end of the evening.

### John Martin's

**Map 6, F4**. 253 Miracle Mile ⓣ 305/445-3777.

Run by two Irishmen, *John Martin's* is refreshingly authentic. In the restaurant section, the food includes potato soup and other hearty Irish staples; in the bar, it's all dark green drapes and wood paneling, where a wide mix of people down pints of

Guinness in a relaxed atmosphere that seems a world away from tony Coral Gables.

### Titanic Brewing Company

5813 Ponce de Leon Blvd ⓣ 305/667-2537, ⓦ www.titanicbrewery.com.

The *Titanic* brewpub offers terrific beers made on the premises, served with deliciously greasy bar food, and often accompanied by live music. Since it's right next to the University of Miami, expect a youngish, mainstream vibe.

## COCONUT GROVE

### Kiss Café

**Map 7, C6**. 2957 Florida Ave ⓣ 305/461-4214.

This funky retro lounge is decked out in modernist reds and whites, and is a welcome addition to the rather mainstream nightlife in Coconut Grove. Drinks are moderately priced, and the crowd is a smooth mix of college kids and young professionals.

## Monty's Raw Bar

**Map 7, E4**. 2550 S Bayshore Drive ⓣ 305/856-3992.
Come to *Monty's* for the views: this outdoor tiki bar overlooks Biscayne Bay and offers stunning panoramas, especially at dusk. Drink prices are reasonable, and the vibe is more partying than posing – though it's a pity that when the house reggae band starts up it's often too loud to chat comfortably.

## Taurus Chop

**Map 7, B6**. 3540 Main Hwy ⓣ 305/443-5553.
Filled with college kids and older locals, this basic establishment – which doubles as a burger joint – has a pub-style restaurant and a dark wood-paneled bar, with a respectable range of beers.

## KEY BISCAYNE AND VIRGINIA KEY

-------------------------

## Jimbo's

**Map 1, F6**. Inside the park at Virginia Key Beach, Virginia Key. No phone.
More like a junkyard with a place to drink attached than a real bar, *Jimbo's* is run-down, ramshackle and renowned throughout Miami. Help yourself to a beer from a wheelbarrow full of ice and settle down on a broken plastic chair in the shade: a bit self-consciously stagey, but good fun nonetheless.

## Rusty Pelican

**Map 1, F6**. 3201 Rickenbacker Causeway, Key Biscayne ⓣ 305/361-3818.
The views from the terrace of the *Rusty Pelican* are superb – an unbroken panorama of downtown Miami's glittering skyscrapers. Buy a drink and settle back to watch one of Miami's sensational sunsets from the deck.

## LITTLE HAITI AND THE DESIGN DISTRICT

-------------------------

## Churchill's Hideaway

**Map 8, D6**. 5501 NE 2nd Ave ⓣ 305/757-1807, ⓦ www.churchillspub.com.
Emblazoned all over with the Union Jack, this utterly out-

of-place bar set deep in the heart of Little Haiti is home away from home for Miami's expat Brits. It serves good tap beer, and satellite soccer and rugby matches are beamed into the main bar; check out the live band performances, too.

**Piccadilly Garden**
**Map 8, C9**. 35 NE 40th St

## HOTEL BARS

You might normally associate hotel bars with middle-aged business travelers nursing a lonely scotch, chatting wearily with the bartender. But in Miami, many of the funkiest spaces are inside hotels: we've listed a few suggestions below, but check *Street Miami* and the *New Times* for one-off events in other places like *Townhouse*, which often uses its glorious rooftop space for parties (see review p.120).

**Banana Bar** *Banana Bungalow*, 2360 Collins Ave, South Beach ☎305/538-1951.
Not only budget-conscious travelers stay at the *Banana Bungalow* – those looking for a cheap drink do as well. The poolside tiki bar is a friendly place to meet fellow travelers, and its happy hour from 4–7pm means a 20-ounce beer is only $2. Drunken and fun.

**The Rose Bar** *Delano Hotel*, 1685 Collins Ave, South Beach ☎305/672-2000.
Weave through the gauzy curtains draped around the Wonderland of a lobby, and head to the back of the main hall. On the right, you'll find the *Rose Bar*, spilling out into the walkway: snag one of the chunky bar stools if you can, and enjoy its seclusion – drinks are pricey, though.

305/573-8221
Open until 3am, this dark, secluded restaurant also serves as the neighborhood's local lounge. The food is good, mainstream American, but since this is one of the few places in the area to drink until dawn, it's especially lively late at night on weekends when the vibe is divey and raucous, as is the crowd.

**The Fallabella** *Albion Hotel*, 1650 James Ave, South Beach
305/913-1000.
Named after the horse relief on one of its walls, this small, curvy bar is a great place for an early evening drink. Enclosed by a wooden wall that folds over like a fortune cookie, this is a relaxing, unpretentious place.

**The Marlin Bar** *The Marlin Hotel*, 1200 Collins Ave, South Beach
305/604-5000.
While the garishness of the *Marlin*'s rooms can be grating, its futuristic, all-silver bar is on the right side of outrageous, with theatrically industrial sculpted steel chairs, among other nice touches. Not the scalding hotspot it once was (come during the week to avoid the Causeway Crowds), but the music's still consistently good.

**The Tides Bar** *Tides Hotel*, 1200 Ocean Drive, South Beach
305/604-5130.
Inside the swanky *1200* restaurant at the *Tides Hotel*, you'll find a small bar with a few sleek stools. There's barely room for it to be busy, but it's a soothing stop-off after the elbow-rubbing crowds at most lounges. Cocktails are splendid, and you can also sample some of the restaurant's signature dishes (try the conch hush puppies). Upstairs, at a small bar by the pool, a pianist plays on weekends.

LITTLE HAITI AND THE DESIGN DISTRICT

# Nightlife

For a city with a hard-partying image like Miami, it's surprising how few true nightclubs there are. Instead, most **nightlife** venues tend toward the hybrid bar-lounge-dancefloor, where you can choose whether to sip a cocktail, kick back or dance – or, conveniently, all three. And, although some bars may wield a tough velvet rope, most nightclub spaces – in an odd reversal – are less snooty. That said, it's always worth looking sharp for an evening out in style-conscious Miami: **doormen** are very label-conscious and intolerant of anyone scruffy.

As for **live music**, the Miami scene is – unsurprisingly – strongest with regard to **Latin** clubs, and there are some good spots for salsa, merengue and modern Latin fusion. On the other hand, the **rock'n'roll** scene is rather moribund, and several classic venues have recently shuttered: as a rule, don't expect world-class quality in the performers, and you'll have fun.

## CLUBS

Most clubs in Miami keep **hours** from 10pm to 5am, although thanks to less restrictive liquor licenses, many of the newer downtown spaces are open even later than that – some even 24 hours a day. It's also worth going out during the week, as that's when the crowd will be most local, especially on South Beach.

---

**Keep an eye out for local big-name DJs like Tracy Young who spin regularly at venues around town.**

---

Generally, **cover charges** will be $15–20, although early in the evening they may be waived. Note also that many clubs in Miami are alcohol- and age-conscious, so you're likely to have problems if you're under 21: call individual venues to check.

---

**As parties and promoters change frequently, be sure to peruse the latest line-ups in the *New Times* or *Street Miami*, or call the phone numbers in the reviews below.**

---

## DOWNTOWN

### Living Room Downtown
**Map 2, D3.** 60 NE 11th St
ⓣ305/531-5535.
Fri–Sun 11pm–dawn.
Owned by the same team as the *Opium Garden* (see p.168), the *Living Room*, with its plush velvet décor, is as much lounge as club. For drinking, come early in the evening, as later it becomes sweatier and clubbier: after-hours sets, beginning at 5am, are hardcore and attract plenty of bartenders and waiters from

the beach keen to party after a long weekend shift.

### Space
**Map 2, D3.** 142 NE 11th St
ⓣ305/372-9378, ⓦwww
.clubspace.com. Fri 10pm–Sat 10am, Sat 10pm–Sun noon.
New York warehouse-style superclub, with more than 30,000 square feet of dancefloor, the after-hours choice for Miami's hardcore clubbers. There are three massive dance areas, and the vibe's furtive and underground – music ranges from two-step to trance.

CLUBS

## SOUTH BEACH AND CENTRAL MIAMI BEACH

----------------------

### Billboardlive

**Map 3, G3**. 1501 Collins Ave
ⓣ305/538-2251,
ⓦwww.billboardlive.com.
Fri–Sat 10pm–5am.

A massive, gleaming nightlife complex incorporating the *Breez* restaurant (see review p.141) plus several bars and dancefloors. The main area's on the second floor, with a members-only VIP room on the fourth level. The musical menu is mainstream, but the sound system is hi-tech and high-quality.

### B.E.D.

**Map 3, F5**. 929 Washington Ave ⓣ305/532-9070.
Daily 8pm–3am.

Primarily a restaurant, this space – like many others in Miami – also doubles as a disco, especially on Wednesday and Sunday nights when there's a live DJ and a lively crowd.

### Club Deep

**Map 3, E6**. 621 Washington Ave ⓣ305/532-1509,
ⓦwww.clubdeep.com.
Wed–Sun 10pm–5am.

Satirized in the spoof novel *Naked Came the Manatee* (see p.296, "Books"), *Club Deep* is a flashy space with exactly one selling point: its dancefloor stands on a 2000-gallon aquarium. Unfortunately, the scene's as obvious as the tanks, so come for the spectacle more than anything.

### Crobar

**Map 3, F4**. 1445 Washington Ave ⓣ305/531-5027,
ⓦwww.crobarmiami.com.
Wed–Mon 10pm–5am.

There's no sign for this club, just a neon sign that reads "Cameo," the place's old name when it was an Art Deco movie theater. Although this *Crobar* isn't much compared to its venerated Chicago sibling, it's still the hardest-partying club on the beach. Expect young, frenetic dancers with a large gay and drag queen element, especially on Sundays for the "Anthem" party.

CLUBS

## Jimmy'z

**Map 4, E4**. 432 41st St
℡ 305/604-9798.
Tues–Sun 10pm–3am.
*Jimmy'z* is best during the
weekly parties on Wednesday
nights, but even then it's not
for ravers: the design here is
sequinned 1980s, and the
crowd is Eurotrash
trustafarians. Good for kitsch
glamour, but not the place to
cut loose.

## Level

**Map 3, F4**. 1235 Washington
Ave ℡ 305/532-1525.
Daily 10pm–5am.
A sprawling nightclub
complex, famous for its
enclosed, 30-foot waterfall,
but musically nondescript,
with programming
dominated by mainstream
house. However, there are
nine rooms on three floors,
so even if it's not the current
hotspot, most people will
find somewhere to boogie.

## Lola

**Map 4, E8**. 247 W 23rd St
℡ 305/695-8697.
Tues, Thurs–Sun 9pm–5am.
*Lola* has one of the best and

biggest dancefloors on South
Beach: it's trendy, but not
oppressively so, and the velvet
rope burns less often than in
many similar places. A
different DJ spins every night,
and once a month there's a live
band. All told, a great place for
a casual groove and a cocktail
or two, with the added bonus
that there's no cover charge.

## Mynt Ultra Lounge

**Map 3, G1**. 1921 Collins Ave
℡ 786/276-6132.
The lounge of the moment is
*Mynt* – although how long it
will remain so depends on
how fast several other
planned superclubs appear.
Deep green walls are washed
in menthol green light, and
delicate scents of mint
supposedly waft through the
air vents – although it's often
hard to tell thanks to the
clouds of cigarette smoke. An
enormous black bar runs the
length of the right-hand side:
unfortunately, though, it's
often understaffed. *Mynt's*
especially popular on Friday
night when even the VIP
room is packed; be prepared
for a ferocious door policy.

CLUBS

167

## Opium Garden

**Map 3, E8**. 136 Collins Ave
℡ 305/531-5535,
ⓦ www.opiummiami.com.
Fri–Sun 11pm–5am.

*Opium Garden* is a massive open-air complex with a vaguely Asian theme that plays fierce, if populist, house. The central dancefloor is enormous and there are plenty of private booths scattered around when it's time to rest the toes. Not a classically clubby crowd, but everyone here knows how to dance.

## Rain Lounge

**Map 4, E8**. 323 23rd St
℡ 305/674-7447,
ⓦ www.rainlounge.com.
Daily 9pm–5am.

This space once housed the fondly remembered *GrooveJet*, but has now been transformed into a thoroughly South Floridian bar-lounge. Half open-air, half under cover, it's filled with leather beds and gauzy white curtains, daubed with sorbet-colored furniture in Starck-lite designs. Though struggling to find a niche and a regular crowd, it's still worth a visit for the large, open-air dancefloor, at its best during the pumping hip-hop nights.

## Rumi

**Map 3, F2**. 330 Lincoln Rd
℡ 305/672-4353,
ⓦ www.rumimiami.com.

Although it's no longer the number one nightspot in town, *Rumi* is still very chic. This restaurant-bar-dance club features a geometric color scheme in ochre, rush and eggshell, plus a small bar upfront that spills over into the restaurant at the rear around 11pm, when tables are cleared for dancing.

# COCONUT GROVE

## Iguana Cantina

**Map 7, C6**. 3390 Mary St
℡ 305/444-8081.
Tues–Sun 4pm–5am.

Both a bar and a club, the *Iguana* hosts an egalitarian, hard-partying crowd. Don't come here for top name DJs; instead, plan to drink plenty, sashay enthusiastically to Latin music, and grind with the flashy, up-for-anything people

**CLUBS**

on the dancefloor. Not for wallflowers or club snobs.

### Oxygen Lounge

**Map 7, C6**. Streets of Mayfair, 2911 Grand Ave ⓣ 305/476-0202, ⓦ www.oxygenlounge.biz.

Daily 6pm–5am.

Enormous lounge-restaurant-club in an unprepossessing setting, with futuristic décor and funky staff uniforms, as well as an onsite waterfall. Although there's a live DJ every night, it's clubbiest on weekends with a house night on Friday and a Middle Eastern fusion DJ on Saturdays. The crowd's dressy and a little self-conscious.

# LIVE MUSIC

Unlike the club scene, which focuses on South Beach and the after-hours strip downtown, **live music** venues are scattered throughout the city: *Club Mystique*, for example, one of the top salsa spots, is inside the Miami Airport *Hilton*, while the indie rock club *Churchill's* is hidden away in Little Haiti.

**Cover charges** vary widely – up to $20 or more for big-names, while local pub bands will run you around $5. Call the numbers we've listed below for up-to-date schedules, or check with the *New Times* and *Street Miami*.

## LATIN, CARIBBEAN AND REGGAE

- - - - - - - - - - - - - - - - - -

### Bayside Hut

**Map 1, F6**. 3501 Rickenbacker Causeway, Virginia Key ⓣ 305/361-0808.

Daily 11am–11pm.

A run-down restaurant that's worth heading out to on weekends, when there's live music with a minimal cover: no big names, but groovy enough. Great views of Biscayne Bay, too.

### Café Nostalgia at the Forge

**Map 4, E4**. 432 41st St, Miami

Beach ☎305/534-4536.
Wed–Sun 9pm–5am.

This legendary nightspot brings a flavor of Old Havana to the beach, showcasing music that's irresistibly danceable, whether from the in-house Cuban jazz band or big-name guest performers. There's also a DJ in the courtyard if you want to dance to Latin crossover pop.

### Casa Panza

**Map 5, C5**. 1620 Calle Ocho, Little Havana ☎305/643-5343.
Mon, Wed 11am–11pm, Tues, Thurs–Sun 11am–1.30am.

*Casa Panza* is a yuppiefied restaurant with a large dancefloor attached: it's liveliest on Tuesdays and Thursdays when there are flamenco shows and a live guitarist. Otherwise, it's open to diners and drinkers every night for salsa and merengue; however, weekends are low-key.

### Club Mystique

**Map 1, C4**. Inside the Miami Airport *Hilton*, 5101 Blue Lagoon Drive ☎305/262-1000, ⓦwww.clubmystique.com.

Thurs, Sun 9pm–4am, Fri 5pm–5am, Sat 9pm–5am.
Don't be put off by *Club Mystique*'s out-of-the-way location – this is one of the premier salsa clubs in the city. And don't worry if you're a beginner: there are free dancing lessons offered on Thursday, given by in-house teachers. Friday and Saturday nights are reserved for big-name performers, but it's busy (and friendly) most every night.

### Club Tropigala

**Map 4, G3**. *Fontainebleau Hilton*, 4441 Collins Ave, Miami Beach ☎305/538-2000. Shows Wed–Sat 8.30pm, Sun 8pm.
This superb supper club is Vegas by way of Latin America, featuring live acts and an orchestra in the grand setting of the MiMo masterpiece the *Fontainebleau Hotel*. Dress to the nines and salsa the night away with a friendly, varied crowd, amid fabulously camp decor.

### Hoy Como Ayer

**Map 5, A5**. 2212 Calle Ocho, Little Havana ☎305/541-2631,

ⓦ www.hoycomoayer.com.
Wed–Sun 9pm–3am.
Enterprising young
promoters recently took over
this classic lounge, once
home to the legendary *Café
Nostalgia* (see p.169). They're
running a creative, intriguing
bar-club that attracts an arty,
eclectic crowd: it's known
especially for its Thursday
Latin fusion night *¡Fuácata!*,
one of the most exciting and
musically adventurous club
nights in the city.

## Mango's

**Map 3, F5**. 900 Ocean Drive,
South Beach ⓣ 305/673-4422.
Daily 11am–5am.
Shamelessly tacky and
gloriously over-the-top,
*Mango's* offers nightly live
pop music and dance shows
by the waiters: the blaring
music spills out onto the
sidewalk – and so does the
crowd. Cheesy, but fun,
especially on weeknights
when the crowd's a little
more local.

# ROCK, R&B AND JAZZ

----------------------

## Churchill's Hideaway

**Map 8, D6**. 5501 NE 2nd Ave,
Little Haiti ⓣ 305/757-1807,
ⓦ www.churchillspub.com.
Daily 11am–3am.
Unmissable, if inconveniently
located, local rock venue
that's nurtured local talent for
twenty years. While the bill is
sometimes hit-and-miss, it's
still an authentic glimpse at
Miami's underground music
scene.

## Jazid

**Map 3, F4**. 1432 Washington
Ave, South Beach ⓣ 305/673-
9372, ⓦ www.jazid.net.
Daily 9pm–3am.
The only R&B and jazz venue
at the heart of club-obsessed
South Beach. A welcome
alternative, if only it had a little
more edge. Granted, there's
nightly music in both the jazzy
downstairs space and upstairs
in the sleek, modern section,
but both décor and music are
bland and toothless – in other
words, *Jazid's* won't please jazz
fanatics.

LIVE MUSIC

## MAJOR PERFORMANCE VENUES

If you're looking to catch big-name acts on world tours, the following four venues are likely where they'll be playing. Miami also offers a chance to catch stadium shows from some Latin superstars who don't tour across the rest of the US.

**American Airlines Arena** 601 Biscayne Blvd, downtown.  786/777-1000,  www.aarena.com.

**James L. Knight Center** 400 SE 2nd Ave, downtown.  305/372-4633,  www.jlknightcenter.com.

**Miami Arena** 721 NW 1st Ave, downtown.  305/530-4400,  www.miamiarena.com.

**Pro Player Stadium** 2269 Dan Marino Blvd, sixteen miles northwest of downtown Miami.  305/623-6100,  www.proplayerstadium.com.

### John Martin's
**Map 6, F4**. 253 Miracle Mile, Coral Gables  305/445-3777. Mon–Sat 11.30am–1am, Sun 11.30am–11pm.
This authentic Irish pub (see review p.160) hosts regular live music – often Irish folk – that's surprisingly enjoyable and high-quality for a pub space. Minimal cover charge.

### Scully's Tavern
9809 Sunset Drive, South Miami  305/271-7404. Mon–Thurs 11am–1am, Fri–Sat 11am–3am, Sun 12pm–1am.

*Scully's*, an unremarkable sports bar in South Miami, hosts local rock bands at 10pm every Friday and Saturday night without a cover – decent, although *Churchill's Hideaway* is more worth the pilgrimage.

### Tobacco Road
**Map 2, D8**. 626 S Miami Ave, downtown  305/374-1198. Mon–Sat 11.30am–2am, Sun 12pm–12am.
This gritty, rather shabby downtown bar features two stages, where nightly live acts

perform. The tunes are mostly blues and R&B, and the place occasionally snags biggish names – so check listings for upcoming performances. On a regular night, the cover's around $7.

## Van Dyke Café

**Map 3, D2.** 846 Lincoln Rd, South Beach ☎ 305/534-3600. Sun–Thurs 8am–12am, Fri–Sat 8am–2am.

Aside from the main restaurant, there's an upstairs jazz lounge with a full bar and high-quality performances seven days a week – and don't come to chat, as enthusiasts will quieten you down if you disrupt the music. It's owned by the same team as the *News Café* (see review p.130) and serves a similar menu; there's a $5 table cover charge at night.

# Performing arts and film

**M**iami's **performing arts** scene is relatively diverse and exciting, considering the city's suntan and cocktails image. **Dance** here is strong, thanks both to fringe Latin American troupes and the nationally-known Miami City Ballet. **Classical music** and **opera** offerings, on the other hand, are average, although the New World Symphony in South Beach often delights with the quality of its performances. As for **theater**, most productions are rather mainstream, leaving little room for avant-garde or experimental work. **Comedy** is the city's weakest link: there are few venues, and the existing companies are hit-and-miss at best. Finally, **film** is perhaps where the city is strongest, with plenty of alternative theaters dotted around, as well as the requisite Hollywood blockbuster cinemas. There are also annual events like the Miami Gay & Lesbian Film Festival (see p.211, "Festivals and events").

For **tickets** to most performing arts shows, contact the ubiquitous Ticketmaster (T 305/358-5885, W www.ticketmaster.com) or the venues directly. Pick up the *Miami Herald*'s Friday edition for details of the following week's concerts, or one of the essential freesheets, the *New Times* or *Street Miami*.

---

The Miami Performing Arts Center – a six-acre complex for drama, music and dance – is scheduled to open in north downtown in 2004. Check Ⓦ www.pacfmiami.org for progress and details.

---

# PERFORMING ARTS

## Actors' Playhouse

**Map 6, F4**. 280 Miracle Mile, Coral Gables Ⓣ 305/444-9293, Ⓦ www.actorsplayhouse.org. Built as a movie theater, this building has been extensively restored, and offers two performance spaces – a small, 300-seat theater upstairs and a larger auditorium with space for 600 downstairs. Many Broadway productions stop off here, and there's an in-house children's theater workshop that performs regularly.

## African Heritage Cultural Center

**Map 1, D4**. 6161 NW 22nd Ave, Liberty City Ⓣ 305/638-6771. This community center offers classes in ethnic dance, drama and art, and there are sporadic performances – often community productions – at the onsite Wendell A. Narasse Theater, a tiny venue with only 200 seats. Call to check the performance schedule.

## Coconut Grove Playhouse

**Map 7, B6**. 3500 Main Hwy, Coconut Grove Ⓣ 305/442-4000, Ⓦ www.cgplayhouse.com. The Coconut Grove Playhouse made its name with the US premiere of Samuel Beckett's *Waiting for Godot*: unfortunately, since then its productions have grown safer, more commercial and less exciting. This is the

PERFORMING ARTS ●

2nd Thursdays is a free arts festival that's held between 6 and 9pm on the second Thursday of each month. The program usually involves music and performance on Lincoln Road on South Beach, as well as special programs at participating museums. Call ⓣ 305/673-7500 for details or visit ⓦ www.2ndthursdays.com.

place to come for broad farce and gentle drama – nothing too taxing, and plenty of Neil Simon.

### Colony Theater
**Map 3, D2**. 1040 Lincoln Rd, South Beach ⓣ 305/674-1026. At the western end of Lincoln Road, this rehabbed Deco building was originally a movie house. Converted to a theater with a 500-seat auditorium, it offers a mixed bag of famous comedians, dance concerts and performances by local theater groups.

### Coral Gables Congregational Church
**Map 6, B5**. 3010 DeSoto Blvd, Coral Gables ⓣ 305/448-7421, ⓦ www.coralgables congregational.org. Built in the Mediterranean Revival style, this church has

a dark interior with fine acoustics, perfect for classical music performances – call or check the website for listings.

### Florida Grand Opera
**Map 5, D8**. 1200 Coral Way, Little Havana ⓣ 305/854-1643 or 1-800/741-1010, ⓦ www.fgo.org. This company produces five operas each year, and performs in both Fort Lauderdale and Miami (at the Miami Dade County Auditorium, 2910 W Flagler St), accompanied by the Florida Philharmonic. As is common with most operas nowadays, English translations are projected above the stage during the performance.

### Florida Philharmonic Orchestra
3401 NW 9th Ave, Fort Lauderdale ⓣ 954/938-6700 or

PERFORMING ARTS

1-800/226-1812, Ⓦ www.floridaphilharmonic .org/miamidade.htm. Headquartered in Fort Lauderdale, the Florida Philharmonic is South Florida's premiere orchestra, performing a mixture of familiar and less well-known classical pieces across the state: its home in Miami is downtown at the Olympia Theater at the Gusman Center for the Performing Arts. Ticket prices start at $17.

## GableStage

**Map 6, B5**. *Biltmore*, 1200 Anastasia Ave, Coral Gables Ⓣ 305/445-1119, Ⓦ www.gablestage.org. Formerly known as the Florida Shakespeare Theater, this company has now made a permanent home in the *Biltmore*, having shuttled around Coral Gables for almost 15 years. Performances take place Thursday–Sunday, and the season usually includes classic plays alongside Florida premieres of Off-Broadway hits.

## Jackie Gleason Theater

**Map 3, F2**. 1700 Washington Ave, South Beach Ⓣ 305/673-7300, Ⓦ www.gleasontheater.com. Its size and beachside location work against the Jackie Gleason Theater, leading most people to presume it'll play host to aging Vegas lounge acts. On the contrary, it's home to the high-profile "Broadway in Miami Beach" program, where shows stop off during national tours on their way to New York City; it's also where the Miami City Ballet performs.

## Miami Chamber Symphony Orchestra

**Map 6, B9**. Gusman Concert Hall, University of Miami, Coral Gables Ⓣ 305/858-3500. A small, local organization, many of whose members also perform with the Florida Philharmonic (see above); it's best known for its unusual performance selections. Call for details of upcoming concerts; tickets cost $12–30.

PERFORMING ARTS

177

There are often classical music performances at alternative venues – for example, the $5 monthly series held at The Barnacle in Coconut Grove (see p.81, "Coconut Grove," and call for up-to-date details).

## Miami City Ballet

**Map 4, E8**. 2200 Liberty Ave, South Beach ⓣ 305/929-7010, ⓦ www.miamicityballet.org. The Miami City Ballet performs at the Jackie Gleason Theater (see above) roughly once every two months: at other times, though, you can stop by to watch rehearsals at its studio. It's among the largest regional companies in the country and the quality of performances is consistently exceptional.

## New Theatre

**Map 6, F7**. 4120 Laguna St, Coral Gables ⓣ 305/443-5909, ⓦ www.new-theatre.org. This 100-seat theater is an arty gem that provides high-quality, adventurous theater: it's dedicated to putting on edgy productions, whether by well-known dramatists like Tony Kushner, of *Angels in America* fame, or by new, local playwrights.

## New World Symphony

**Map 3, E2**. Lincoln Theater, 541 Lincoln Rd, South Beach ⓣ 305/673-3330, ⓦ ww.nws.org. Lincoln Theater, one of the best venues in the city, is home base for the New World Symphony, a company composed of graduate students from across the country who endure rigorous auditions to secure a place on the Symphony's three-year fellowship program. It's a training ground for future orchestral superstars, and the quality of the performances is superb. Ticket prices vary, but can be as low as $12.

## Olympia Theater

**Map 2, E6**. Gusman Center, 174 E Flagler St, downtown ⓣ 305/374-2444, ⓦ www.gusmancenter.org. This kitschy performance space (see p.21, "Downtown Miami" for details) – arguably one of the best venues in the city – is home to a highbrow but eclectic program: there's classical music, dance and offbeat touring productions.

It's not all earnest worthiness, though – it recently hosted a season of *Sing-A-Long Sound of Music*.

# FILM

### Absinthe House Cinemathèque

**Map 6, F3**. 235 Alcazar Ave, Coral Gables ⓣ 305/446-7144. This tiny cinema is a reliable option when you're looking for independent or foreign language films. The space is also home to the Teatro Avante company (ⓣ 305/445-8877, ⓦ www.teatroavante.com), which produces Spanish language plays (with English supertitles) as well as overseeing the International Hispanic Theater Festival each June.

### AMC CocoWalk 16

**Map 7, B6**. 3015 Grand Ave, Coconut Grove ⓣ 305/466-0450.

### AMC Sunset Place 24

**Map 1, C6**. 5701 Sunset Drive,

South Miami ⓣ 305/466-0450. Two of the many mall-based megaplexes, these are both reasonably close to central Miami. Both have the usual stadium seating and booming speakers to go along with all the latest releases.

### Bill Cosford Cinema

**Map 6, B9**. University of Miami Memorial Building, University of Miami campus, Coral Gables ⓣ 305/284-4861.
Named after the long-time film critic at the *Miami Herald*, this is an artsy, surprisingly plush cinema that specializes in foreign language and indie films. The program is set by University of Miami professors, so expect an academic slant to its schedule.

### Mercury Theatre

**Map 8, E6**. 5580 NE 4th Court,

**FILM**

179

north of the Design District ⓣ 305/759-8809.

Operated by the same group that runs the Absinthe Cinemathèque in Coral Gables (see above), this 100-seat movie theater is next to the restaurant *Soyka* on the borders of the Design District. On its single screen it shows a mixture of independent arthouse films and quirkier commercial movies.

### Regal South Beach 18

**Map 3, D2**. 1100 Lincoln Rd, South Beach ⓣ 305/673-6766. Massive multiplex on South Beach showing the usual range of Hollywood blockbusters. It's well located for the nearby municipal parking at 17th Street.

### Tower Theater

**Map 5, C5**. 1508 Calle Ocho, Little Havana ⓣ 305/644-3307, ⓦ www.thetowertheater.com. A landmark Deco building, this cinema was purchased by the city of Miami to show Hollywood movies with Spanish subtitles as a cultural service to Little Havana. Aside from that, it also hosts themed mini-seasons of Spanish films.

# COMEDY

### Dreamers Theater

**Map 6, G4**. 65 Almeria Ave, Coral Gables ⓣ 305/69-FUNNY, ⓦ www.justthefunny.com. The Dreamers Theater is home to one of the few comedy improv troupes in town, Just The Funny, which puts on a show for $10 every Friday and Saturday night at 11pm.

### The Improv Comedy Club

**Map 7, C6**. Streets of Mayfair 3rd level, Coconut Grove ⓣ 305/441-8200, ⓦ www.miamiimprov.com. Miami branch of a nationwide supper/comedy club: the food's mediocre, but the talent is not. One of the few places to see quality, big-name comics in the city.

COMEDY

# Gay and lesbian Miami

For over two decades now, Miami has been viewed as one of the top **gay** destinations in the country, with the scene focused squarely on **South Beach**. It doesn't quite live up to the hype: while there's a definite gay-friendly vibe in the city, and the beach is still the epicenter of gay life in Miami, things have slowed since the frantic, musclebound party atmosphere of the early 1990s. Pressure from the area's increasingly mainstream tourism has pushed many gay locals to Fort Lauderdale or Key West, and the actions of Andrew Cunanan, who mingled unnoticed in neighborhood bars before shooting designer Gianni Versace in broad daylight (see p.37), sent shockwaves through the gay community. During the mammoth **White Party** each November, gay life wholly subsumes straight life, but for the rest of the year – and certainly away from the beach – there's a limited number of clubs and bars for such a mythic gay hot spot.

# INFORMATION AND RESOURCES

There are plenty of free **newspapers** and **magazines** that illuminate what's going on in the gay and lesbian scene around Miami. For events around town, the standard resource is *TWN* (Ⓦ www.twnonline.org), a well-known, newsy freesheet. The glossy *Hot Spots* (Ⓦ www.hotspots magazine.com) and *Outlook* (Ⓦ www.outlook.com) cover the whole of Florida, with a heavy focus on the party scene, while *The Express* (Ⓦ www.expressgaynews.com) is geared to gay tourists and residents of Fort Lauderdale. The large-format glossy *She* (Ⓦ www.shemag.com) is a women-centric publication that spotlights the lesbian scene in the Sunshine State. Lastly, the *Miami Herald* is unusual in having a reporter assigned to cover gay and lesbian issues – but if you really want to find smart coverage of gay news and politics in Miami, visit Ⓦ www.outinmiami.com online.

In addition, the South Beach Business Guild has good information at ☎ 305/534-3336 or 1-888/893-5595; alternatively, contact the Miami-Dade Gay & Lesbian Chamber of Commerce at ☎ 305/534-3336. There's also the local Dade Human Rights Foundation (Ⓦ www.dhrf.com), which was set up in 1994 to support education about, and public awareness of, gay and lesbian issues.

# ACCOMMODATION

There's plenty of **accommodation** in Miami specifically geared to gay and lesbian travelers, especially on South Beach: for information or bookings, call the **South Florida Hotel Network**, 1688 Meridian Ave (☎ 1-800/538-3616 or 305/538-3616). You'll also find that most mainstream hotels are gay-friendly: those listed below are especially so.

---

Reviews below are coded by price (for example, ⑤) – for the key, see the box on p.114 in the "Accommodation" chapter.

---

## GAY ACCOMMODATION

### European Guesthouse
**Map 3, D6**. 721 Michigan Ave, South Beach ⊤ 305/673-6665, Ⓦ www.europeanguesthouse .com.
This secluded, clothing-optional B&B is rather out-of-the-way on the western side of South Beach. Rooms are eclectically furnished but comfortable; note that it's very male-dominated and women may prefer to stay elsewhere. ⑤

### The Island House
**Map 3, F4**. 1428 Collins Ave, South Beach ⊤ 305/534-0547 or 1-800/382-2422, Ⓦ www.islandhousesouthbeach .com.
Nothing special, the *Island House* is notable only as one of the larger gay guesthouses in the area. Rooms are standard, if a little shabby, but its rates are excellent and it's a decent option, especially in high season. ②

### Jefferson House
**Map 3, D5**. 1018 Jefferson Ave, South Beach ⊤ 1-877/599-5247 or 305/534-5247, Ⓦ www.thejeffersonhouse.com.
Rooms here are tastefully decorated with a motley assortment of antiques, and in-room facilities even stretch to VCRs. There's a two-night minimum in season, and a five-night minimum during White Party week. ⑤

### South Beach Villas
**Map 3, D5**. 1201 West Ave, South Beach ⊤ 305/673-9600 or 1-888/GAY-SOBE, Ⓦ www.southbeachvillas.com.
Catering to gay men and women, this is an upscale, low-key resort that brings Key West to mind more than Miami, thanks to its wooden verandahs and leafy tropical garden. The rooms are a little overwrought, festooned with antique furniture, but it's less

ACCOMMODATION

183

cruisey and more comfortable than most other gay hotels in the area. ⑥

## GAY-FRIENDLY ACCOMMODATION

### Doubletree Surfcomber

**Map 3, G2**. 1717 Collins Ave, South Beach ℡305/532-7715 or 1-800/222-TREE, ⓦwww.doubletree.com

The hotel is an active supporter of the White and Winter parties, so book well ahead if you want to stay here then; for more, see review on p.116. ⑥

### Grove Inn Country Guesthouse

22540 SW Krome Ave, Redland ℡305/247-6572 or 1-877/247-6572, ⓦwww.groveinn.com. Gay-owned and -operated, this is a charming guesthouse

that makes a welcome – if inconveniently located – alternative to the South Beach scene. That said, it's a good base for many of the city's outer district attractions, though there's little nightlife nearby. ③

### Hotel Ocean

**Map 3, F4**. 1230 Ocean Drive, South Beach ℡305/672-2579, ⓦwww.hotelocean.com. Rooms in this French-owned hotel are offbeat, charming and European-style, with tiled floors, mismatched antique furniture and light switches that only operate when you insert a room key. Its location opposite the primarily gay 12th Street Beach section makes it a convenient choice, although it's a little overpriced for the amenities it offers. ⑦

# BARS AND CLUBS

### Billboardlive Tea Dance

**Map 3, G3**. 1500 Ocean Drive, South Beach ℡1-888/777-8886, ⓦwww.jeffreysanker.com.

Held every other Sunday, this afternoon tea dance is hosted by local circuit superstar Jeffrey Sanker; the enormous

*Billboardlive* complex has several dancefloors, both indoor and outside. Cover is $10 before 7pm, $15 afterwards.

### The Boardwalk

**Map 1, G1**. 17008 Collins Ave, Sunny Isles Beach ⓣ 305/949-4119.

This strip bar may have buff boys on hand every night, but the crowd's less appealing – the vibe's a little seedy, and it's far out from South Beach. However, it's the only such strip joint in town.

### Cactus

**Map 1, E5**. 2041 Biscayne Blvd, downtown ⓣ 305/438-0662.

This neighborhood lounge is one of the few gay bars that's not on the beach, and the crowd's mostly young professionals, both male and female. It's known for its Friday night happy hours and for Saturday night's "Ay Papi" party, with a heavily Latin crowd, Cuban drink specials and a drag show – cover is $3.

### Crobar

**Map 3, F4**. 1445 Washington Ave, South Beach ⓣ 305/531-5027, ⓦ www.crobarmiami.com.

This satellite branch of the legendary Chicago club is housed in the old Cameo Theater: décor is industrial-theatrical, and the sound system is arguably the best in town. The crowd's varied, but youngish, with plenty of drag queens. It's known for the Sunday night party, "Anthem," hosted by local drag star Kitty Meow, where the cover is $25.

### Laundry Bar

**Map 3, E2**. 721 Lincoln Lane, South Beach ⓣ 305/531-7700.

Stylish, glass-fronted laundromat-bar, where you can sip a beer while your bedlinens dry. The clientele here is young and pretty, and it's one of the few places that has a good mix of girls and boys.

### Level

**Map 3, F4**. 1235 Washington Ave, South Beach ⓣ 305/532-1525.

A massive nightclub complex, famous for its enclosed 30-foot

BARS AND CLUBS

waterfall. Friday is the big gay night, called "Federation," with music that's mainly tribal and trance; cover is $20.

## Loading Zone

**Map 3, C4**. 1426a Alton Rd, South Beach ⊤ 305/531-5623. About as tough as South Beach gets, this earthy leather bar is well-hidden, marked only by a neon yellow arrow visible from the sidewalk. The crowd here is older and less waxed than at most other bars on the beach.

## O'Zone

**Map 1, C6**. 6620 SW 57th Ave, South Miami ⊤ 305/667-2888. A huge suburban club with a sunken dance floor and a predominantly Latin muscle-boy crowd, *O'Zone* is grooviest at the weekends when there's salsa and house music, as well as drag shows. Cover varies from $5 to $15.

## Pump

**Map 3, E6**. 841 Washington Ave, South Beach ⊤ 305/538-7867.
An after-hours club open until 9am Friday to Sunday, *Pump* serves juices and water, but no alcohol. The music's Hi-NRG and house, served up to two floors of cruisey young guys still buzzing at 6am. $15 cover.

## Salvation

**Map 3, C2**. 1771 West Ave, South Beach ⊤ 305/673-6508. *The* place for buff boys and those who love them. A pumped-up crowd (in both senses) crams onto the dance floor every Saturday night and parties till dawn: although it's 100% male on Saturdays, Friday's more mixed with women and a few straight clubheads. Cover is $15 before midnight, $20 afterwards.

## Score

**Map 3, E2**. 727 Lincoln Rd, South Beach ⊤ 305/535-1111. Local video bar, with the usual amenities like a pool table and patio, plus a martini lounge. Open from 1pm, it's a good place to get an afternoon coffee and sit outside to watch the Lincoln Road runway. Wednesday

BARS AND CLUBS

night features an amateur strip contest.

### Twist
**Map 3, E5**. 1057 Washington Ave, South Beach ⊤305/538-9478.
A labyrinthine bar that just keeps expanding: there are two dancefloors, video screens in the main lounge downstairs and a garden bar out back. The all-male crowd's friendly and more diverse than most South Beach watering holes. In addition, go-go boys perform in the garden bar Fridays, Sundays and Mondays.

# SHOPS

### Body Body Wear
**Map 3, F5**. 943 Washington Ave, South Beach ⊤305/531-6325.
Miami branch of the circuit clothing chain masterminded by designer Stephen Sandler. Body Body Wear sells skintight tops and pants, plus underwear, all made from performance fabrics that will keep you cool in the hottest club or gym.

### Lambda Passages Bookstore
**Map 8, E3**. 7545 Biscayne Blvd, near Little Haiti ⊤305/754-6900.
This gay and lesbian bookstore – and unofficial community center – may be a little out-of-the-way, but it has a wide range of fiction and non-fiction, as well as a video rental library of classic films.

### The Pink Palm Company
**Map 3, E2**. 737 Lincoln Rd, South Beach ⊤305/442-7373.
A stationery and trinkets megastore on Lincoln Road with a wide selection of gay greeting cards, as well as a small selection of furniture and fun, kitschy gifts.

### Whittall & Shon
**Map 3, F4**. 1319 Washington Ave, South Beach ⊤305/538-2606, ⓦwww.whittallshon.com.
Whittall & Shon is an orgy of

SHOPS

●

feather boas and flouncing hats for boys and girls, as well as a smaller selection of clubbers' clothing. Great, campy fun.

### Zoo14

**Map 3, F5**. 933 Washington Ave, South Beach ⊤ 305/538-4273, Ⓔ zoo14florida@aol.com. Zoo 14 sells clothes from a variety of designers, but it's especially known for its selection of skimpy swimwear: not the coolest store, perhaps, but more accommodatingly mainstream than Whittall & Shon. Branch: 918 N Federal Hwy, Fort Lauderdale ⊤ 954/462-7373.

# GYMS

### Club Body Center

2991 Coral Way, Little Havana ⊤ 305/448-4357, ⓦ www.clubbodycenter.com. Nominally a gym, but working out comes second to making out at this growing chainlet. There's super-cruisey nude sunbathing by the pool, and plenty of social events to help encourage mingling – plus it's open 24 hours year-round.

### David Barton Gym

**Map 3, G2**. Inside the *Delano* hotel, 1685 Collins Ave, South Beach ⊤ 305/674-5757. Small and lush, this gym's decorated with orchids and plenty of celebrities. It's less musclebound than most other gyms around, and has plenty of free weights, as well as yoga classes.

### Idol's Gym

**Map 3, E2**. 715 N Lincoln Ln, South Beach ⊤ 305/532-0089. A good budget option, since a day pass here costs only $10 – and it's open 24 hours a day during the week. The workout room, decorated with a trashy mural, is crowded with machines and looks out directly onto the street: like most gyms on the beach, Idol's is packed with superpumped muscleboys.

Branch: 5556 NE 4th Ct, just south of Little Haiti ☏ 305/751-7591.

### South Beach Ironworks
**Map 3, C3**. 1676 Alton Rd, South Beach ☏ 305/531-4743, Ⓦ www.southbeachironworks .com.

Massive gym on the west side of South Beach, less sceney than others and with extensive classes available: a day pass is $15.

# GAY BEACHES

There are no officially designated **gay beaches** in the city – however, look for the densest crowds on the South Beach seafront, and you'll find the **12th Street Beach**, a popular gay hangout that stretches for several blocks of sand. In addition, the northern reaches (stations 27–29) of the nude beaches at **Haulover Park** (see p.56) are less predominantly gay but, oddly, cruisier.

# EVENTS

### The Winter Party
Early March

A huge week-long event, the Winter Party is the springtime counterpart to November's White Party (see below), with special nights at most major South Beach venues. The festivities climax with an outdoor club on the beach at 14th St and Ocean Drive; ☏ 305/572-1841, Ⓦ www.winterparty.com.

### Miami Gay & Lesbian Film Festival
Late April

Two weeks of gay-themed film programming at the Colony Theater in South Beach: there's a mixture of amateur and professional movies, in both documentary and drama genres; ☏ 305/534-9924, Ⓦ www .miamigaylesbianfilm.com.

---

**For up-to-date gay and lesbian information, check online at
Ⓦ www.circuitnoize.com, or pick up one of the free
magazines like *Outlook* (see p.182).**

---

## Aqua Girl
Mid-May

One of the few women-centric events in the city, this four-day party of cocktails and clubbing raises money for the Dade Human Rights Foundation; Ⓣ 305/572-1831, Ⓦ www.aquagirl.org.

## Pride Miami
May

The local Pride celebrations usually take place off-season in May – check out Pride South Florida in March in Fort Lauderdale, too, which is larger and livelier; Ⓣ 305/358-8245, Ⓔ pridemiami@aol.com.

## The White Party
Thanksgiving

The godfather of all circuit parties, this is a week when what few clothes people wear must be white, and takes in hotels and bars across South Beach. Don't miss the debauched, surreal White Party itself when the neo-Italian Villa Vizcaya is transformed into gay Miami's fabulous answer to the Venice Carnival, all to raise funds for local HIV-related charities; Ⓦ http://whiteparty.net.

EVENTS

# Shopping

**M**iami provides plenty of opportunities to drop your dollars **shopping** for clothes, music, souvenirs and beauty treatments – though the pickings are fairly mainstream. The biggest disappointment in Miami's retail landscape is its dearth of bookstores, pitifully few for a city this size. At least most shops generally stay open late, especially at the beach, so you can browse before dinner.

**South Beach** is undeniably the place to head if you're looking for quirky, smaller boutiques, its outdoor spaces a welcome antidote to overly air-conditioned malls. Collins Avenue and Lincoln Road hold the largest number of browsable stores, while further north on the beach, **Bal Harbour** is home to the city's densest selection of designer names, albeit in an unflattering setting.

Check out **Coconut Grove** for some unusual gift stores, especially in the triangle made by Commodore Plaza, Grand Avenue and the Main Highway; otherwise, its much-ballyhooed shopping centers are rather disappointing. **Coral Gables** has plans to reinvigorate its Miracle Mile, although at the moment most shops seem to offer older ladies' fashions with window displays that look unchanged since 1983. Around the city, a large number of **suburban malls** essentially replicate one another's offerings with branches of The Gap, Express and Victoria's Secret.

In **Little Havana**, all the retail action is along Calle Ocho: come here for cigars and Cuban knickknacks, as most of the other storefronts house mini-markets or cafés. The **Design District** has most of its notable housewares stores on 40th Street. Finally, **downtown** Miami is barren except for an odd assortment of a dozen or so fabric peddlers, plenty of cheap shoe stores, and numerous electronics outlets, blaring music onto the sidewalk and hooking passers-by with deals that seem too good to be true – and they are.

## BOOKS

It's surprisingly hard to find a good **bookstore** in the city; listed below are all the major ones close to the center: the newly opened Fifteenth Street Books is perhaps the only one with a sizeable selection of secondhand titles.

**Barnes & Noble**
Map 6, G4. 152 Miracle Mile
ⓣ 305/446-4152,
ⓦ www.bn.com.
Located in the heart of downtown Coral Gables, this is the only nearby branch of the book megachain – it stocks the usual wide selection of books and music,

plus a large Spanish-language section of both novels and non-fiction.

## Books & Books

**Map 3, D2**. 933 Lincoln Rd, South Beach ☎305/532-3222, ⓦ www.booksandbooks.com. The city's signature book-store, Books & Books is pleasant enough, and the café's good, too. This branch is smallish and filled with coffee table books, but it's the only place on the beach for reading material other than the rundown Kafka's Kafé (see overleaf). Branch: 265 Aragorn Ave, Coral Gables ☎305/442-4408.

## Borders

**Map 7, C6**. Streets of Mayfair, Coconut Grove ☎305/447-9890, ⓦ www.borders.com. Chain megastore that offers good discounts on new hardcovers and has a strong selection of local interest books. It also sells CDs and hosts author readings – call or drop by for schedules.

## B. Dalton

**Map 7, B6**. CocoWalk, Coconut

Grove ☎305/444-5143. A smaller store, part of the large Barnes & Noble group, that focuses on popular titles, including a wide selection of thriller and romance paperbacks.

## Downtown Book Center

**Map 2, E6**. 247 SE 1st St, downtown ☎305/377-9939. Tiny, bilingual bookstore, strong on popular fiction, thrillers and romance.

## Eutopia

**Map 3, D3**. 1627 Jefferson Ave, South Beach ☎305/532-8680. This small bookstore stocks first editions and rare books – not exactly beach reading, but a joy for connoisseurs.

## Fifteenth Street Books

**Map 6, G3**. 296 Aragon Ave, Coral Gables ☎305/442-2344 Lots of art books and old hardcovers in top condition. It may not be a bargain hunter's paradise, but it's well stocked by the knowledgeable, friendly owner, who was the original founder of nearby Books & Books.

BOOKS

### Kafka's Kafé

**Map 3, F4**. 1464 Washington Ave, South Beach ⓣ 305/673-9669.

Rather ratty selection of used books – and don't come here looking for anything specific as the filing system is erratic. Budget paperbacks are good beach throwaways, although that's all they're good for; on the plus side, there's a wide selection of magazines and it's open until midnight.

### Murder on Miami Beach

**Map 1, G2**. 16850 Collins Ave, Sunny Isles Beach ⓣ 305/956-7770

Unsurprisingly, this store stocks a wide selection of murder and mystery books, both new and used, plus signed first editions and gimmicky murder-related gifts.

### Ninth Chakra

**Map 3, E2**. 811 Lincoln Rd, South Beach ⓣ 305/538-0671, ⓦ www.9thchakra.com.

New age bookstore and gift shop that's rather out-of-place in the strutting retail palace of Lincoln Road. There's a wide selection on everything from reiki healing to regression; though it's a pity about the disinterested staff.

## CLOTHES: NEW

The **high fashion** zone in Miami stretches along two blocks of Collins Avenue on South Beach, between 5th and 8th streets. Here, side by side, you'll find many of the big-name, mid-price designers: the upscale stuff is in the Bal Harbour shops. Strangely for a town as funky and fashion-conscious as Miami, there are few homegrown designers: the closest South Beach comes is with its club-wear stores.

### Agnès b

**Map 3, D2**. 640 Collins Ave, South Beach ⓣ 305/604-8705.

Chic, slim-fit French fashions with an emphasis on muted gray, black and navy. The

---

**If you need anything altered, skip the pricey in-store rates: Maria's Alteration Shop (1622a Alton Rd, South Beach ⓣ 305/674-1552) is reliable and reasonably priced – although few of the staff speak fluent English.**

---

men's selection is especially strong with patterned, Paul Smith-esque shirts, as well as minimalist suits and exclusive sneaker designs.

### Base

**Map 3, E6**. 939 Lincoln Rd, South Beach ⓣ 305/531-4982, ⓦ www.baseworld.com. Urban clothes for men and women, conceived by British choreographer-turned-designer Steven Giles – sexy, showy fashions with an Asian edge that aren't for the self-conscious. It's a lifestyle store, too, stocking the designer's capsule range of sleek homewares, plus music and beauty supplies.

### Betsey Johnson

**Map 3, E6**. 805 Washington Ave, South Beach ⓣ 305/673-0023, ⓦ www.betseyjohnson.com. For every girl's inner Cyndi Lauper, Betsey Johnson

makes clothes that are wacky, fun and feminine. She's known for her crazy color combinations, but the real reason the clothes sell is because they're so figure-flattering.

### FunkySexy

**Map 3, E2**. 637 Lincoln Rd, South Beach ⓣ 305/532-2649, ⓦ www.funkysexyonline.com. Trashy, goofy clubwear for men and women – a great pitstop if you're caught short with one too few tube tops or a need for just one more skin-tight T-shirt.

### Intermix

**Map 3, E6**. 634 Collins Ave, South Beach ⓣ 305/53-5950. This New York boutique's Miami outpost hosts the same quirky, girly mix of designers alongside wardrobe staples like Earl Jeans. Great for handbags, too.

**CLOTHES: NEW**

## Laundry Industry

**Map 3, F6**. 666 Collins Ave, South Beach ⓣ 305/531-2277. Here, simplicity is everything: this store borrows its style from Donna Karen – pure cotton T-shirts and loose pants for women in a monochrome palette, with the occasional splash of color.

## Metro

**Map 3, F5**. 915 Washington Ave, South Beach ⓣ 305/673-6878.
Perhaps not the subtlest store, but quintessentially Miami, this clubwear boutique is for those with more moxie than money, filled with skimpy clothes for clubbing and strutting.

## Nicole Miller

**Map 3, F6**. 656 Collins Ave, South Beach ⓣ 305/535-2200. Nicole Miller's line is classy, floaty, and just fashionable enough. Great for glamorous clothes that don't reveal too much skin.

## Santini Mavardi

**Map 3, F5**. 935 Washington Ave, South Beach

ⓣ 305/538-6229, ⓦ www.santinimavardi.com. For the South Beach Cinderella, this store stocks a small line of clothes, but is best known for its glitzy shoes – they run the gamut from rhinestone-studded, super-stiletto-heeled and custom-made.

## Seize Sur Vingt

**Map 3, F5**. 203 11th St, South Beach ⓣ 305/695-1779, ⓦ www.16sur20.com.
The New York shirtmaker's first branch outside Manhattan offers custom-made shirts that are understated, expensive and fit like a glove. Recently, it's also begun bespoke suit tailoring, and its made-to-order cashmere sweater is the ultimate luxury.

## Theory

**Map 3, F6**. 610 Collins Ave, South Beach ⓣ 305/673-8825. Long known in department stores for its stretchy lycra shirts with a killer fit, this newly opened stand-alone boutique offers sexy but elegant clothes for women.

CLOTHES: NEW

There's also a small but attractive collection for men, including shirts, casual jackets and jeans.

## CLOTHES: VINTAGE AND THRIFT

There's a good selection of **vintage** shops in South Beach, but true retro devotees should make the pilgrimage to Liberty City. There, you'll find half a dozen warehouses piled high with supercheap bargains – there's even a strip mall housing nothing but thrift stores.

### Beatnix
**Map 3, F5**. 1149 Washington Ave, South Beach ⊤305/532-8733.
Alongside the vintage, Beatnix keeps technicolor wigs, enormous feather boas and plenty of rubber clubwear: half drag, half dress-up, and definitely fun.

### Before Dark
**Map 3, F4**. 1321 Washington Ave, South Beach ⊤786/276-6888.
Before Dark's specialty is uniforms and outerwear: heavy overcoats that aren't much use in Miami are bargain-priced, and it feels a little more authentically vintage than many of the other stores around the beach – just don't be put off by its ramshackle appearance.

### Consign of the Times
**Map 3, D3**. 1635 Jefferson Ave, South Beach ⊤305/535-0811.
Here, Miami's obsession with designer labels pays off – locals offer their Gucci cast-offs for sale, splitting the profits with the store. Granted, there's plenty of flashy trash, but also the occasional find if you're prepared to sift through the racks.

### Douglas Gardens Thrift Store
**Map 1, D4**. 5713 NW 27th St, Liberty City ⊤305/638-1900
One of several vast warehouses clustered together, there's an enormous selection at rock-bottom prices – in fact, chi chi vintage stores

from New York and LA regularly arrive with vans to scour for stock. Keep in mind that this isn't the greatest part of town, so it's best to visit by car or not at all.

**Recycled Blues**
**Map 3, F3**. 1507 Washington Ave, South Beach Ⓣ 305/538-0656, Ⓦ www.recycledblues.com. The largest thrift store on the beach, this shop has a great selection of cool merchandise (especially denim) – its biggest drawback is the premium prices.

## DEPARTMENT STORES AND MALLS

Miami has a large number of **malls**, both traditional and open-air – though all tend to house the standard crop of shops and department stores, as well as plenty of Burdine's, the local variety (see p.22).

For details on one of the best and biggest outlet malls in the country, see "Out of the City: Fort Lauderdale," p.234.

**Aventura Mall**
19501 Biscayne Blvd, Aventura Ⓣ 305/935-1110. North of Miami, just off I-95 (take the Miami Gardens Drive exit and follow the signposts), you'll find Aventura, the local megamall that essentially sprouted a town around it. There are several department stores here, as well as an enormous food court and the usual mall branch shops.

**Bal Harbour Shops**
**Map 1, G3**. 9700 Collins Ave, Bal Harbour Ⓣ 305/886-0311, Ⓦ www.balharbourshops.com. The Bal Harbour Shops house every well-known designer name, from Gucci to Prada, plus an enormous Saks Fifth Avenue – and an oddly incongruous branch of The Gap. The mall itself is singularly unappealing, housed in a clunky concrete building.

## Bayside Mall

**Map 2, F5**. 401 N Biscayne Blvd, downtown ⊤ 305/577-3344, Ⓦ www.baysidemarketplace.com. This waterfront complex features stores much like any other: there's a large branch of the upscale jeanswear company Guess?, funky teen shoe store Skechers, and a Sharper Image.

## Burdine's

**Map 2, D6**. 22 E Flagler St, downtown ⊤ 305/577-2410, Ⓦ www.burdines.com. Florida's signature department store differs little from department stores everywhere: downtown, the tattered flagship branch sells homewares, clothes from the usual designer names and plenty of perfume. The outpost at 1777 West Ave in South Beach (⊤ 305/825-7351) is smaller and more architecturally interesting, complete with ornamental palm trees.

## CocoWalk

**Map 7, B6**. 3015 Grand Ave, Coconut Grove ⊤ 305/444-0777, Ⓦ www.cocowalk.com. When it opened in the early 1990s, this shopping center revitalized Coconut Grove. Now, the pleasant but unremarkable Mediterranean Revival architecture, with its covered walkways and plenty of eateries, houses the usual names like Victoria's Secret and The Gap, as well as a branch of bookseller B. Dalton's.

## The Falls Shopping Center

**Map 1, C7**. 8888 SW 136th St, South Miami ⊤ 305/255-4570. Enormous open-air shopping complex, sporting a waterscape punctuated with waterfalls, and a funky sculpture by artist Romero Britto (see p.202). It has more than 100 stores and is a little more upscale than most: there's a massive Bloomingdales, plus stylish homewares from Crate & Barrel, Pottery Barn and Williams-Sonoma – and sexy women's wear from BCBG and Bebe.

## Streets of Mayfair

**Map 7, C6**. 2911 Grand Ave,

Coconut Grove ⓣ 305/448-1700, ⓦ www.streetsofmayfair.com. Positioned as CocoWalk's posher sister, this oddly designed and unappealing mall is filled with copper statues and mosaics, but oddly empty of people. There's a men's-only branch of Banana Republic, plus The Limited, Ann Taylor's Loft, United Colors of Benetton and a huge Borders bookstore.

## Shops at Sunset Place

**Map 1, C6**. 5701 Sunset Dr, South Miami ⓣ 305/663-0482. A mammoth outdoor mall in South Miami that's notable for its large Niketown, as well as Miami's only Virgin Megastore, plus substantial branches of Barnes & Noble and Urban Outfitters.

## ETHNIC SPECIALTIES AND CRAFTS

Stores across the city claim to sell authentic souvenirs of Miami's two dominant immigrant cultures – Cuban and Haitian – but the ones listed below offer the real thing.

### El Credíto Cigar Factory

**Map 5, E5**. 1106 Calle Ocho, Little Havana ⓣ 305/858-4162. It's easy to understand why this is the best known smokeshop in the city. Here, you'll see rows of *tabaqueros* (cigar rollers) making juicy cigars by hand, using top-quality tobacco – it's generally agreed that this store's *La Gloria Cubana* cigar is one of the best available.

### Haitian Art Factory

**Map 8, F2**. 835 NE 79th St, Little Haiti ⓣ 305/758-6939, ⓦ www.haitianartfactory.com. This eccentric shop, attached to a doctor's office, carries

In addition to El Credíto, there are plenty of good, authentic cigar shops in Key West – see p.259, "Out of the City: The Florida Keys."

ETHNIC SPECIALTIES AND CRAFTS

fine wood carvings and crafts from Haiti – admittedly alongside plenty of tat. Call ahead to check if it's open, as hours can be erratic.

### Halouba Botanica

**Map 8, C6**. 101 NE 54th St, Little Haiti ⊤ 305/751-7485. One of many *botanicas* on the *voudou* strip, this store is spacious and a little less daunting than some of the others (see box, p.101). There's a large temple onsite, which holds regular ceremonies ministered by the husband-and-wife team that runs the store.

### La Casa de las Guayaberas

**Map 1, C5**. 5840 Calle Ocho, Little Havana ⊤ 305/266-9683. This shop's specialty is the unmistakably Cuban *guayabera* shirt – cool in the tropical heat and billowy in the wind. The tailor-owner is one of the earliest Cuban-American refugees, and everything is hand-sewn by his team: he offers inexpensive options

starting at $15 to $20, as well as pricey, custom-made designs starting at $250.

### La Casa de las Piñatas

**Map 5, B5**. 1756 Calle Ocho, Little Havana ⊤ 305/649-4711. *Piñatas*, the gaudy party favors bashed by guests until they'll spill their candy-stuffed guts, are sold here in any shape or size: hundreds hang from the ceiling. If your Spanish is good, and you've time and money, you can even commission custom-made shapes.

### Libreri Mapou

**Map 8, D5**. 5919 NE 2nd Ave, Little Haiti ⊤ 305/757-9922, ⓦ www.librerimapou.com. The place to go if you want to dig deeper into Little Haiti, offering a wide selection of books on the history and politics of the Caribbean nation, as well as Haitian novels in English, French and Creole, French magazines and Haitian newspapers.

# FOOD AND DRINK

You don't have to splurge on every meal if money's tight: there are branches of the supermarket chain Publix everywhere in the city. Also, ask about local **farmers markets** – one of the best is held every Saturday in Coconut Grove, at the junction of Grand Avenue and Margaret Street, selling sumptuous local produce, much of it organic. There are also plenty of liquor stores – although note that recently enacted local ordinances limit the sale of alcohol after 10pm on the beach.

### Epicure Market
**Map 3, C3**. 1656 Alton Rd, South Beach ⊤ 305/672-1861. A gourmet market offering high-quality – but expensive – foodstuffs like hand-made biscotti, plus fresh fish and meats. There's an interesting beer selection, as well as a small, but fresh, flower stand.

### Wild Oats Community Market
**Map 3, C5**. 1020 Alton Rd, South Beach ⊤ 305/532-1707, ⓦ www.wildoats.com. Delicious and healthy, this enormous supermarket offers more than just granola and tofu – among other things, there are freshly baked cakes, exotic juices and organic produce. A terrific picnic lunch stop-off.

## GIFTS AND ODDITIES

### Britto Central
**Map 3, D2**. 818 Lincoln Rd, South Beach ⊤ 305/531-8821. Local artist Romero Britto paints colorful, cartoony images on everything from ties to handbags, available at this gallery-cum-store. There's something sweet, trashy and deliciously Miami about his work.

### Pink Palm Company
**Map 3, E2**. 737 Lincoln Rd,

South Beach ⊤ 305/538-8373 or 1-877/538-8373, ⓦ www.pinkpalm.com.
The best card store in the city, with a wide range of greeting cards both traditional and funky, as well as an eclectic mix of candles, notebooks and other small gifts.

## Pop

**Map 3, F5**. 1151 Washington Ave, South Beach ⊤ 305/604-9604, ⓦ www.popsouthbeach.com.
An eclectic mix of toys, greeting cards and a few clothes, all chosen with the same wacky sense of style and humor, Pop is a great place for unusual gifts – check out the bootleg CDs from local circuit parties, as well as pristine 1980s memorabilia.

## Toy Town

**Map 1, F7**. 260 Crandon Blvd, Key Biscayne ⊤ 305/361-5501.
Forget Toys'R'Us and F.A.O. Schwarz – this is a traditional, family-owned toy store that's the best in the city. It sells simple, nostalgic toys like train sets, board games and stuffed animals, perhaps as novel to today's kids as it is familiar to their parents.

## HEALTH AND BEAUTY

### Brownes & Co. Apothecary

**Map 3, D2**. 841 Lincoln Rd, South Beach ⊤ 1-888/BROWNES, ⓦ www.brownesbeauty.com.
Stock up on sumptuous skincare lines like Kiehls and Fresh, as well as top-name make-up brands here. The Some Like It Hot salon (⊤ 305/538 7544) upstairs is renowned for great, if pricey, manicures.

### Massage by Design

**Map 3, E8**. 100 Collins Ave, South Beach ⊤ 305/532-3112.
At the tip of South Beach is a locals' favorite: this spa offers combo massages, including shiatsu and reflexology, as well as hot stone rubs, all in feng shuied surroundings.

GIFTS AND ODDITIES • HEALTH AND BEAUTY

The staff are personable, and you can also arrange for manicures and waxing.

### Oribe Salon

**Map 3, D3**. 1641 Jefferson Ave, South Beach ☏ 305/538-7661. One of the top salons on the beach, with prices to match; the place for an emergency cut-and-color.

### Russian Turkish Bath

**Map 1, G4**. *Castle* hotel, 5445 Collins Ave, Miami Beach ☏ 305/867-8313. The facilities here are a little less lush than at other spas,

but it's a place utterly devoid of attitude; there's a gym, steam rooms, and a salt-water jacuzzi.

### Sephora

**Map 3, F6**. 721 Collins Ave, South Beach ☏ 305/532-0904, Ⓦ www.sephora.com. A beauty supermarket where fragrances are grouped not by fashion house but alphabetically. There are fewer pushy sales staff and testers for every product – and it's open late: great for a pre-dinner pit-stop if you forgot to spritz at home.

## HOUSEWARES

For **housewares**, the main drag is inevitably along 40th Street in the Design District – although there you'll find as much furniture as ornaments. If you do fall in love with something large and unpackable, most stores will be happy to ship it to you anywhere in the world – at a price, of course.

### Holly Hunt

**Map 8, D9**. 3833 NE 2nd Ave, Design District ☏ 305/571-2012. Beyond chic, this showcase for multiple homeware lines is the last word in classic

design. There's little that's daring or avant-garde (and definitely no bargains), but it's a sumptuous space with luxurious furniture – great for browsing.

## Lamartine

**Map 3, F3**. 421 Española Way,
South Beach Ⓣ 305/695-0903.
Amid the tourist tack of
Española Way, Lamartine is a
small, stylish store that stocks
groovy Alessi homewares,
many of them the brainchild
of Philippe Starck.

## Real Life Basic

**Map 3, E2**. 643 Lincoln Rd,
South Beach Ⓣ 305/604-1984,
Ⓦ www.reallifebasic.com.
Next to pots, pans and
cookbooks, this store stocks
quirky gifts and fun kitchen
gadgets that are anything but
basic, from funky fondue sets
to marabou-trimmed velvet
wine bottle slipcovers.

## MUSEUM STORES

There's little imaginative buying at most **museum stores**,
but those listed below are fun enough places to browse.

---

The Bass Museum has a terrific bookshop with a wide
selection of art books that should be even better when the
museum refit is finally completed (see p.45, "South Beach").

---

## Art Deco Welcome Center

**Map 3, F5**. 1001 Ocean Drive,
South Beach Ⓣ 305/672-2014,
Ⓦ www.mdpl.org.
This lobby store is a treasure
trove of offbeat trinkets, from
unique embossed metal
postcards to a wide range of
gifts and books on all things
Deco.

## Miami Art Museum Gift Shop

**Map 2, C6**. Metro-Dade
Cultural Center, 101 W Flagler
St, downtown Ⓣ 305/375-1700,
Ⓦ www.miamiartmuseum.org.
Superb downtown gift shop
with a funky edge. Alongside
the usual books and arty
cards, you'll find design-
conscious housewares at
better prices than in most
rarefied museum stores.

MUSEUM STORES

# MUSIC

-------------------------------------------------

For dance and club **music** in the city, there's nowhere to beat the stores on South Beach. If your taste is a little more eclectic, there are superb stores in Little Havana and Little Haiti for Caribbean and Latin American music.

### Grooveman Music

**Map 3, F3**. 1543 Washington Ave, South Beach ☎ 305/535-6257, Ⓦ www.groovemanmusic.com. A DJ's dream, this store stocks underground house and trance – kept dark during the day and night, the place throbs with loud music and is usually packed with local club kids.

### Les Cousins

**Map 8, D2**. 7858 NE 2nd Ave, Little Haiti ☎ 305/754-8452. Blasting laid-back Haitian tunes out onto the street, this record shop offers rare and hard-to-find Caribbean music at good prices.

### Spec's Music

**Map 3, F7**. 501 Collins Ave, South Beach ☎ 305/534-3667. Miami's sorely lacking the usual glut of Sam Goody and FYE music stores that pepper most American cities: the best local alternative is Spec's Music. Its beach location is good for singles and dance music, and there's an up-to-date import section – just don't look for any obscure artists. Another location downtown at 202 SE 1st St (☎ 305/577-6167).

### Uncle Sam's

**Map 3, E5**. 1141 Washington Ave, South Beach ☎ 305/532-0973, Ⓦ www.unclesamsmusic.com. Standard record store with an ample selection of popular music, as well as a secondhand section, posters for sale, and mountains of flyers and freesheets – a good place to check out what's happening music-wise in the next few weeks around the city.

# Festivals and events

**M**iami is always looking for an excuse to party, and plenty of **festivals** and **events** cater to that need throughout the year. The greatest number of events take place during peak season, from January through April; the only time when there's little, if anything, on offer is during the sticky summer months of July and August. The Orange Bowl in January whips the city into a frenzy, while the three events which put extra strain on accommodation are the **Boat Show** in February, the **Winter Music Conference** in March, and the **White Party** in November.

The list below is by no means comprehensive, but includes a range of widely different activities – for detailed information, call the phone numbers listed. Otherwise, contact the Greater Miami Convention and Visitors Bureau, 701 Brickell Ave (Mon–Fri 8.30am–6pm; ☎305/539-3000, ⊛www.tropicoolmiami.com).

Other good sources for festival listings are the alternative weeklies, the *New Times* and *Street Miami*, available free on most street corners.

## JANUARY

---

### Orange Bowl Festival

January 1

Miami is crazy about college football, and the Orange Bowl Parade is the height of the madness. There are floats, marching bands and even an Orange Bowl Queen. If you want to watch for free, snag a spot early on the parade route along Biscayne Boulevard; otherwise, bleacher seats start at $12; ☎305/371-4600, ⓦwww.orangebowl.org.

### Three Kings Day Parade

Early January

This celebration of the Three Wise Men is one of the biggest Latin events in the country, with crowds of up to half a million. It all takes place along Calle Ocho between 4th and 27th avenues; ☎305/445-4020.

### Art Deco Weekend

Third weekend in January

Ocean Drive is completely taken over with booths and bands for this celebration of all things Deco. The Miami Design Preservation League arranges multiple tours of the historic district as part of the festival; ☎305/672-2014, ⓦwww.mdpl.prg and www.artdecoweekend.com.

### Art Miami

Mid-January

Thanks to Miami's vibrant art scene, this massive exhibition at the Miami Beach Convention Center often showcases interesting and innovative work by local artists; entrance fee is $12; ☎305/553-8924, ⓦwww.art-miami.com.

### Martin Luther King Day Parade

January 16

This march through Liberty City commemorates the slain civil rights leader; ☎305/247-9306.

### Taste of the Grove

Late January

Coconut Grove's lively restaurants join together to stage this event in Peacock Park, each with a booth that offers samples from their menu. There's also live music;

ⓣ 305/444-7270,
ⓦ www.coconutgrove.com.

## Key Biscayne Art Festival

**Late January**
Crandon Boulevard hosts a small but fun party, celebrating Key Biscayne's artists; ⓣ 305/361-0049, ⓦ www.key-biscayne.com.

## Miami Film Festival

**Late January–early February**
Recently taken over by Florida International University, this festival includes arthouse and mainstream films from the USA and overseas, especially Cuba. Films are shown in three locations – the Colony Theater and the Regal Cinema on South Beach, and the Gusman Center downtown; ⓣ 305/377-3456, ⓦ www.miamifilmfestival.com.

# FEBRUARY

## Scottish Festival and Games

**Early February**
In nearby Pembroke Pines,
this festival includes country dancing and an evening *ceilidh,* as well as Scottish pipe bands and highland food. Entrance fee is $12; ⓣ 305/756-8335, ⓦ www.sassf.com.

## Homestead Championship Rodeo

**Early February**
Here you can see professional rodeo cowboys competing in steer wrestling, bull riding, calf roping and bareback riding competitions; ⓣ 305/247-3513, ⓦ www.homesteadrodeo.com.

## Miami International Boat Show

**Mid-February**
A massive luxury exhibition, showcasing top-range boats for potential buyers from around the world; ⓣ 305/531-8410, ⓦ www.boatshows.com.

## Coconut Grove Arts Festival

**Mid-February**
Fittingly eccentric for Coconut Grove, you're as likely here to find alternative

**FEBRUARY**

crafts – such as talking mirrors – as you are traditional painting; a lively, fun festival; ☎305/447-0401, ⓦwww.coconutgroveartsfest .com.

# MARCH

-------------------

## Miami Grand Prix
### Early March
The season opener for the Indy Racing League, the Miami Grand Prix takes place at the Homestead track, south of Miami. Tickets cost from $25–45; ☎305/230-5000 for information or 230-RACE for tickets, ⓦwww .homesteadmiamispeedway .com.

## Carnaval Miami
### Early March
A nine-day celebration of Latin culture, held across the city. It culminates in a parade at the Orange Bowl Stadium, while a Little Havana offshoot showcases Cuban arts, crafts and cooking along Calle Ocho; ☎305/644-8888, ⓦwww.carnaval-miami.org.

## Asian Arts Festival
### Early March
This festival features Asian crafts, cuisine and martial arts, as well as fashion shows and acrobatic displays; ☎305/595-1353.

## Winter Music Conference
### Late March
Bringing together producers, managers and promoters at the Miami Beach Conference Center, this is one of the highlights of the electronic music industry's year. Performances at South Beach clubs by scores of top-name DJs draw a huge crowd, and hotel space is often tight; ☎954/563-4444, ⓦwww.wmcon.com.

## The Ericsson Open
### Late March
One of Miami's major sporting draws, the Open attracts marquee players to the fifth-largest tennis tournament in the world. It's held on Key Biscayne at the Crandon Park Tennis Center (see p.221) and tickets start at $25; ☎305/446-2200 for

information or 442-3367 for tickets, Ⓦ www.ericsson-open.com.

## APRIL

### Miami Gay & Lesbian Film Festival

Late April

Overseen by the director of the classic gay documentary *Beyond Stonewall*, this festival takes place at the Colony Theater in South Beach, and features amateur as well as professional submissions; Ⓣ 305/534-9924, Ⓦ www.miamigaylesbianfilm .com.

## MAY

### The Great Sunrise Balloon Race

Early May

A surreal and spectacular race, where dozens of brightly colored balloons compete for charity at Kendall-Tamiami airport; Ⓣ 305/275-3317, Ⓦ www.sunrisegroup.org.

### Hip Hop Weekend

Memorial Day weekend

Recent years have seen an unofficial Hip Hop Festival held on South Beach during Memorial Day weekend – expect plenty of makeshift clubs, name DJs and personal appearances by a handful of well-known performers.

## JUNE

### Goombay Festival

Early June

This celebration of Bahamian culture takes over Peacock Park in Coconut Grove with colorful stalls and music; Ⓣ 305/372-9966.

### International Hispanic Theater Festival

Mid-June

Held at El Carrusel Theater in Coral Gables, this festival marks Hispanic achievement in the theater arts with performances by companies from around the world; Ⓣ 305/445-8877.

APRIL–JUNE

## JULY

### America's Birthday Bash
July 4

Independence Day features both fireworks and a laser show, with a three-stage music concert at Bayfront Park; ⊺305/358-7550. The *Biltmore* hotel in Coral Gables also hosts a July 4th celebration, which is pricey but spectacular.

### Tropical Agriculture Fiesta
Mid-July

A chance to sample dozens of different varieties of mango, as well as other exotic fruits at the Fruit and Spice Park – see p.106; ⊺305/278-4185, ⊛www.tropicalag.org.

## AUGUST

### Miami Reggae Festival
First Sunday in August

Jamaican Independence Day is commemorated in Bicentennial Park, with a full roster of local, national and international musical acts;

⊺305/891-2944.

## SEPTEMBER

### International Ballet Festival of Miami
Early September

Ballet's big stars come to town for a two-week-long program that is spread among the Colony and Jackie Gleason theaters in South Beach, and the Manuel Artime Theater in Little Havana. It's overseen by the Miami Hispanic Ballet, so there's a strong Latin American slant; ⊺305/549-7711.

### Festival Miami
Mid-September to mid-October

The University of Miami sponsors this festival, with almost four weeks of mostly classical concerts in and around Coral Gables; ⊺305/284-4940, ⊛www.music.miami.edu.

### Sportsman Fishing Show
Late September

Held in the Dade County

Fairgrounds, this show features nearly everything to do with angling, from cat netting and fly casting demonstrations to actual fishing seminars. Entrance fee for visitors is $7; ℡ 813/839-7696, Ⓦ www.floridasportsman.com.

## OCTOBER

### Hispanic Heritage Festival
Throughout October
One of the largest events of the year, with concerts, fairs and parades throughout Little Havana. There's also the "Discovery of America" day, and the Miss Hispanidad pageant; ℡ 305/541-5023.

### Columbus Day Regatta
Early October
Held on the weekend nearest Columbus Day, this two-day race begins at Dinner Key Marina in Coconut Grove and heads out to Elliott Key in Biscayne National Park; Ⓦ www.columbusdayregatta .net.

### Lincoln Road Halloween
October 31
Although there's little officially organized for Halloween in the city, the place to see the wildest costumes (and most outrageous behavior) in Miami is along Lincoln Road on South Beach. Grab a spot at one of the outdoor cafés and watch the impromptu parade.

## NOVEMBER

### Miami Book Fair International
Mid-November
Enormous fair attracting every publisher you could name to set up stalls for the weekend on the campus of Miami-Dade Community College downtown; ℡ 305/237-3258, Ⓦ www.miamibookfair.com.

### Harvest Festival
Weekend before Thanksgiving
Organized by the Historical Museum (see p.22, "Downtown Miami"), this festival celebrates the agricultural tradition of South

Florida. There are stalls, quilting demonstrations and even historical re-enactments at the Dade County Fairgrounds in West Dade; ☎305/375-1492, ⓦwww.historical-museum.org.

### The White Party
Late November

Centered on South Beach, this is one of the largest HIV/AIDS fundraisers in America – a largely gay, six-day extravaganza of clubbing and cocktail parties where white clothing is *de rigeur*. It peaks with the decadent ball at Villa Vizcaya, where the white costumes are almost all elaborate, skimpy affairs. Tickets for events start at $25, while tickets for the ball start at around $100; ☎305/667-9296, ⓦwww.whiteparty.net.

## DECEMBER

- - - - - - - - - - - - - - - - - - - -

### Indian Arts Festival
Late December

The Miccosukee Village in the Everglades plays host to Native American artists from across America who come to show and sell their work; ☎305/223-8380.

### King Mango Strut
Late December

Begun twenty years ago by a rejected would-be marcher in the Orange Bowl Parade, the Strut is a campy parade through Coconut Grove, whose participants take aim at topical events with their bizarre costumes; ☎305/401-1171.

# Sports, fitness and ocean activities

**M**iami's climate makes it ideally suited to most **sports**, and there's plenty on offer, whether you want to stay fit by playing or just lounge around and watch. The city hosts franchises from each of the three major sports – **football** team the Miami Dolphins have been around the longest and are the most consistently successful, while the Miami Heat draw the hoops crowd and the Florida Marlins the **baseball** fans. **College football** and **basketball** are also fanatically followed, thanks to the perennial success of the University of Miami Hurricanes. In addition, Miami hosts top-name **tennis** and **golf** tournaments on its numerous, quality facilities, probably best in Key Biscayne – and most greens and courts are open to the public.

For those who don't just like to watch, **biking** is popular, as is **rollerblading**, the patron sport of South Beach. In addition, many people casually fish off the jetties at the beach; a better, though pricey, option is a charter deep-sea fishing trip. There are also plenty of shops that run **diving** and **snorkeling** outings but, other than the coral reef in

Biscayne National Park (see p.109), the best regional diving spots are dotted along the Keys less than two hours away.

An authentic local experience is to watch (or even attempt) a game of **jai alai**, a fast, frenzied sport that arrived in Miami from Spain via Cuba. Alternatively, take in a day at the **greyhound track**, undeniably an experience.

## BASEBALL

The **Florida Marlins** are less than a decade old and talk has already begun of relocating – or even disbanding – the team. In its brief history the Marlins have managed to win a World Series (1997), but the top stars were sold off almost immediately after and the team has struggled to remain competitive since.

The season runs April–October, and ticket prices range from $4 to $55. The Marlins play at the Pro Player Stadium, at 2269 Dan Marino Blvd, sixteen miles northwest of downtown Miami (information ☎305/623-6100, tickets ☎305/350-5050, ⓦwww.flamarlins.com). Tickets can also be bought in person from the satellite ticket office at 3701 Calle Ocho, Little Havana (Mon–Fri 9am–5pm).

## BASKETBALL

The **Miami Heat** basketball team is defined by larger-than-life coach Pat Riley; while the team has never won a championship, they have at least been fairly solid over the years, and star players like Alonzo Mourning guarantee good crowds and loyalty from the locals.

The season runs October–April, and ticket prices range from $8 to $160. The Heat plays at the American Airlines Arena, 601 Biscayne Blvd, downtown (see p.28) – call ☎786/777-4328 for tickets, or visit ⓦwww.heat.com.

In the late 1990s, the NBA tested a women's league that enjoyed moderate success; it was at least profitable enough to allow for the addition of four expansion teams in 2000. One of these was the **Miami Sol**, which also plays at American Airlines Arena; the WNBA season begins around the time the men finish. Ticket prices range from $6 to $52 (tickets ☎ 786/777-4765, ⊛ www.miami-sol.com).

Finally, **college basketball** is certainly popular in Miami, and the UM Hurricanes attract a good – if less fanatical – following than their football team. The hoops season runs from November to March at the Miami Arena, 701 Arena Blvd, downtown (☎ 305/530-4400).

## FOOTBALL

-----------------------------------------------

The **Miami Dolphins** have a storied past, closely associated with (now-retired) star quarterback Dan Marino, the league's all-time leading passer, and ex-coach Don Shula, who led the team to the only perfect season in recent league history (in 1972). Unfortunately, though, the team has not appeared in the Super Bowl since 1984.

The season runs from September to January, and ticket prices range from $27 to $47. The Dolphins play at the Pro Player stadium when the Marlins are out of season (see above) – call ☎ 305/573-8326 for tickets, or visit ⊛ www.miamidolphins.com. Tickets can also be purchased in person at Gate G onsite at the stadium (Mon–Fri 8.30am–5.30pm, Sat 10am–4pm).

On the collegiate level, the University of Miami **Hurricanes** are one of the top football teams in the country, and local devotion to them is as passionate as to the Dolphins. The regular season runs September–November, and ticket prices start at $15. The 'Canes, as they're known, play at the Orange Bowl Stadium, 1400 NW 4th St, Little Havana (☎ 305/284-2263, ⊛ www.hurricanesports.com).

**FOOTBALL**

## GREYHOUND RACING

There's no horse racing in Miami, so for those who enjoy a day at the track, the only option is the **greyhound races**. It's certainly not the most posh attraction in town, but the dog races can still be great fun and oddly exciting. The only venue in the city is the Flagler Greyhound Track, 401 NW 38th Court, at the corner of 37th Avenue and NW 7th Street (season June–Nov; ☎305/649-3000, ⓦwww.flagler dogs.com). Matinee races are held Tuesday, Thursday and Saturday at 1pm, and evening races every day at 8pm – and as an added bonus, general admission is free.

## JAI ALAI

Derived from the Basque game of *pelota*, **jai alai** (pronounced "high-uh-lie," meaning "merry festival" in Basque) arrived in Cuba from Spain late in the nineteenth century. It quickly made the leap across the water to Miami, and there are now more jai alai *frontons* (or courts) in Florida than anywhere else in the world. It's a brutal, breakneck sport: a bullet-hard ball ricochets around the court at speeds up to 150mph, and players try to catch it in a *cesta* (basically a lacrosse basket attached to a baseball mitt). Until a star player suffered an accident in the late 1960s, helmets weren't even mandatory, and each fifteen-minute match is a thrilling, if dangerous, spectacle. The Miami Jai Alai is where the pros play: it's located at 3500 NW 37th Ave, near the airport, where you can watch matches Wednesday–Monday noon–5pm and Friday–Saturday 7–12pm. General admission is $1, reserved seating $2; ☎305/633-6400.

## BIKING AND ROLLERBLADING

**Biking** through downtown Miami is configured only for

the bravest – there are few cycle lanes, and the slipknot of freeways that crisscross the city make it even tougher on two wheels. A bike is a good option, though, in South Beach, where car parking is both pricey and congested; even better are the cycle routes in Coconut Grove (a fourteen-mile path down to South Miami) and Key Biscayne, which is especially worthwhile: not only are the parks beautiful, but scant public transport makes getting around any other way almost impossible.

Reliable stores for **bike rental** include: Mangrove Cycles, 260 Crandon Blvd, in the Square Shopping Center, Key Biscayne (Tues–Sat 9am–6pm, Sun 10am–5pm; $15/day, $30/3 days; ℗305/361-5555); Miami Beach Bicycle Center, 601 5th St, South Beach (Mon–Sat 10am–7pm, Sun 10am–5pm; $20/24 hrs; ℗305/674-0150). The *Banana Bungalow* hostel also rents bikes from its activities desk ($4/hour; ℗305/538-1951, ⑩www.bananabungalow.com).

As for **rollerblading**, it's arguably Miami's signature sport: the payoff for days spent perfecting your body in the gym is a couple of hours cruising along the beach on a pair of blades. Don't be put off, though, even if you're a neophyte – rollerblading through South Beach's oceanfront parks is a glorious way to see the sights, well worth the occasional tumble. For **rollerblade rental**, try Fritz's Skate Shop, 730 Lincoln Rd, South Beach (daily 10am–10pm; $7.50/hr, $22/day; ℗305/532-1954), which also rents bikes at the same rates.

## GOLF

Miami's large enough and warm enough to mean that there are plenty of options for **golf** in and around the city. Greens fees vary widely, but the most lush and best-known course, site of the Genuity Championship, is at the Doral Golf Resort & Spa, 4400 NW 87th Ave, downtown ($105 to

$275 for 18 holes; ⊤305/592-2030, ⊛www.doralresort
.com). There's also Crandon Park, a top-ranking public
course that's the site of the Royal Caribbean Classic, at
6700 Crandon Blvd, Key Biscayne ($52 to $131;
⊤305/361-9129). Alternatively, you can tee off at the luxurious, historic Biltmore Golf Course, 1210 Anastasia Ave,
Coral Gables ($76; ⊤305/460-5364 or 305/669-9500), or
the Normandy Shores course out on Miami Beach, 401
Biarritz Drive at 71st Street ($25 to $55; ⊤305/868-6502,
⊛www.geocities.com/normandyshoresgc).

---

**For those on tight budgets, the suburbs offer
substantial savings on a round of 18: a good choice is the
Palmetto Golf Course, 9300 SW 152nd St, South Miami
($13.90 to $22.15; ⊤305/238-2922).**

---

## TENNIS

---

The climate in Miami suits **tennis** as much as it does golf,
and there are plenty of public courts. Most of them operate
on a first-come, first-served basis and charge only nominal
fees – the list below is by no means exhaustive: for other
options in different neighborhoods, contact the City of
Miami Parks & Recreation Department (Mon–Fri
8am–5pm; ⊤305/416-1308, ⊛www.ci.miami.fl.us) or the
City of Miami Beach Parks & Recreation Department
(Mon–Fri 8.30am–5pm; ⊤305/673-7730, ⊛www.ci.miami
-beach.fl.us).

---

**For professional matches, Key Biscayne is also home to the
Ericsson Open at the Crandon Park Tennis Center – see
p.210, "Festivals and events," for details.**

---

Courts include Flamingo Park, 1000 12th St, South

TENNIS

Beach ($5.33/hr; ☎305/673-7761) and a larger number of courts at Haulover Park in northern Miami Beach ($2.12/hr; ☎305/947-3525). Finally, Crandon Park, 4000 Crandon Blvd on Key Biscayne has a wide range of surfaces (hard $3/hr daytime, $5/hr night, grass and clay $6/hr; ☎305/365-2300).

## GYMS

Miami has no shortage of **gyms** for South Beach body-toning, or just general fitness; the following all offer day pass memberships – remember to bring two forms of ID, including one with a photograph: Crunch, 1259 Washington Ave, South Beach (☎305/674-8222); David Barton Gym at the *Delano*, 1685 Collins Ave, South Beach (☎305/674-5757); Gables Personal Fitness, 1350 S Dixie Hwy, Coral Gables (☎305/667-0106); and The Fitness Company, 2901 Florida Ave, Coconut Grove (☎305/441-8555).

## DIVING AND SNORKELING

Much is made of **diving** and **snorkeling** in Miami, and most hotels will offer some form of aquatic trips. However, most locals agree that diving in Miami comes a far second to dive sites in the Keys like Looe Key (see p.257) or the more remote but spectacular Dry Tortugas (see p.269). The one exception is the reef at Biscayne National Park near Homestead, a massive underwater park with fantastic coral formations. When booking a trip, ask whether it's better for snorkelers or scuba divers – some trips may head out to deep waters, making observation from the surface difficult.

If you do decide to dive around Miami, the following operators run both diving and snorkeling trips at reasonable prices: Bubbles Dive Center, 2671 SW 27th Ave, North

Miami (☎305/856-0565); South Beach Divers, 850 Washington Ave, South Beach (☎305/531-6110 or 1-888/331-DIVE, ⓦwww.southbeachdivers.com); Tarpoon Lagoon, 300 Alton Rd at Miami Beach Marina, South Beach (☎305/532-1445, ⓦwww.tarpoondivecenter.com).

## FISHING

Tearing into your own fresh catch for dinner is a satisfying experience, and plenty of anglers come to Miami for the **fishing** – although, as with underwater sports, the Keys are probably a better bet for variety and volume of fish. Plus, the only public fishing pier in the city is up in Sunny Isles at 16701 Collins Ave, next to the *Holiday Inn Crowne Plaza Hotel* ($3; ☎305/949-1300 ext 1266).

If you've more money or less experience, a great option is a day out on a boat **deep-sea fishing**: expect to pay around $500 for a half day, and $750 for a full day of private charter, including bait, supervision and fish-gutting. For confident anglers, there are public boats, which cost $40 and up for the ride only. Try Sonny Boy Sportfishing, Key Biscayne Marina (☎305/361-2217, ⓦwww.sonnyboysport fishing.com); Mark the Shark at Biscayne Bay Marriott Marina, downtown (☎305/759-5297, ⓦwww.striker-1 .com); or Reward Fishing Fleet, 300 Alton Rd at Miami Beach Marina, South Beach (☎305/372-9470, ⓦwww .fishingmiami.com).

# Directory

**Airlines** Air Canada ℡ 1-888/
247-2262, ⓦ www.aircanada.ca;
AirTran ℡ 1-800/AIR-TRAN,
ⓦ www.airtran.com; American
Airlines ℡ 305/1-800/433-7300,
ⓦ www.aa.com; British Airways
℡ 1-800/247-9297, ⓦ www
.britishairways.com; Continental
℡ 1-800/525-0280, ⓦ www
.continental.com; Delta ℡ 1-
800/221-1212, ⓦ www.delta-air
.com; JetBlue ℡ 1-800/JET-
BLUE, ⓦ www.jetblue.com;
Northwest Airlines ℡ 1-800/
225-2525, ⓦ www.nwa.com,
ⓦ www.klm.com; Spirit Airlines
℡ 1-800/772-7117, ⓦ www
.spiritair.com; United ℡ 1-800/
241-6522, ⓦ www.ual.com; US
Airways ℡ 1-800/428-4322,
ⓦ www.usair.com; and Virgin
Atlantic ℡ 1-800/862-8621,
ⓦ www.virgin-atlantic.com.

**American Express** Branches
are located at: 100 N Biscayne
Blvd, downtown ℡ 305/358-
7350 or 1-800/365-9870; 32
Miracle Mile, Coral Gables
℡ 305/446-3381; and Bal
Harbour Shops, 9700 Collins
Ave ℡ 305/865-5959.

**Area code** Miami has two
prefixes – the original code
(℡ 305), and a newer code to
accommodate demand for
additional lines (℡ 786). Note
that although numbers in the
Keys share the same prefix as
Miami, the call is charged as
long distance, not local.

**Banks and exchange** There
are foreign exchange desks at
the Miami International Airport
and at the following banks:
Bank of America, 100 SE 2nd
St ℡ 1-800/299-2265 and 1 SE

3rd Ave ☎ 305/350-6350; First Union National Bank, 200 S Biscayne Blvd ☎ 305/599-2265; SunTrust Bank, 777 Brickell Ave ☎ 305/591-6000; and Citibank International, 201 S Biscayne Blvd ☎ 305/347-1600.

**Boat rental** If you've a yearning to explore the waters round Miami on your own, boats can be rented by the hour from Beach Boat Rentals, 2400 Collins Ave, Miami Beach ☎ 305/534-4307. Rates start at $89 for two hours.

**Car rental** Major car rental companies include: Alamo (toll-free ☎ 1-800/GO-ALAMO), at 3885 SW 8th St, Coral Gables ☎ 305/476-0904 or the Miami International Airport ☎ 305/633-4132; Budget (toll-free ☎ 1-800/527-0700), at the *Loews Hotel*, 1601 Collins Ave, South Beach or 3655 SW Coral Way, Coral Gables; Dollar (toll-free ☎ 1-800/800-3665), at the *Eden Roc* hotel, central Miami Beach ☎ 305/532-5359 or the Miami International Airport ☎ 305/894-5020; Hertz (toll-free ☎ 1-800/654-3131), at 1619 Alton Rd, South Beach ☎ 786/276-1121 or the Miami International Airport ☎ 305/871-0300.

**Children** Miami's not especially configured to entertain children – there are few traditional amusement parks or kids' museums. However, Parrot Jungle (see p.50), the Miami Metrozoo (see p.105) or the Seaquarium (see p.91) have plenty of animals and stage shows throughout the day designed for kids. Key Biscayne's beaches, free from undertow and pristinely kept, are also a good option; on South Beach, the most family-friendly area is the stretch of sand at 3rd Street and Ocean Drive. The traditional Toy Town store on Key Biscayne (see p.203, "Shopping") is a Nintendo-free zone, and a refreshing place to browse.

**Coastguard** ☎ 305/535-4313.

**Consulates** Countries include: Canada, 200 S Biscayne Blvd, Suite 1600 ☎ 305/579-1600; Denmark, PH 1D, 2655 Le Jeune Rd ☎ 305/446-0020; France, 1 Biscayne Tower, Suite 1710 ☎ 305/372-9798; Germany, Suite 2200, 100 N Biscayne Blvd ☎ 305/358-0290;

DIRECTORY

Netherlands, 800 Brickell Ave, Suite 918 ⓣ 305/789-6646; UK, 1001 Brickell Bay Drive, Suite 2800 ⓣ 305/374-1522.

**Dentist** For a referral, call ⓣ 305/667-3647 or 1-800/336-8478.

**Doctor** To find a physician, call ⓣ 305/324-8717.

**Emergencies** ⓣ 911.

**Film processing** All have one-hour service (though you'll pay extra): Coconut Grove Camera, 3317 Virginia St, Coconut Grove ⓣ 305/445-0521; Deco Photo, 1238 Washington Ave, South Beach ⓣ 305/532-6552; Bayside Photo, Bayside Marketplace, downtown ⓣ 305/377-3686; Eckerd Drug, 1160 South Dixie Hwy, Coral Gables ⓣ 305/663-8697.

**Helplines** Crisis Counseling Hotline ⓣ 305/358-4357; Miami Beach Tourism Hotline ⓣ 305/673-7400.

**Hospitals** In Miami: Jackson Memorial Medical Center, 1611 NW 12th Ave ⓣ 305/585-1111; Mercy Hospital, 3663 S Miami Ave ⓣ 305/854-4400. On Miami Beach: Mt Sinai Medical Center, 4300 Alton Rd ⓣ 305/674-2121;

South Shore Hospital, 630 Alton Rd ⓣ 305/672-2100.

**Internet access** Surf the web or check email at: *Kafka's Kafé*, 1464 Washington Ave, South Beach ⓣ 305/673-9669 (daily 8.30am–midnight); *Cybr Caffe*, 1574 Washington Ave, South Beach ⓣ 305/534-0057, ⓦ www.cybrcaffe.com (Mon–Fri 10am–12.30am, Sat–Sun 11am–12.30am); *Kaffe and Net*, Bayside Marketplace, downtown ⓣ 305/374-2668 (daily 10am–10pm); the Public Library (see below), which offers 45 minutes free; and the no-charge access at the Museum of Science (see p.87, "Coconut Grove").

**Laundromats** Many hotels will likely have some form of laundry service; otherwise, try the Wash Club of South Beach, 510 Washington Ave ⓣ 305/534-4298; Clean Machine, 226 12th St, South Beach ⓣ 305/534-9429 (open 24 hrs); or the Coconut Grove Laundry & Cleaners, 3101 Grand Ave ⓣ 305/444-1344.

**Library** Miami-Dade County Public Library, 101 W Flagler St, downtown ⓣ 305/375-2665 (Mon–Sat 9am–6pm, Thurs until 9pm; Oct–May also Sun 1–5pm).

**Lost & found** Metro-Dade Transit Lost & Found ⓣ 305/375-3366 (Mon–Fri 8.30am–4.30pm).

**Pharmacies** Usually open from 8 or 9am until 9pm or midnight. 24-hour pharmacies include Eckerd, 200 Lincoln Rd, South Beach ⓣ 305/673-9502 and Walgreens, 5731 Bird Rd, Coral Gables ⓣ 305/666-0757 and 1845 Alton Rd, South Beach ⓣ 305/531-8868.

**Police** For non-emergency ⓣ 305/673-7900; emergency ⓣ 911.

**Post office** In downtown Miami, 500 NW 2nd Ave ⓣ 305/373-7562; in Coral Gables, 251 Valencia Ave and 20 Miracle Mile, both ⓣ 305/443-2532; in Coconut Grove, 3191 Grand Ave ⓣ 305/529-6700; in Homestead, 739 Washington Ave ⓣ 305/247-1556; in Key

Biscayne, 951 Crandon Blvd ⓣ 305/361-7884; and in Miami Beach, 1300 Washington Ave and 445 W 40th St, both ⓣ 305/538-2708. All are open Mon–Fri 8.30am–5pm and Sat 8.30am–12.30pm.

**Rape hotline** ⓣ 305/585-7273.

**Road conditions** ⓣ 305/470-5277.

**Tax** Sales tax is 6.5 percent; room tax 3 percent, except in Surfside and Bal Harbour, where it's 4 percent.

**Time** Miami is on Eastern Standard Time, five hours behind Greenwich Mean Time and three hours ahead of Pacific Standard Time. Daylight savings takes place between the first Sunday in April and the last Sunday in October.

**Weather/surf information** ⓣ 305/324-8811 or 229-4522.

**Wire transfers** Western Union has offices all over the city – for the nearest location, call ⓣ 1-800/325-6000, or log onto ⓦ www.westernunion.com.

# OUT OF THE CITY

---

OUT OF THE CITY

# Fort Lauderdale

After a long beach-party hangover, **Fort Lauderdale** is developing – albeit slowly – a distinctive, more sophisticated atmosphere, thanks to its revitalized Historic District and a growing gay scene, comprised largely of refugees from South Beach. The city divides roughly into two areas: **downtown** and **beachside**, through which run two main arteries: Hwy-1 (also known as the Federal Highway), which cuts north–south through the center of the city and, parallel to that, Hwy-A1A which follows the length of the beachfront. Though the beaches here may not be as glossy as Miami's imported sands, they're pleasant enough and often quieter, especially out of season.

Fort Lauderdale began its life as a military fortification against a Seminole Indian attack – though by the end of the nineteenth century it had grown into a thriving trading post. It wasn't until the 1930s, though, when swim teams began coming here for meets, that the town's hard-partying reputation began to form – cemented by the 1960 film *Where the Boys Are*, which made Fort Lauderdale synonomous with college students' spring break. However, by the 1990s, Fort Lauderdale was making aggressive, ultimately successful, efforts to slough off its somewhat tawdry image – although some say that the students took much of the city's verve with them when they decamped north to Daytona Beach.

# ARRIVAL, INFORMATION AND CITY TRANSIT

Arriving by bus or train, you'll end up in or near downtown – the **Greyhound** bus station is at 515 NE 3rd St (℡954/764-6551), and the **Tri-Rail** station is at 200 SW 21st Terrace (Amtrak ℡1-800/872-7245; TriRail ℡954/728-8445 or 1-800/TRI-RAIL).

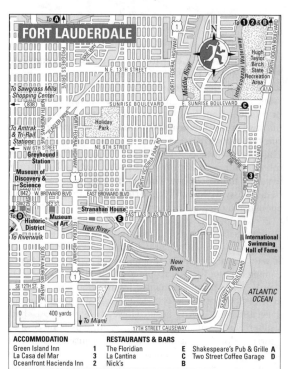

| ACCOMMODATION | | RESTAURANTS & BARS | |
|---|---|---|---|
| Green Island Inn | 1 | The Floridian | E |
| La Casa del Mar | 3 | La Cantina | C |
| Oceanfront Hacienda Inn | 2 | Nick's | B |
| | | Shakespeare's Pub & Grille | A |
| | | Two Street Coffee Garage | D |

As for getting around, **yellow cabs** can be hailed or booked by calling ☎954/565-5400, while the **water taxis** that wind through the intracoastal waterway (daily 6.30am–12.30am; $4 one-way, $5/day pass; ☎954/467-6677, ⓦwww.watertaxi.com) make a scenic, if slow, sight-seeing alternative.

For up-to-date Fort Lauderdale information, look for the maps and brochures produced by the **Convention & Visitors Bureau**, out in Port Everglades, at 1850 Eller Drive, suite 303 (Mon–Fri 8.30–5pm; ☎954/765-4466, ⓦwww.sunny.org). Also, for Historic District information, seek out the main office of the **Fort Lauderdale Historical Society**, at 219 SW 2nd Ave (Wed–Fri 10am–4pm, Sat noon–4pm; free; ☎954/463-4431, ⓦwww.oldfortlauderdale.org).

---

To find out what's going on around town, call the entertainment and attractions hotline at ☎954/527-5600.

---

# ACCOMMODATION

### La Casa del Mar

3003 Granada St, Beachside
☎954/467-2037,
ⓦwww.lacasadelmar.com.
There are only 10 rooms at this secluded beachside B&B, and each is uniquely furnished. *La Casa del Mar* also has a pool, a small garden and a good breakfast buffet. ❹

### Green Island Inn

3300 NE 27th St, Beachside
☎954/566-8951 or 1-888/505-8951, ⓦwww.greenislandinn.com.
Charming, family-run inn,

For an explanation of price codes (for example, ❹) see the box on p.114, "Accommodation."

ACCOMMODATION

with bright, homely rooms and kitchenettes, set in a leafy garden. There's a small pool, plus ample parking. **2**

**Oceanfront Hacienda Inn**
1924 N Atlantic Blvd, Beachside
Ⓣ954/564-7800 or 1-800/562-

8467, Ⓦwww.oceanfronthacienda.com.

Rooms are simple, but rates are reasonable considering its oceanfront location – and there's a glorious tropical garden and pool that face the ocean. **3**

# DOWNTOWN AND THE HISTORIC DISTRICT

Tall, anonymous, glass-fronted buildings make an uninspiring first impression, but **downtown Fort Lauderdale** – a thin rectangle bounded by NW 7th Avenue to the west, NE 8th Avenue to the east, Broward Boulevard to the north and Las Olas Boulevard to the south – has an outstanding modern art museum and is close to the **Riverwalk** area, a pedestrian shop'n'stroll complex packed with the standard stores and restaurants; it's a little soulless, but usually full with people.

More interesting is the **Historic District**, a small but growing collection of buildings within – but not of – downtown, located around SW 2nd Street and SW 3rd Avenue. One of these, the **New River Inn**, at no. 231 (Tues–Sun noon–5.30pm, tours Wed & Fri 2pm & 3pm; $5), was the city's first tourist hotel in 1905, and now houses a varied collection of documents and artifacts on the history of Fort Lauderdale. The sports room is especially good, as is the video that shows clips from the dozens of movies (including *Porky's* and *Body Heat)* that were filmed or set locally. Next door, at no. 229, there's the **King-Cromartie House** (Sat tours 1pm, 2pm, 3pm; $5), built in 1907, and housing an unremarkable museum of early settler life; the building itself, though, is a good example of Florida Pioneer architecture with its simple, well-ventilated design.

## Stranahan House

Oct–May Wed–Sat 10am–4pm, Sun 1–4pm, compulsory tours begin on the hour; $5.

East from the Historic District stands a more complete reminder of early Fort Lauderdale life: the **Stranahan House**, at 335 SE 6th Ave. With a lovingly restored interior that belies its unprepossessing exterior, this was the home of Frank Stranahan, so-called Father of Fort Lauderdale, who set up the first trading post here and accrued substantial wealth through trade with the Seminoles.

The Florida frontier-style house gives a good idea of what life was like for wealthy pioneers, crammed as it is with antique ephemera. Note too the wraparound porch, raised from the ground but open on all sides much like a *chickee* (Seminole hut), where Native Americans would spend the night during trading expeditions to the area.

## Museum of Discovery and Science

Mon–Sat 10am–5.30pm, Sun noon–6.30pm; $13 including admission to one IMAX film.

At the end of the Riverwalk, you'll find the creative, fun **Museum of Discovery and Science** at 401 SW 2nd St (☎954/467-6637, ⓦwww.mods.org) – great for the kid in everyone. The interactive exhibits are engaging and educational, including "Gizmo City" on the 2nd floor, which explains the principles of physics through everyday machines; and the "Florida EcoScapes" exhibition near the atrium, which houses native Everglades critters such as fish and turtles, plus a huge living coral reef. There's also an IMAX theater onsite that shows a rotating schedule of 3-D films; call for showtimes and current movies (☎954/463-4629).

## Museum of Art

Daily Tues–Sun 10am–5pm, free tours Tues and Thurs 1.30pm; $10.

A smallish exhibition space that houses unique temporary shows, the **Museum of Art** at 1 E Las Olas Blvd (T954/525-5500, Wwww.museumofart.org) also displays a rotating choice from its permanent collection, including marquee modern names like Andy Warhol, plus plenty more Pop Art. It's best known, though, for its exhaustive survey of work from the short-lived CoBrA movement of the early 1950s – the unwieldy acronym derives from the three cities (Copenhagen, Brussels and Amsterdam) where its artists were most active. With a desire to create without inhibitions, the CoBrA clique's Abstract Expressionism is marked by a focus on intense color, making their canvases an eye-popping, if acquired, taste. The museum also has a fine shop that sells stylish souvenirs.

# THE BEACHES

The main route to the Fort Lauderdale **beaches** is Las Olas Boulevard, lined with shops and reasonably priced restaurants, and taking you past the swanky residences of **the Isles**. The beachfront may be less brash than it was in its spring break heyday, but there are still plenty of theme

## SAWGRASS MILLS

Forty minutes west of Fort Lauderdale's beachfront is the discount retail palace of Sawgrass Mills, at 12801 W Sunrise Blvd (Mon–Sat 10am–9.30pm, Sun 11am–8pm; T954/846-2300, Wwww.sawgrassmillsmall.com), which claims to be the world's largest designer outlet mall. Alongside Gap and Levi's outlets, it's crammed with higher-end discounters like Neiman Marcus Last Call and Saks Off Fifth.

restaurants and rowdy bars. As for the beach itself, it's hemmed in by swaying palm trees, and usually easy to stake out a spot in the sun; the most popular area is the beach found just north of the International Swimming Hall of Fame (see below).

---

Facilities at the beach include restrooms and picnic tables at the junction of Sunrise Boulevard and Hwy-A1A, and showers at the junction of Las Olas Boulevard and Hwy-A1A.

---

Of the tacky beachside amusements, none really stand out, unless you're a diehard swim enthusiast – in which case, head for the **International Swimming Hall of Fame**, at 1 Hall of Fame Drive (daily 9am–7pm; $3; ☏954/462-6536, ⊛www.ishof.org), which showcases great swimmers and divers from every country across the world. But, disappointingly, time seems to have stopped here ten years ago: there's no mention of any Olympic Games since Seoul in 1992, rendering the whole place somewhat irrelevant.

# EATING AND DRINKING

### The Floridian
1410 E Las Olas Blvd, downtown ☏954/463-4041. Inexpensive.
Old Fort Lauderdale at its finest: formica furniture, peeling autographed pictures lining the walls, and outstanding diner food at rock-bottom prices. Unpretentious and enormous, which means never having to wait for a table.

### La Cantina
2870 E Sunrise Blvd, Beachside ☏954/565-3839. Moderate.
Giant 46oz. margaritas for $9 and enormous, cheap portions of authentic Mexican food make this a good stop on the beach. Try the *enchiladas tultecas*, filled with *chorizo* (spicy Mexican

sausage) or the unusual *machaca burrito*, filled with beef and eggs.

### Nick's

3496 N Ocean Blvd, Beachside
☎954/563-6441. Moderate.
Low-key Italian restaurant that's open until 4am, serving fresh, hefty portions of pasta. Come here late (it's open until 4am), as it's a scene by 1am, when waitstaff from surrounding restaurants descend for their own dinner.

### Shakespeare's Pub & Grill

1015 NE 26th St, north of downtown ☎954/563-7833.

Inexpensive.
With thirty beers on tap, including ciders and a food menu, this is the local favorite pub from which most crawls originate.

### Two Street Coffee Garage

209 SW 2nd Ave, Historic District ☎954/523-7191.
Inexpensive.
Groovy, laid-back coffee house with art on the walls, plus plenty of comfy seating. The café's signature drink is a Thai latte flavored with plum, mango or green tea, and served with gooey rice balls.

# GAY AND LESBIAN FORT LAUDERDALE

Often eclipsed by the glitz of Miami, **gay** Fort Lauderdale is laid-back and not very hedonistic, but still has great beaches and nightlife: call the Gay & Lesbian Community Center (☎954/563-9500, ⓦwww.glccftl.org) for information on what's happening, or pick up freesheets like *Scoop* or *Hotspots*.

There is plenty of gay and gay-friendly **accommodation** in Fort Lauderdale: try the luxurious *Pineapple Point Guesthouse*, at 315 NE 16th Terrace, downtown (☎1-888/844-7295 or 954/527-0094, ⓦwww.pineapplepoint.com;

❻), or go for the simpler rooms and lower prices at *Orton Terrace*, 606 Orton Ave, Beachside (☎954/566–5068 or 1-800/323–1142, ⓦwww.ortonterrace.com; ❸).

---

**Unofficial gay beaches in Fort Lauderdale can be found along Hwy-A1A at NE 18th Street and Sebastian Street.**

---

As for **nightlife**, *The Copa* is a local clubbing institution, located near the airport at 2800 S Federal Hwy (☎954/463–1507, ⓦwww.copaboy.com); there's also the cruiser and cooler *Cathode Ray*, at 1105 E Las Olas Blvd, downtown (☎954/462–8611, ⓦwww.cathoderayusa.com).

# The Everglades

*"The Everglades is a test. If we pass, we get to keep the planet."*
Environmentalist Marjory Stoneman Douglas

Little more than an hour from the condos and clubs of Miami, **Everglades National Park** is breathtakingly wild. Although the land is on the same latitude as the Sahara, more than one third of the park is made up of marine areas and underwater estuaries, and sawgrass covers nearly four million acres of swampy prairie. Both water and land teem with wildlife, from rare crocodiles to raccoons, as well as dozens of species of birds.

Despite this raw vastness, the Everglades exists in a delicate and endangered ecosystem. The area was originally formed by natural water drainage from the region around Orlando, flowing south to collect on the oolitic limestone table of Florida's swampy tip. In the last half century, though, developers have diverted this precious water source east to cities like Miami, Fort Lauderdale and Palm Beach, leaving the Everglades ecosystem thirsty and shrinking.

Marjory Stoneman Douglas was one of the first local lobbyists against such eco-vandalism – many say that her book *The Everglades: River of Grass* kickstarted the conservation movement in South Florida. Now, there are dozens of organizations dedicated to safeguarding this unique ecosystem – though of course none could prevent the wreckage caused by Hurricane Andrew more than a decade ago, from which northern portions of the park are only now beginning to recover.

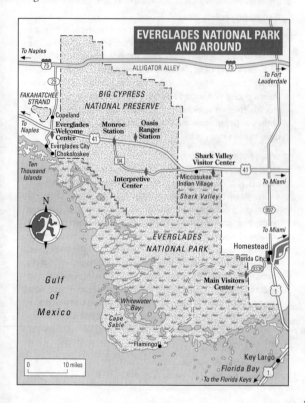

EVERGLADES NATIONAL PARK
AND AROUND

When **exploring** the Everglades, the worst thing to do is rush around. Although the speed limit on most roads is 55mph, you'll see and enjoy far more if you travel slowly

## EVERGLADES PRACTICALITIES

### Getting around

The park is almost impossible to reach without a car, as there's no public transport to or within the Everglades. The busy Hwy-41 (Tamiami Trail) cuts through the top half of the park, providing direct access to Everglades City and Shark Valley. To reach Flamingo, drive through Homestead and look for the poorly signposted Rte-9336 (or just turn left at the ramshackle "Robert is Here" fruitstand), which leads to the main entrance. Once inside the boundaries, it's roughly a 40-minute drive to the settlement.

### When to visit

Most people come during the dry season (Nov to April), when the park is at its most active, and the mosquitoes at their least. At this time, there are larger numbers of birds, and receding water levels leave the animals a reduced number of watering holes, thus concentrating wildlife activity; plus, there are more activities for people offered by the park and its concessionaires.

A visit in wet season (May to Oct) is only for the dedicated: the park receives at least sixty inches of rain each year, ninety percent of which falls between May and November, and insects abound – especially if the preceding winter was very dry, killing off the fish that eat bug larvae. If you come during a shoulder season (late April to early May or late Oct to early Nov), it's a risk, as the weather may still be poor, but there will be fewer crowds.

### Information and permits

There are five visitor's centers in the park: the Ernest F. Coe

and look for nature's subtleties: notice, for example, that the water everywhere is tea-brown, thanks to the tannic acid that leeches out of fallen leaves.

Center at the main entrance is the largest and most informative (daily 8am–5pm; ☎305/242-7700, ⊛www.nps.gov/ever), and a likely first stop-off for anyone arriving here from Miami. There are satellite offices at Royal Palm (daily 8am–4.15pm; ☎305/242-7700 ext 7237), Flamingo (Nov–Apr daily 7.30am–5pm; May–Oct daily 8am–5pm; ☎239/695-2945), Shark Valley (daily 8.30am–5pm; ☎305/221-8776) and the Gulf Coast near Everglades City (Nov–Apr daily 7.30am–5pm; May–Oct daily 8.30am–5pm; ☎239/695-3311). All entrances are open 24 hours a day except Shark Valley (daily 8.30am–6pm).

A seven-day general permit costs $10 per vehicle ($8 at Shark Valley) and $5 per person for cyclists ($4 at Shark Valley). Backcountry permits are also available from any visitors center, and are $10 for up to 6 people for up to 2 weeks; backcountry campgrounds throughout the park are little more than tended clearings, unless marked as a *chickee* (raised platform with a roof, open on all sides) on the map available from the visitor's center.

## What to bring

Whatever and whenever your plans, bring plenty of insect repellent. Year-round the mosquitoes are numerous, and especially ferocious during the summer wet season. If you're camping, you might also encounter sand gnats, or "no-see-ums," tiny insects that inflict painful bites. There's also little shade, so sunblock is essential. For backcountry camping, bring flashlights, a compass and water in hard containers – raccoons can (and will) tear through soft cartons.

EVERGLADES PRACTICALITIES

In the northwest region of the park, around Everglades City, all activities are aquatic: there's good **fishing**, **boat tours** and **canoeing**. Conversely, at Shark Valley, located in the northeastern corner of the park, there's a landbound trail too long to hike in its entirety, but accessible via bike or tram. Down south, Flamingo offers something for everyone: superb saltwater fishing and excellent birdwatching sites, plus boat tours, canoeing, kayaking and hiking. As for wildlife spotting, early in the morning is the best time; during the dry season, make it a point to come during the week, as busy weekends on the waterways drive animals undercover during the day.

# ROUTE 9336: THE ROAD TO FLAMINGO

Just southwest of Homestead, **Route 9336** enters the park at the main visitor center, leading to some of the best and most accessible sights in the Everglades, before eventually arriving at **Flamingo**, the only settlement inside the park proper. Several of the trails along this route are former roads, while others are specially constructed boardwalks. Soon after entering the park, take a turn south toward the **Royal Palm Visitor Center**, where there's access to both **Anhinga Trail**, a half-mile concrete path through sawgrass marsh that's a dependable site for wildlife viewing, and **Gumbo Limbo Trail**, which offers a glimpse of the Paradise Key hardwood hammock. Back on the main road, before Rte-9336 takes a turn south, is the **Pa-hay-okee viewing platform**, well worth a stop for the panoramic views across the sawgrass plain. Further south, **Paurotis Pond** becomes a wading bird rookery in January, when egrets, woodstorks, and occasional spoonbills come to breed; while **Nine Mile Pond** is a good, manageable canoe trail choice, appropriate for amateurs. On the other hand, **Hells Bay Trail**, about five miles from here, is a well-signposted adventure for more experienced canoeists – maps of these and other canoe trails are available from the visitor center.

On the home stretch to Flamingo, dedicated birdwatchers should head south along **Snake Bight Trail** – just watch out for the armies of mosquitoes. In addition, nearby **Mrazek Pond** should not be missed in February, when the area's at its liveliest due to receding waters which concentrate the fish population and draw dozens of hungry birds to feed; amateur hikers should seek out **Eco Pond Trail**, just past the Flamingo Visitor Center.

**Boat tours** run from the marina at Flamingo (☏239/695-3101); choose either the two-hour Pelican Backcountry Cruise (daily 8am, 10.30am, 1.30pm, 4pm, fewer trips out of season; $16) which journeys into Coot Bay and offers plenty of reptile-spotting, or the 90-minute Bald Eagle Florida Bay Cruise (daily sunrise, 10am, 12.30pm, 2.30pm, fewer trips out of season; $10), a can't-miss for bird watchers. You can rent kayaks ($27 half day/$43 full day) and canoes ($22 half day/$32 full day), as well as charter a fishing boat ($250 half day/$350 full day) from the marina, too.

# SHARK VALLEY

Highway 41 enters the northeastern corner of the park near the **Shark Valley Visitor Center**. There's only one lengthy **trail** from here, a fourteen-mile-long loop that's off-limits to cars and a tough hike: it's paved, though, so it makes for a pleasant, if shadeless, cycling trip. Rent bikes from the Shark Valley Tram Tour Company (daily 8.30am–4pm, last rental 3pm; $4.75/hour; ☏305/221-8455) and head for the 50-foot observation tower at the trail's mid-point. A more leisurely way to see the trail is on a **tram tour** (daily 9am–4pm, on the hour; $11; ☏305/221-8455), where park rangers point out notable wildlife and stop regularly for viewings – alligators and turtles are plentiful, and the birdwatching is a twitcher's paradise. Those determined to set out on foot can enjoy two short rambles from the visitor center: the **Bobcat Boardwalk** runs through sawgrass marsh, and the rough limestone **Otter Cave trail** snakes into tropical hardwood hammock.

# EVERGLADES CITY AND TEN THOUSAND ISLANDS

The northwest edge of the preserve is known for its **Ten Thousand Islands**, where the coastline shatters into mangrove island shards that are excellent fishing sites. To reach **Everglades City**, the logical base for exploring this area, leave Hwy-41 at Rte-29 and head three miles south. Continue through the city to the end of Rte-29 until you reach the dock at Chokoloskee Causeway, site of the official visitor center and boarding point for most **boat trips**.

Everglades National Park Boat Tours is one of the few park-sanctioned operators (daily 9.30am–5pm; ℡239/695-2591 or 1-800/445-7724, ⓦwww.evergladesnatlboatours .com), offering two trips: the 2-hour Ten Thousand Islands Tour ($13), which heads for the outer islands bordering the Gulf of Mexico, or the 2-hour Mangrove Wilderness Tour ($16), which journeys inland through the winding red mangrove waterways. Boats leave every half hour year-round from the docks at Chokoloskee. Canoes can also be rented from the same company (daily 8.30am–5pm; $24/day).

# ACCOMMODATION

**Everglades Hostel**
20 SW 2nd Ave, Florida City
℡305/248-1122 or 1-800/372-3874,

ⓦwww.evergladeshostel.com.
A clean, budget option in Florida City with the usual amenities (laundry room,

## CAMPING

Rangers will tell you that Long Pine Key campground – west from the Ernest F. Coe Visitor Center and south from Rte-9336 – has the fewest bugs, but that it's worth braving the mosquitoes at Flamingo for its views and its facilities, such as hot and cold showers. Camping is $14 per night, and reservations (☎1-800/365-2267 or ⊛http://reservations.nps.gov) are recommended from November to April.

kitchen, internet access) that also runs various excursions into the park. Dorm beds $13/night, private rooms $33, plus $3 fee for non-members.

### Flamingo Lodge

1 Flamingo Lodge Hwy, Flamingo ☎239/695-3101 or 1-800/600-3813, ⊛www.flamingolodge.com. At the end of the long road through the park lies *Flamingo Lodge*, a convenient base for most Everglades activities. Rooms are standard but comfortable, plus there's a screened-in pool and a restaurant. The staff live onsite, and give friendly, knowledgeable recommendations on what to do. $95

### Ivey House Bed & Breakfast

1077 Camellia St, Everglades City ☎239/695-3299, ⊛www.iveyhouse.com.
Open Nov–April.
A charming B&B with reasonable rates, especially in its older building where the simple rooms share baths; the new addition has plusher rooms with private baths. Family-style dinners are also served each evening. $50 without private bath in old building, $90 with private bath in new building.

ACCOMMODATION

# The Florida Keys

**T**he **Florida Keys** are a dash of the Caribbean in America, as distant from the US in attitude as geography. Beginning with the small islands in Biscayne National Park and ending with the Dry Tortugas, the Keys form a broken necklace of land that stretches for more than 200 miles from Florida's southern tip. Roughly 125,000 years ago, they were a living coral reef, created when water levels rose dramatically, flooding low-lying areas. As the waters gradually receded, the upper reaches of reef were exposed, and limestone islands were formed from the dying coral. At the same time, the lower areas of the reef to the west survived, which now make for spectacular snorkeling and diving.

Aside from the shipping hub in Key West and a short-lived settlement on Indian Key (see p.253), the islands remained sparsely populated by European settlers until well into the twentieth century, in part due to harsh, humid summers and legions of insects. However, after Henry Flagler's railroad connected the Keys with Miami, communities grew up in clusters, supported mostly by fishing and smuggling – indeed, the narcotics trade here was endemic until well into the 1980s. Today, though, both pursuits have given way to tourism as the overwhelming local industry.

The Keys are more or less divided into three sections.

THE FLORIDA KEYS

Gulf of Mexico

40 miles

N

EVERGLADES
NATIONAL PARK

Flamingo

CARD SOUND ROAD

905

OVERSEAS HWY

Miami
(30 miles)

North
Key Largo

JOHN
PENNEKAMP
CORAL REEF
STATE PARK

1

UPPER KEYS

Key Largo
Dolphin Cove

Tavernier
Plantation

Florida Keys
Wild Bird Center

Islamorada
Lignumvitae Key
Botanical State Park

Indian Key
Historic State Park

Florida Bay

LONG KEY STATE
RECREATION AREA

MIDDLE KEYS

1

Marathon

OVERSEAS HIGHWAY

BAHIA HONDA STATE
RECREATION AREA

Key Deer
Refuge

Big Pine
Key

SEVEN MILE
BRIDGE

Big Torch
Key

Little Torch Key

Cudjoe
Key

Sugarloaf
Key

Ramrod
Key

LOOE KEY
MARINE
SANCTUARY

LOWER KEYS

Big Coppitt
Key

OVERSEAS HIGHWAY

1

KEY WEST ISLAND

Key
West

Dry Tortugas
National Park
(70 miles)

ATLANTIC OCEAN

The **Upper Keys**, which include the towns of Key Largo and Islamorada, are used as bases for fishing and diving in the John Pennekamp State Park – though there's a definite uneasiness in the locals' relationship with tourism, and the famously laid-back local attitude is less prevalent here.

## OCEAN ACTIVITIES IN THE KEYS

### Beaches

The better Keys beaches are in Bahia Honda State Park, as well as Sombrero Beach near Marathon and Anne's Beach just past Islamorada. Around Key West, there are few options – the best is probably the beach at Fort Zachary Taylor Historic State Park.

### Snorkeling and diving

The John Pennekamp State Park (see p.252) has several notable reefs and is very popular; however, there's livelier wildlife and more to see at Looe Key Marine Sanctuary (see p.257) or at Biscayne National Park (see p.109). Fort Jefferson in the Dry Tortugas has spectacular coral formations and plenty of fish less than 100 yards off its western shores.

Operators include the Coral Reef Park Company at the John Pennekamp Visitor Center (daily 8am–5pm; ☎305/451-1621, ⊛www.pennekamppark.com), which runs glass-bottomed boat tours at 9.15am, 12.15pm and 3pm for $18, or snorkel trips at 9am, noon and 3pm for $30, including equipment. Its branch in Bahia Honda State Park runs snorkeling trips to Looe Key (daily 8am–5pm; ☎305/872-3210, ⊛www.bahiahondapark.com) at 10am and 2pm for the same price.

In the Lower Keys, the friendly staff at Underseas, MM 30.5-oceanside, Big Pine Key (snorkel trips start at $30; ☎305/872-2700 or 1-800/446-5663, ✉diveusaeas@aol.com), run enjoyable trips out to Looe Key – a good choice for first-timers. The

Centered on the settlement of Marathon and the remarkable Seven Mile Bridge, the **Middle Keys** are more welcoming. Marathon has good amenities, plus access to clean beaches and well-stocked fishing sites nearby: for the casual traveler, this is the best base for exploring the area. South

leisurely alternative for coral viewing is by glass-bottomed boat: try the two-hour trip on the *Key Largo Princess*, MM 100-oceanside (daily 10am, 1pm, 4pm; $18; ⊤305/451-4655).

### Fishing

A good independent bait shop is the World Class Angler, at MM 50, Marathon (⊤305/743-6139), where the staff is knowledgeable, and can make good local fishing site recommendations. The deluxe option is to take a personal charter trip – in Marathon, try Captain Tina Brown ($375/half day, $475/full day; ⊤305/743-7150, ℮tina824@aol.com), who's renowned for her helpfulness with less experienced anglers, or Captain Brian Yates (⊤305/745-7337). In the Upper Keys, Robbie's, at MM 77.5-bayside, Islamorada, also runs larger group trips (9.30am–1.30pm and 1.45–5.45pm is $28, plus $3 rod rental; 7.30pm–12.30am is $33, plus $4 rod rental; ⊤305/664-8498, ⓦwww.robbies.com).

### Kayaking

Florida Keys Kayak & Sail at Robbie's Marina, MM 75.5-bayside, Islamorada (⊤305/664-4878), runs escorted kayak tours to Indian and Lignumvitae keys, as well as the chance to see wildlife in the mangrove swamps nearby (from $39 per person). Kayak rentals without a guide start at $30 per half day. In the Lower Keys, try Sugarloaf Marina, MM 17-bayside, Sugarloaf Key (⊤305/745-3135), where a half day's rental starts at $25.

OCEAN ACTIVITIES IN THE KEYS

from here, the **Lower Keys**, beginning at Big Pine Key, are rewarding for landlocked wildlife-watching – most notably, the rare key deer.

Finally, there's fabled **Key West**, the prime target for most visiting the Keys. Old Town is now a feast of wooden colonial houses and winding streets, less blighted by tourism than some contend, and with much of the sleepy grace that first attracted visitors thirty years ago; it's also one of the gayest towns in America, due to liberal local attitudes plus pure chance.

## Arrival, information and getting around

Greyhound runs a limited service connecting Miami and Key West with stops in major centers along the route ($31.25 one-way; trip takes approx. 5 hours; departures at 6.20am, 12.20pm, 3.50pm, 6.50pm; ☏1-800/231-2222, ⓦwww.greyhound.com). Even so, since there's no local public transportation, it's almost impossible to see or enjoy most of what the Keys has to offer without a **car** (see p.224 for rental information). Driving though is easy, as the islands are joined by a single road: **Hwy-1**, also known as the **Overseas Highway**, which connects Key West with Florida City, continuing on up the East Coast. To avoid tourist traffic, do as the locals do and branch off from Hwy-1 south of Homestead onto Card Sound Road, also known as Hwy-905A ($1 toll) – it's slightly longer, but the views of the Florida Bay are worth it.

**Addresses** in the Keys are given using the Mile Marker (MM) system, which begins with 0 in Key West at the junction of Whitehead and Fleming streets and ends just south of Homestead. The only islands large enough to require street addresses in the Keys (aside from Key West) are Big Pine and Marathon.

There are several **visitor centers** scattered along Hwy-1.

The largest is the **Florida Keys Visitor Center** (MM 106-bayside, Key Largo; daily 9am–6pm; ℡305/451-1414 or 1-800/822-1088), which provides information on the Keys in general. The **Islamorada Chamber of Commerce** is unmissable in its bright red roadside caboose and good for the Upper Keys (MM 82.5-Bayside; Mon–Fri 9am–5pm, Sat 9am–4pm, Sun 9am–3pm; ℡305/664-9767); while the **Marathon Chamber of Commerce** has ample information on the Middle Keys (MM 48.5-bayside, Marathon; daily 9am–5pm; ℡305/743-5417 or 1-800/262-7284, ⓦwww.floridakeysmarathon.com). Further along Hwy-1, there's the **Lower Keys Chamber of Commerce** (MM 31-oceanside, Big Pine Key; Mon–Fri 9am–5pm, Sat 9am–3pm; ℡305/872-2411 or 1-800/872-3722).

---

When visiting the Keys, don't forget to bring plenty of insect repellent: ravenous mosquitoes are plentiful no matter the time of year.

---

# The Upper Keys

The **Upper Keys** is made up of three major communities. Driving south along Hwy-1, the first you'll come to is Key Largo, perhaps the most unappetizing of all the settlements in the Keys. There's little reason to spend much time here, though nearby is the 80-acre underwater coral reef in the **John Pennekamp State Park**, as well as the **Florida Keys Wild Bird Center** further south in Tavernier, the second major community.

The third, **Islamorada** (pronounced eye-lah-more-RAH-dah), is actually a chain of four small islands:

Plantation, Windley, and Upper and Lower Matecumbe. It's one of the larger fishing hubs in the Keys, and makes a good base for exploring both **Indian Key** and **Lignumvitae Key**. The easiest way to reach both of them is by **boat** from Robbie's Marina, located at MM 75.5-bayside, Islamorada (daily 9am & 1pm; $15; ☎305/664-8498, ⓦwww.robbies.com).

# JOHN PENNEKAMP STATE PARK

Daily 8am–sunset; $4 per car, plus 50¢ per person, $1.50 pedestrians.

The enormous, underwater **John Pennekamp State Park**, at MM 102.5-oceanside, Key Largo (☎305/451-1202) is, frankly, a little overrated – the beaches are far better at Bahia Honda, and the coral formations more spectacular in Biscayne National Park (see p.109) or the Dry Tortugas. However, for **wreck diving**, it's worth a detour: there are two Coastguard cutters near **Molasses Reef** that were deliberately sunk in 1987, while just off **Cannon Beach** are the remains of an early Spanish shipwreck. Finally, the algae-soaked **Christ of the Deep** statue, a nine-foot bronze memorial to sailors who lost their lives at sea – arguably one of the weirdest sights in the Keys – lies 20 feet down at Key Largo Dry Rocks.

---

For details on snorkeling, diving and boat trips, see the box on p.248.

---

# FLORIDA KEYS WILD BIRD CENTER

24 hours a day; self-guided tours; $5 suggested donation.

Just south along Hwy-1 from the John Pennekamp State

Park you'll find the **Florida Keys Wild Bird Center** (93600 Overseas Hwy; ☏305/852-4486, ⓦflorida-keys.fl.us/flkeyswildbird.htm). Located in small, homely Tavernier, this hospital and sanctuary receives wounded birds from around the Keys. The staff nurse most until they can be returned to the wild, while animals too badly injured remain in specially constructed habitats. A visit here is a great way to get close to many of the local species – an eco-friendly walkway made from recycled materials snakes through the aviary, and many long-term residents are tame enough to approach.

# INDIAN KEY HISTORIC STATE PARK

Further south along Hwy-1, past Islamorada, a trip to the wilderness of **Indian Key Historic State Park** (ⓦwww.dep.state.fl.us/parks) is well worth it: the ruins of what was once the last inhabited outpost on the journey down to Key West are an evocative, if crumbling, reminder of early settler life in the Keys – take special note of the grassy paddock that was once the town square. Seek out the observation tower, too, which gives spectacular views across the island's lush and jumbled foliage.

Much like the vegetation here, Indian Key's history is also jumbled. In 1831, a rogue wrecker named Jacob Housman, driven out of Key West in disgrace, bought the island to build his own fiefdom. Less than ten years later, Indian Key had become a busy trading port when Henry Perrine, a plant-mad doctor, arrived to begin experiments in cultivating agave cacti. However, a brutal Seminole attack in 1840 leveled the town, ending the island's habitation as quickly as it had begun. Although the doctor himself was killed, his flora still thrive – the island's now choked with agave plants.

# LIGNUMVITAE KEY BOTANICAL STATE PARK

Tours Thurs–Mon 9.30am, 1.30pm; $1.

On the north side of Hwy-1, roughly opposite Indian Key on the south side, the **Lignumvitae Key Botanical State Park** (T305/664-2540, Wwww.dep.state.fl.us/parks) is the best remaining example of original Florida Keys tropical hammock. Named for the medicinal hardwood *lignumvitae* (meaning "water of life") tree, the park is full of exotic vegetation, and knowledgeable rangers lead tours that provide thorough background on all the indigenous plants. Note that the island's ravaged by mosquitoes, so wear long sleeves and long pants, and bring plenty of insect repellent if you decide to make the trip.

# UPPER KEYS PRACTICALITIES

Two good **accommodation** options for the Upper Keys are in Islamorada: the fancier of which, the *Chesapeake*, at MM 87.5-Oceanside (T305/664-4662, Wwww.chesapeake-resort.com; ❺), has standard rooms with large balconies, some of which face the ocean. Its strongest selling point, though, is the private beach, only yards from the main building, as well as onsite tennis courts and a sparkling, if small, swimming pool. A cheaper option is the *Key Lantern/Blue Fin*, at MM 82.1-Bayside (T305/664-4572, Wwww.keylantern.com; ❷), which has basic – if a little frayed – rooms. If you have a choice, take a room in the *Blue Fin*, as these have been redone more recently.

Islamorada also has a couple of good choices for **eating**. Try *Papa Joe's*, at MM 79-Bayside (T305/664-5300; moderately priced), which serves decent seafood in a basic setting; the real reason to come here, though, is the outdoor bar hidden on a jetty at the back, perfect for a cheap beer and some appetizers at sunset. *Squid Row*, at MM 82-Oceanside (☎305/664–9865; moderately priced), is a casual, diner-style eatery with a brightly lit bar. Serving plenty of seafood and known for its conch burgers, it's a true local hangout that gives a sense of everyday life in the Keys.

# The Middle and Lower Keys

Between Islamorada and Key West lie the **Middle** and **Lower keys**, split in half at the western end of the **Seven Mile Bridge**. The one major settlement in the Middle Keys is **Marathon**, an appealingly blue-collar town with ample amenities that makes a terrific base for exploring; **Bahia Honda State Recreational Park** is just twelve miles south from here. The Lower Keys are much larger, and heavily residential: it's worth pausing here before racing on to Key West, especially on Big Pine Key for the **Key Deer Refuge**, as well as trips out to the **Looe Key Marine Sanctuary**.

## SEVEN MILE BRIDGE

Connecting Marathon to the Lower Keys is the **Seven Mile Bridge**, a stunning feat of engineering when built nearly a century ago, and equally impressive now. Eschewing landfill in order to preserve the deep Moser Channel for commercial shipping, Henry Flagler sought to bridge the unthinkable seven-mile gap between Key Vaca and Bahia Honda Key, thereby providing a course for extending his railroad. Using his own in-house technicians, he oversaw the completion of the bridge in only four years at a staggering cost of $22 million. Although the railway was soon wiped out by the hurricane of 1935, the bridge itself held. By 1982, though, it was superseded by a wider, modern structure, built to better allow trucks passage back and forth along the highway. In testament to its craftsmanship, Flagler's century-old bridge is as strong as ever, while the parallel bridge is already corroding and in need of repair less than twenty years after its construction.

# BAHIA HONDA STATE RECREATIONAL PARK

Daily 8am–sunset; $4 per car plus 50¢ per person, $1.50 pedestrians.

The new Seven Mile Bridge leads you right to the **Bahia Honda State Recreational Park**, at MM 37-Oceanside (☎305/872-2353, ⓦwww.dep.state.fl.us/parks/district5/bahiahonda), which features a glorious two-mile-long white sand beach, one of the few natural beaches in the Keys. Take care when swimming in the deep waters off the park's southern tip, as currents can be strong; if you're snorkeling, there's a concession at the marina where you can rent equipment ($10). Otherwise, the park's known for its rare and unusual plants, such as the endangered silver palms, and there's a pleasant nature trail that weaves along the coast through the tropical hardwood hammock. Self-guiding leaflets are available at the entrance, or join a ranger-led tour (Tues 11am). If you want to stay here, there's a choice of camping or one of three raised cabins on the waterfront: for these, book well ahead, as they're very popular in season – call ☎1-800/326-3521 or visit ⓦwww.reserveamerica.com for reservations.

# KEY DEER REFUGE

Park open daily sunrise–sunset, visitor center in Big Pine Shopping Center open Mon–Fri 8am–5pm; free.

The 8400-acre **Key Deer Refuge**, at MM 33-Bayside (☎305/872-0774, ⓦnationalkeydeer.fws.gov), stretches across Big Pine and adjacent No Name Key and is the only home of the Key Deer, a rare subspecies of white-tailed deer. Sometimes called toy deer because of their small stature, there are now only 300 left, all of which live in the refuge. The best time to spot them is at sunrise or sunset, when the deer take advantage of their sharp eyesight and come out to forage in safety. Don't miss the **hiking trails** here, either – Blue Hole is a large freshwater lake that's home to plenty of soft-shelled turtles and alligators, and a good place for bird spotting.

---

Nearby No Name Key is notable as the staging ground for the failed Bay of Pigs invasion; the remnants of a decaying airstrip can be made out in a clearing on the south of the Key.

---

# LOOE KEY MARINE SANCTUARY

Named after the British frigate *HMS Looe* that sank here – just off Ramrod Key – in 1744, there's no Looe Key landmass. Instead, the **Looe Key Marine Sanctuary** (☎304/292-0311, ⓦwww.fknms.nos.noaa.gov) consists of five square miles of protected coral reef that makes for some of the best and easiest snorkeling in all the Keys. The water ranges in depth from 8 to 35 feet, and the coral formations are enormous – look for showy elkhorn and star coral, not to mention deadly but shortsighted barracuda. Don't come to see a sunken ship, though: the *HMS Looe* has long since disintegrated, and all that's left are a few hard-to-spot ballast stones.

------------------------------------------------

**For details on dive operators, see the box on p.248.**

------------------------------------------------

# MIDDLE AND LOWER KEYS PRACTICALITIES

In the Middle and Lower keys, Marathon is your best bet for **accommodation**: there's *Banana Bay*, at MM 49.5-Bayside (℡305/743-3500 or 1-800/BANANA-1, Ⓦwww .bananabay.com; ❹), a lush, palm-crowded resort with airy, tropical rooms and good onsite amenities; the *Flamingo Inn*, at MM 59.3-Bayside (℡305/289-1478 or 1-800-439-1478, Ⓦwww.flamingoinnflakeys.com; ❸), an old-style motel with big, clean rooms engagingly painted in lurid pinks and greens; and the *Sea Dell Motel*, at MM 50-Bayside (℡305/743-5161 or 1-800/648-3854; ❷), which features spotless, simply furnished, bright, white and turquoise rooms – one of the best budget options in the Keys.

As for **eating**, two good choices in Marathon are the *Castaway Restaurant*, at 1406 Oceanview Ave, near MM 47.5-Oceanside (℡305/743-6247; moderately priced), a local place known for its tasty and unusual alligator tail dishes – you can also bring your own fish for cooking – and *Porky's BBQ*, at MM 47.5-Bayside (℡305/289-2065; moderately priced), a thatched-roof shack that serves inexpensive BBQ platters. Also worth seeking out is the devilishly hard-to-find *No Name Pub*, at MM28-Bayside, about a quarter mile south of No Name Bridge on Big Pine Key (℡305/872-9115, Ⓦwww.nonamepub.com; inexpensive): the freshly made pizzas are particularly good.

# Key West

The southernmost point of the continental United States is in **Key West** – and it shows. An easy blend of Caribbean and American cultures, its Old Town is packed with ice cream-colored colonial houses and unhurried locals, washed over with a sense that this could be the town at the edge of the world.

Key West has had a checkered history, tumbling from commercial pre-eminence at the turn of the twentieth century, when trains took over from ships and little Lemon City transformed into Miami; although Flagler's railroad looked likely to reinvigorate Key West, it didn't work and was washed away in the 1935 hurricane. But the locals – or conchs, as they're called – don't seem to care: whatever happens in life, people here seem determined to remain unruffled. It's partly this supine tolerance that has allowed a huge, quietly integrated gay population to accumulate in Key West in the past twenty years.

Compact but not small, **Old Town** – at the western end of the island – is where most major sights can be found: it's best to rely on walking as you'll see more local color and worry less about finding parking on the cramped streets. **Mallory Square**, the old wreckers' dock, is the heart of tourist Key West, hosting the well-known sunset celebrations and with many museums close by; while **Duval Street**, the main drag, extends south from here.

The city's military history is clear in the **Truman Annex**, once a naval base and now an enclave of the swankiest homes in town. Close by, and very different, the Caribbean contribution to Key West's growth is evident in the old workmen's homes of the **Bahama Village**, a great place to saunter round on a hot, lazy afternoon – and the **Hemingway House**, for devoted fans of the author, is just

●

outside the Bahamian quarter. Finally, east from the town center you'll find **East Old Town**, home to a large wooden historic district.

# CITY TRANSIT AND TOURS

As the sights in Key West Old Town are virtually crammed together, the area is easily navigable on foot – though renting a bike is a good alternative option. There's also a **bus**

## THE CONCH REPUBLIC

Key West is also known as the "Conch Republic," and the story behind its nickname shows the town's savvy and sense of humor. After the Mariel Boatlift catalyzed resentment towards illegal immigrants in South Florida, Keys residents began to be seen by some as complicit in smuggling Cuban refugees into America. In response, the border patrol erected a roadblock at the start of the Keys, searching every car for illegal aliens.

Traffic backed up for miles, deterring tourists and severely crippling the local economy. In a fusion of marketing savvy and media flair, the government of Key West declared that if it was treated like a foreign country, it would become one, seceding from the United States and promptly declaring a one-minute war on April 23, 1982. Its immediate surrender was followed by a demand for $1 billion in foreign aid to rebuild.

A publicity stunt, yes, but one that worked – fast-selling bumper stickers declared "I made it to the Conch Republic!" and "We seceded where others failed," and the story put the Keys on television news across the country. The economy rapidly revived, and every year in April during Conch Republic Days the city still commemorates its fleeting moment of independence.

service, with two routes that loop through town (75¢ exact change; ℡305/292-8164, ⒲www.keywestcity.com).

The best **guided tours** are with local historian Sharon Wells – call ℡305/294-8380 for prices and schedule, or pick up her superb free self-guided walking tour brochure from the **Key West Chamber of Commerce** at 402 Wall St (daily 8.30am–6.30pm; ℡305/294-2587, ⒲www.keywest chamber.org). Local ghostbuster David Sloan also runs fun "haunted" tours, which leave from the *Holiday Inn* at 430 Duval St ($18; ℡305/294-9255, ⒲www.hauntedtours.com).

# ACCOMMODATION

If you're staying in Key West proper, it's worth the extra cost to stay downtown: the hotels scattered along Hwy-1 as you approach the Old Town may be slightly cheaper, but there is little public transport and parking is nightmarish in high season.

A good lodging resource is the Key West Innkeepers Association, headquartered at 922 Caroline St (℡305/295-1334 or 1-888/KEY-INNS, ⒲www.keywestinns.com): more than 60 guesthouses and B&Bs in Old Town are members, and the helpful staff should be able to guide you to the right accommodation for price and location.

---

**For an explanation of the price codes below, see the box on p.114, "Accommodation."**

---

### Budget Inn

1031 Eaton St ℡305/294-3333. Tucked away north of the Old Town near the seaport, this is a rare find in Key West, with low prices, pleasant rooms and good location. Onsite amenities may be minimal, but the rooms themselves are delightful, with refrigerators and large bathrooms. ❸

## Key Lime Inn

725 Truman Ave ⓣ305/294-5229 or 1–800/549-4430, ⓦwww.keylimeinn.com.
There are various different accommodations in this cluster of cottages near the center of Old Town. A good buffet breakfast is served by the pool, and the ample onsite parking is a major plus. Room décor is Key West tropical – splurge on one of the bungalows for the seclusion and the verandah. ❹–❻

## Marrero's Guesthouse

410 Fleming St ⓣ305/294-6977 or 1-800/459-6212, ⓦwww.marreros.com.
Reputed to be haunted, this fancy but friendly hotel has rooms crammed with antique furniture. Ghost-hunters should ask for room 18, where most paranormal activity has been reported. Regular room ❹, room 18 ❻

## Paradise Inn

819 Simonton St ⓣ305/293-8007 or 1-800/888-9648, ⓦhttp://theparadiseinn.com.
A sumptuous choice for anyone who wants to live the high life, Key West-style. Cigar makers' cottages and Bahamian houses have been transformed into country luxury rooms, dotted among a lush garden. There's a pool, jacuzzi and on-site parking. ❼–❾

# DUVAL STREET

Jammed with tacky T-shirt and souvenir shops, especially at its northern end, **Duval Street** is often held up as a prime exhibit in the spoiling of Key West. Despite appearances, though, there are some surprisingly good restaurants and bars dotted along its length, as well as Key West's most famous watering hole, **Captain Tony's Saloon**, at 428 Greene St (ⓣ305/294-1838, ⓦwww.capttonyssaloon.com), where Hemingway drank back when it was called *Sloppy Joe's*. Confusingly, another bar named *Sloppy Joe's*, laden with Hemingway memorabilia, is just across the street.

Southeast along Duval are more traditional sights, like the salty **Wrecker's Museum** and the comprehensive, Cuban-focused **San Carlos Institute**. Take a right onto South Sreet as you near Duval's southern tip, where just offshore you'll see the **Southernmost Point** marker. The red, black

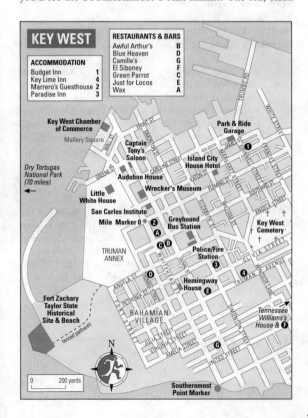

**KEY WEST**

**ACCOMMODATION**
| | |
|---|---|
| Budget Inn | 1 |
| Key Lime Inn | 4 |
| Marrero's Guesthouse | 2 |
| Paradise Inn | 3 |

**RESTAURANTS & BARS**
| | |
|---|---|
| Awful Arthur's | B |
| Blue Heaven | D |
| Camille's | G |
| El Siboney | F |
| Green Parrot | C |
| Just for Locos | E |
| Wax | A |

Key West Chamber of Commerce

Mallory Square

Dry Tortugas National Park (70 miles)

Park & Ride Garage

Captain Tony's Saloon

Island City House Hotel

Audubon House

Wrecker's Museum

Little White House

San Carlos Institute

Mile Marker 0

Greyhound Bus Station

Key West Cemetery

TRUMAN ANNEX

Police/Fire Station

Fort Zachary Taylor State Historical Site & Beach

Hemingway House

BAHAMIAN VILLAGE

Tennessee Williams's House &

fenced pathway

N

0    200 yards

Southernmost Point Marker

**DUVAL STREET**

and yellow barrel is an irresistible photo opportunity – but be advised that if you accept the offer of any helpful "passers-by" to take your picture, they'll demand a tip in return.

## Wrecker's Museum

Daily 10am–4pm; $5.

Built in 1829 when Florida was still a territory, the **Wrecker's Museum** (☎305/294-9502) is located in the oldest house in town, at no. 322. Hokey but entertaining, the museum presents the history of wrecking via artifacts and models, as well as the posh furniture of Captain Watlington, one of the house's first inhabitants. There's more than a little poetic license to many of the sea dog yarns the museum offers, and the saintliness of the selfless wreckers is unintentionally hilarious, given how often they were accused of encouraging, rather than just responding to, lucrative wrecks.

## San Carlos Institute

Tues–Fri 11am–5pm, Sat 11am–5pm, Sun 11am–6pm; $3.

Nicknamed *La Casa Cuba*, the **San Carlos Institute** at no. 516 (☎305/294-3887) was founded in 1871 by Cuban expats who wanted to celebrate the language, ideals and culture of the Cuban people – it now offers a sturdy survey of Cuban presence in the US. The neo-baroque building stands out amid the simpler structures elsewhere in the Old Town; it's also notable as the site of the first racially integrated school in the States, having from its inception educated children of all races together.

# MALLORY SQUARE

**Mallory Square** was originally the hub of Key West's wrecking industry, its buildings used for the storage and auction of goods salvaged from wrecked ships. Now, it's the hub of Key West's tourist trade, filled with market stalls and street performers. Nearby there's also the excellent museum and tropical gardens at the **Audubon House**.

At night, the **sunset celebration** sweeps over the area, when jugglers, fire-eaters and assorted loose-screw types create a merry backdrop to the day's end. The party began with a group of hippies in the 1960s, but it's not quite the countercultural hangout it once was: even so, it's still worth a stop for the spectacular sunsets over the water and the general liveliness.

## Audubon House & Tropical Gardens

Daily 9.30am–5pm; $8.50.

The restoration of the **Audubon House**, at 205 Whitehead St (☎305/294-2116, ⓦwww.audubonhouse.com), kickstarted the local preservation movement in 1958. Built by Captain John Geiger, one of the most successful wreckers in Key West in the early nineteenth century, this grand house was named for the famous ornithologist John James Audubon, who visited here in 1832. As with many homes in the Old Town, it's constructed using shipbuilding techniques, making it more flexible in high winds. Inside is a superb museum, with an evocative audio tour that captures Key West's wrecking heyday; there's also a small on-site gallery of pricey Audubon prints for sale.

# TRUMAN ANNEX

The **Truman Annex**, which encompasses much of the northwest corner of Key West, was originally part of a naval base established in 1822 to curb pirate activity in the area; it later became a favored place for flight training thanks to wide uninterrupted air space and clear, predictable local weather. Although the base was decommissioned in the

1970s, the charming old houses here were significantly restored when purchased by a developer in 1986. It's now the site of some of the most luxurious homes in Key West – pick up a free map from one of the boxes dotted throughout the complex.

---

**The Truman Annex also provides access to Fort Zachary Taylor (see below) via a fenced path.**

---

The area is named after its most famous former resident, President Harry S. Truman, who first came here on doctor's orders in March 1946 to recuperate after World War II. He quickly adopted Key West as a second home and spent most of his visits in **The Little White House**, at 111 Front St (daily 9am–5pm; $10, admission only by guided tour; ☎305/294-9911), which has now been restored to its Truman-era heyday, and is open as a museum. There's not much to see inside, other than mid-twentieth century ephemera, although the knowledgeable docents make it a worthwhile stop.

---

**At the corner of Fleming and Whitehead streets is Mile Marker 0, the starting point for the Keys' idiosyncratic address system.**

---

## Fort Zachary Taylor State Historical Site

Daily 8am–sunset; $1.50 pedestrians and cyclists, $2.50/1 person plus car, $5.00/2 people plus car, 50¢ each additional person; ☎305/292-6713

Conceived in the 1840s as part of a coastal defense system that also included Fort Jefferson in the Dry Tortugas, **Fort Zachary Taylor**'s glory days came during the Civil War, when as a Union stronghold it was used to block maneuvers

TRUMAN ANNEX

by the Confederate navy. Eventually, though, the fort fell into disrepair and disuse, before being turned over to the Navy as a historic site in 1947. The park offers informative guided tours (every day at 12pm & 2pm), where rangers provide detailed history on the fort. But for many visitors, the **beach** is the real reason to come here: it's the best in Key West, and there are full facilities onsite, including showers.

# BAHAMIAN VILLAGE

One of the few places that still has the feel of old Key West, unrestored and untouristed, the **Bahamian Village**, just southeast of the Truman Annex, sprang up in the 1820s after a law was passed making it illegal for vessels salvaged in US waters to be taken elsewhere. Many who worked in the salvage trade were Bahamian, and their temporary homes in Key West became permanent ones.

Quite a few of the small buildings here are bedraggled and a little rundown, a refreshing contrast to much of the over-elegant restoration in Old Town. Most of the reason for coming here is to get a feel for the laid-back vibe – witness the locals relaxing out on their porches while chickens roam the streets. The lone tourist sight here is eminently avoidable, the tacky Bahama Village Market, at 318 Petronia St.

# HEMINGWAY HOUSE

Daily 9am–5pm; $9.

Just outside the Bahamian Village quarter lies the **Hemingway House**, at 907 Whitehead St (℡305/294-1136, Ⓦwww.hemingwayhome.com). Even if there's much controversy over the true story of Hemingway's life in (and love for) Key West, his former home is one of the most enjoyable sights in town. His study – where he wrote two of his most famous novels, *For Whom the Bell Tolls* and *To Have and Have Not* – is compact and practical, set apart from the rest of the house in its own smaller outbuilding. Restoration of this and the main home has ostensibly taken the two back to how they looked during the time Hemingway was here – although his former secretary strongly contests the authenticity of much of the furnishings.

To see inside, join one of the regular **tours** (every 10 minutes, 30 minutes duration) led by true Key West eccentrics, who do a good job of spinning stories that play into the writer's macho myth – but take everything they say with a grain of salt.

## EAST OLD TOWN

Northeast from the Hemingway House lies Key West's **wooden historic district**, the largest of its kind in the US, bigger than better-known settlements in Savannah, Georgia or Charleston, South Carolina. The conch house style found here is a Colonial-Victorian fusion, and there are some excellent examples along William Street between Caroline and Angela streets. Shored up by a foundation of coral slabs, the houses themselves were built cheaply and quickly, fanning out from the earliest settlements around the port (now Mallory Square). The reason these houses have lasted so well is that many were put up by shipwrights using boat-building techniques, so they sway in high winds and weather extremes of climate handily. A fine example of this early Key West architecture is the **Island City House Hotel**, at 411 William St – built in the 1880s, it's the oldest hotel in town.

Twenty minutes' walk from the center of Old Town stands the Tennessee Williams House at 1431 Duncan St – however, as per the playwright's will, his house has never been open to visitors.

## DRY TORTUGAS NATIONAL PARK

Almost 70 miles out from Key West, the seven islands of the Dry Tortugas – named by Ponce de Leon in 1513, who found *tortugas*, or sea turtles, plentiful here – are exhilaratingly isolated and a birdwatcher's paradise; in particular, Bush and Long keys serve as sanctuaries for sooty terns and frigate birds. In addition, coral reefs here are close to the beach, especially on the western coast, making for sensational snorkeling; plus, the ruins of Fort Jefferson – an old Union Civil War stronghold – are fun and easy to explore. If you plan to stay overnight, the camping fee is $3 per person, but bring everything you'll need – including fresh water – as facilities are very basic. Call ⊤305/242-7700 for information, or visit ⓦwww.nps.gov/drto.

The only way to make the trip here is by boat or plane: the *Yankee Freedom* leaves daily from the dock at the end of Margaret St on Key West at 8am ($109 daytrip, $130 overnight; ⊤305/294-7009 or 1-800/634-0939, ⓦwww.yankeefleet.com), returning at 5pm. However, northerly winds can make for an extra-bumpy ride, so those with wobbly sea legs might prefer to spend a little extra and fly: try Seaplanes of Key West, located at 3471 S Roosevelt Blvd ($179/half day, $305/full day; ⊤305/294-0709 or 1-800/950-2FLY, ⓦwww.seaplanesofkeywest.com).

# EATING, DRINKING AND NIGHTLIFE

There are plenty of good **restaurants** in and around Duval Street, even if at first glance they may all seem rather tacky. It's also worth dipping into the Bahamian Village for cheap, authentic Caribbean food. For Cuban coffee and sandwiches, check out the streetside lunch counters – two worth trying are *Sandy's Café* at the M&M Laundry, located at 1026 White St (⊤305/295-0159), and Five Brothers Grocery, at 930 Southard St (⊤305/296-5205). Every restaurant in town offers its take on **key lime pie**: give it a try at the *Blond Giraffe*, at 629 Duval St (℗305/293-6998), which in years past won "Best Key Lime Pie" in a town-wide bake-off.

As for **drinking**, many hotels offer good deals on drinks during happy hour (usually 5-7pm), and there are some good run-down bars in the Old Town, many of which also showcase **live music**.

### Awful Arthur's Seafood Company

628 Duval St ℗305/293-7663.
Moderate.
This casual fish shack offers excellent-value nightly specials, such as All You Can Eat Snow Crab for $20, not to mention crisp, tangy french fries and cheap beer.

### Blue Heaven

729 Thomas St ℗305/296-8666.
Expensive.
Serving outstanding food in a relaxed setting, this Bahamian Village landmark has a large outdoor seating area that diners share with local chickens that wander around undisturbed. Open all day, the breakfasts are fine (try the lobster benedict), but lunch and dinner are better, especially when capped off with one of the sumptuous desserts.

### Camille's

1202 Simonton St
℗305/296-4811,
Ⓦwww.camilleskeywest.com.
Moderate.
*Camille's* is known as one of the best places in town for breakfast, thanks to luxurious specials like French toast with Godiva chocolate sauce or cashew nut waffles with coconut milk. Dinner's less exciting, though.

### Captain Tony's Saloon

428 Greene St ℗305/294-1838,
Ⓦwww.capttonyssaloon.com.
This bar was the original *Sloppy Joe's* that Hemingway frequented; now, it's a grimy yellow shack where you can catch live music most nights. Not the most atmospheric place in town, but worth a quick drink.

## El Siboney

900 Catherine St ⓣ305/296-4184. Inexpensive.

Crammed with tables and jammed with people, this large Cuban restaurant on the eastern side of the Old Town has cheap food and vast portions; the pork tenderloin is especially tasty.

## Green Parrot

601 Whitehead St ⓣ305/294-6133, ⓦwww.greenparrot.com.

Grubby old-time pub centered on an enormous square bar that's been a landmark for more than a century. Drinks are cheap, it's full of locals, and there are antique bar games alongside the pool tables. There's often live music at weekends on its small stage.

## Just for Locos

517 Truman Ave ⓣ305/296-1177. Inexpensive.

A roadside shack café with a laid-back, punky Cuban vibe, serving giant bargain sandwiches. One of the best places in town to sample a *café con leche*.

## Wax

422 Appelrouth Lane ⓣ305/296-6667, ⓦwww.waxkeywest.com.

The closest Key West comes to a traditional nightclub: overstuffed red sofas and bead curtains decorate a chic, dimly lit space. Come here only if you're determined to dance, as the music's way too loud to talk.

# GAY AND LESBIAN KEY WEST

For a town that's lauded as one of the **gay** meccas in America, the scene in Key West is surprisingly small – perhaps because the gay and straight communities are so integrated here. Accommodation-wise, almost every hotel and restaurant will be gay-friendly: stop by the **Gay and Lesbian Community Center** at 1075 Duval Square (ⓣ305/292-3223, ⓦwww.glcckeywest.org) for information and leaflets on specific hotels, or try the **Key West Business Guild** at 728 Duval St (℡305/294-4603 or 1-800/535-7797, ⊛www.gaykeywestfl.com).

---

**The unofficial gay beach is Higgs Memorial Beach at the southern end of Reynolds Street.**

---

To cruise on water rather than land, take one of the day or evening **boat trips** – one of the best is Tea on the Sea, run by Sebago Watersports (Tues & Sat $30, men only; Thurs $35, women only, including unlimited wine and beer; ℡1-800/507-9955, ⊛www.sebagokeywest.com), which leaves at 9pm from the dock at the end of William Street. For information on gay and lesbian goings-on in Key West, pick up a copy of the free *Southern Exposure* magazine or check out *Celebrate! Key West* (⊛www.celebratekeywest.com), a newsier, more informative freesheet.

## Bars and clubs

### 801 Bourbon Bar
801 Duval St, ℡305/294-4737. Drag shows are held upstairs every night at 11pm, while downstairs there's a nondescript bar with a mixed, slightly older crowd that opens out onto the street, so you can watch passers-by. Friendly, if bland, atmosphere.

### Bourbon St Pub
724 Duval St ℡305/296-1992, ⊛www.bourbonstreetpub.com.

A huge video bar with five bars, seven screens and a pleasant garden. There are go-go boys every night, and happy hour until 8pm. This pub attracts both locals and tourists and, as with most bars in town, the crowd's diverse and chatty.

### Diva's
711 Duval St ℡305/292-8500, ⊛www.divaskeywest.com. Twice-nightly drag shows (at 10pm and 11.30pm) here are

hit-and-miss, although some performers are spectacular. There's a raised lounge with good views of the stage, and a big dancefloor.

# CONTEXTS

---

# A brief history of Miami

## Early natives and European settlement

The Miami area's earliest residents were **Tequesta Indians** who made their home some 10,000 years ago near what's now the Deering Estate in Cutler, just south of Miami. The Tequesta, likely responsible for the mysterious Miami Circle, lived and farmed the land alone until joined by the **Seminole Indians** in the 1400s, and were soon after completely wiped out by European settlements.

The **first European sighting** of Florida is believed to have been made by brothers John and Sebastian Cabot in 1498, when they chanced upon what's now Cape Florida on Key Biscayne. Fifteen years later, **Ponce de León**, former governor of the Spanish possession of Puerto Rico, was dispatched by his king to find the fabled Fountain of Youth. Instead, he "discovered" land during *Pascua Florida*, the Spanish Easter festival, and so named the area *La Florida*, or "Land of the Flowers."

De León continued on, sighting the Florida Keys, which he named *Los Martires*, the land fragments resembling to him the bones of Christian martyrs, and the Dry Tortugas, which he called *Las Tortugas* after the hundreds of turtles he found there.

## Spanish colonial rule and beyond

After Ponce de León's claim in 1513, Florida remained a **Spanish possession** until the late eighteenth century. During this time, England had been aggressively colonizing the southern seaboard of America and, in the process, seized Havana, Spain's colonial jewel. Eager to recapture the Cuban capital, Spain traded Florida to Britain for the return of the city in 1763.

However, after the American War of Independence was fought and won twenty years later, the 1783 Treaty of Paris – which recognized American independence – had the newly formed United States return Florida to Spain in return for the country's support during the war.

This second spate of Spanish rule turned out to be short-lived. Spain ceded Florida back to the US to relieve itself of the $5 million owed in land grants to American settlers (though the money was never repaid). The US settlers mostly coveted northern and central Florida for its rich land and had little interest in the southern reaches for the time being.

## The birth of a city

In the late 1830s, during the Second Seminole War – the first had been quickly subdued in 1818 – a trading post and plantation called **Fort Dallas** was established along the Miami River, marking the first permanent white settlement in the Miami area. In 1842, at the end of the bloody seven-year war, Colonel William English decided to stay in Fort Dallas and further develop the post, beginning the first of

Miami's many real estate advertising campaigns, designed to sell plots of land to homesteaders.

With Florida's entry into **statehood** on March 3, 1845, prospects for the nascent city indeed looked bright, but ten years later, a third Seminole War broke out, lasting for three years, soon to be followed by the Civil War. Together, these conflicts delayed any significant development, other than the building of a post office and a few other structures.

It wasn't until the arrival later that century of three visionary pioneer settlers from Ohio that Miami truly began to take shape. Wealthy entrepreneur **William Brickell** arrived with his wife **Mary** in 1870: they built a grand home and set up an Indian Trading Post just south of the Miami River. Meanwhile, Brickell's friend and rival Ephraim Sturtevant came down from Cleveland and purchased land along Biscayne Bay. Sturtevant was often visited by his daughter, **Julia Tuttle**, who quickly realized the area's immense potential, and so purchased acres of land along the river. By 1891, she'd moved her family to Florida, taken over her late father's lands north of the river, and bought the remains of William English's plantation as her home.

Just a few miles down the road, **Coconut Grove** was in the midst of establishing its own identity, helped along by characters such as Ralph Middleton Munroe, an eccentric sea captain-cum-architect. Munroe encouraged others to invest and build there, including Charles and Isabella Peacock, business owners who came over from England and erected South Florida's first hotel in the Grove, the *Bay View House*, in 1882.

## The railroad arrives

Despite the inroads made by the various real estate magnates of the late 1800s, Miami still had little contact with the outside world. This would change with a deal between railroad tycoon **Henry Flagler**, who had made his fortune as a partner in John D. Rockefeller's Standard Oil Company, and Julia Tuttle.

In the apocryphal story, Flagler was resistant to extending his existing railroad from Palm Beach south to Miami – that is, until Julia Tuttle sent him a package full of fresh orange blossoms on the heels of the 1894–95 winter, nicknamed the "Big Freeze," which had destroyed most citrus crops in northern Florida. Thinking that such a tropical climate would attract northern vacationers, Flagler began to revise his plans, and agreed to the extension in exchange for land from Tuttle and the Brickells.

On this land, Flagler built the magnificent *Royal Palm Hotel*, while simultaneously gouging out an easy shipping channel for the Port of Miami – the waterway between South Beach and Fisher Island now known as Government Cut.

Meanwhile, the **railroad** took just over a year to arrive, and in April 1896, the first passenger train entered the city, bringing with it excited refugees from elsewhere in the state. Two months later, on July 28, the city was formally incorporated: voters eventually settled on the name Miami, believing – erroneously – that it was the Tequesta word for "sweet water."

## The building boom

The biggest obstacle to widespread settlement in South Florida was its swampy, low-lying land. By 1908, developers began addressing that problem head-on, systematically dredging the water-soaked inland areas in a desperate race to keep up with consumer demand: many let their staff sell faster than they dredged, leading to reputations of offering "land by the gallon."

Despite some shady sales practices, the **building boom** in Miami was in full swing. In 1912, the department store Burdine's became the city's first "skyscraper," at five stories high, while millionaire James Deering was building the opulent neo-Renaissance Villa Vizcaya. Mary Brickell, assisted by her husband, planned the wide vista of Brickell Avenue to connect Miami with Coconut Grove. It quickly became known as **Millionaires' Row** when wealthy new residents, including presidential candidate William Jennings Bryan, built enormous mansions there. By 1920, the new city had more than 30,000 inhabitants: five years later, Miami tripled its size by annexing Coconut Grove and Lemon City, an early settlement located where Little Haiti now lies.

The fuel for this expansion was largely hot air: Miami was the first American city built equally on hype and high hopes. Everest G. Sewell was one of the first masters of public relations, responsible for the relentless sloganeering of the city, including taglines like "Miami: Where the Summer Spends the Winter," and, simply, "Stay through May." The local chamber of commerce funded lavish holidays for journalists who wrote for wire services, to ensure good press in papers across the country.

Meanwhile, in a flight of idealistic megalomania, George Merrick began the most ambitious building project of all: **Coral Gables**. Inspired by the City Beautiful movement (see box p.290), he envisioned a European-style town with civic amenities and civilized settlers. By 1925, less than four years after its inception, and nourished by the local flair for publicity, Coral Gables was a viable city that had earned its founder almost $150 million.

## Miami and the beach

The development of Miami's mainland would soon be

superseded by a piece of land that was mere swamp only decades before. In 1882, **John Collins** had bought a fetid strip of property directly east of downtown Miami, in the hopes of turning it into a fruit-and-vegetable plantation. The only problem was that the land was in effect an off-shore island, three miles east of Miami proper with nothing connecting it to the mainland. Collins set out to construct a rudimentary bridge, but ran out of money halfway through.

His vision was carried out some thirty years later by **Carl Fisher**, millionaire and Indianapolis racetrack designer, who saw a lucrative goldmine in Collins' island and agreed to finance the project in exchange for two hundred acres of oceanfront property. Fisher constructed Miami's first cause-way in 1913, a more durable structure than Collins', and **Miami Beach** was born, incorporated into the city of Miami two years later.

## A hurricane, the Great Depression, and the building bust

In September of 1926, a **hurricane** with winds up to 125mph came ashore in South Florida, passing directly over Miami; it destroyed 5000 homes, flooded downtown, and vitually obliterated Miami Beach. Already hurting financially from the inflation that accompanied the recent building boom, the city plunged into economic crisis. The Wall Street crash of 1929 and the **Great Depression** that followed further hobbled Miami's progress. The commercial airline business provided the only glimmer of hope in these times; **Pan American Airlines** moved its headquarters from Key West to Coconut Grove's Dinner Key in 1928 and immediately connected Miami to 32 Central and South American countries.

## Art Deco, World War II, and the tourism revival

With Miami in the economic throes of the Depression, Roosevelt's New Deal and the Florida citrus industry saved Miami from total bankruptcy and allowed the city to begin a slow recovery. Miami Beach was actually the main beneficiary, with hundreds of hotels, residences and other buildings thrown up in the mid-to-late 1930s, to keep pace with a tourist industry that was again thriving. Many of these structures were designed in the modern **Art Deco** style, led by the designs of architects L. Murray Dixon and Henry Hohauser.

**World War II**, when it arrived, sped the recovery process along, bringing 70,000 soldiers to the city for training. Almost 150 hotels were used as barracks, and the *Biltmore* hotel in Coral Gables was converted into a military hospital. After the war, these soldiers, who were said to have gotten "sand in their shoes" during training, flocked back as civilians. Capping the decade in 1949, the *Raleigh* hotel made a visionary investment in a central air-conditioning machine. No longer would the summers be too stifling for visitors – Miami was now a year-round destination. At a national convention in the early 1950s, travel agents figured out that Miami Beach had built more hotels since the war than all other resorts worldwide put together.

## The 1950s and 1960s: racial tension and Cuban immigration

As elsewhere in the American South, voters supported enforced **segregation**, and local blacks were sent to live in an area that became known as Coloredtown. Even after the Supreme Court ruled in favor of desegregation in 1954, economic discrimination continued. The situation did not improve in the 1960s, as the Miami local government displaced more than 20,000 residents from Coloredtown (renamed Overtown) in order to build a massive freeway through the area. Payback came in race riots that ignited in Liberty City in 1968 and again in 1980.

Racial tensions were exacerbated by the repercussions of the 1959 Cuban Revolution, in which **Fidel Castro** came to power. Many of the immigrants who came to Miami over the next five years were members of Cuba's elite, tossed out because of the potential threat they posed. They imagined their stay would be temporary until the joint blow of the botched Bay of Pigs invasion in 1961 and the Cuban Missile Crisis – a tense standoff between the US and the USSR over Soviet nuclear missile bases on the island – a year later effectively barred their return home. In reaction to anti-Communist outrage from Cuban expats and Americans alike, the US began so-called Freedom Flights in 1965. They ran for eight years, bringing more than 300,000 Cubans to Miami, where many settled west of downtown in the Jewish area of Riverside, soon to be known as Little Havana. An odd group to be refugees, these doctors, lawyers and entrepreneurs started out working menial jobs, but were soon re-establishing themselves in the professions they'd followed back home.

Still, the impact of this wave of immigration on the city was abrasive. Under the Cuban American Adjustment Act of 1966, permanent residency was granted to any Cuban who'd lived in the United States for at least one year, a luxury afforded no other immigrant group before or since – and still a source of resentful friction with other ethnic minorities, like the Haitians.

## The 1970s: economic decline and architectural preservation

The 1970s were a quiet, if bleak, period in Miami history: as elsewhere across the nation, **economic decline** continued, and the city struggled to retain tourist dollars. In addition, during this period Dade County declared itself bilingual in 1973, in response to massive Spanish-speaking immigration. The move was highly controversial, and was rescinded after the infamous Mariel Boatlift (see below).

The bright spot of the 1970s was the establishment of the **Miami Design Preservation League** by Barbara Baer Capitman, who defended the decaying Art Deco structures in Miami Beach against the wrecking ball, and kickstarted a reassessment of their architectural value (for more information, see the box "Decoding Art Deco", on p.38).

## The Mariel Boatlift

The first wave of middle-class Cuban immigrants were joined by a totally different kind of refugee thanks to the **Mariel Boatlift** in May 1980, an event which tore Miami apart. After a spat with the Peruvian government over a group seeking asylum in Havana's Peruvian embassy, Castro opened the port of Mariel and announced that anyone who wished to leave the island was free to do so. And they did: 125,000 Cubans arrived in Miami in less than three days. But Castro's seemingly capricious gesture proved a masterstroke: numerous refugees were fresh from Cuban jails, and many others were mentally ill. The local government in Miami created a tent city under Interstate 95 and struggled to find somewhere to house the new arrivals. Many ended up in then-rundown South Beach.

## The rest of the 1980s and the 1990s

The 1980s represented the nadir of Miami's reputation, when the city was synonymous with **cocaine** and **crime**. At this time it was estimated that one quarter of the cocaine that entered America arrived through Florida; and at one point, the murder rate in Miami was so high that the local medical examiner rented a refrigerated truck for corpses, as the 30-body capacity of the cooler in the central morgue was regularly maxing out. In addition, the now-decrepit hotels on South Beach, already filled with the old and infirm, living their last years in the warm weather (earning the area the nickname "God's Waiting Room"), added the *Marielitos* to their ranks, transforming the area into a hub for local criminal activity. The bubblegum cop show *Miami Vice*, set on the beach, added an unrealistic, glossy sheen to the grubby district.

Corruption and crime continued into the 1990s, even as South Beach was discovered by fashion photographers and enjoying a throbbing renaissance. From 1992 to 1998, forty public officials were indicted on bribery and corruption charges, while tourist violence reached its height in 1994 and 1995, prompting then-governor Lawton Chiles to create a Task Force on Tourist Safety, as well as providing special tourist-oriented police and more easily visible roadside signage for vacation-goers. To a large degree, his measures worked: petty crime today is down, and tourist violence minimal.

## Miami today

Present-day Miami is still struggling to live up to the glossy reputation it's created for itself. One major success, though, is its banking industry: after the city was grazed by **Hurricane Andrew** in 1992 (districts further south were not so lucky), the city emerged as an important banking center, with dozens of gleaming downtown office blocks as proof of its economic vitality.

Politics and race remain contentious issues, especially with regard to Cuba: even if the federal government's concern for the communist nation is cooling, the ire of local exiles is boiling hotter than ever. Nowhere was that better illustrated than in the recent case of **Elián González**. After his mother was killed trying to reach America with Elián in tow, the boy was returned – by the federal government, and by force – to his father in Cuba. Few involved in this sad mess escaped unblighted – not least Bill Clinton (already reviled by Cuban exiles for not being tough enough on Castro's regime), who supported Elián's repatriation, and Florida attorney general Janet Reno, who had final say in the matter. Tellingly, though, Manny Diaz, the lawyer who defended Elián's right to stay in America, is now the mayor of Miami.

Later in the year, the **2000 presidential election** debacle turned all eyes to South Florida again, when the right to the White House hung on a few hard-to-read votes in Miami-Dade County. Charges of corruption still ripple: some claim that the ballots were oddly designed and confusing, and the fact that the brother of George Bush – who was eventually awarded the presidency by the Supreme Court – was state governor at the time only stokes the fires of conspiracy.

Economically the city is enduring a few worries, too; though tourism remains strong, South Beach has lost a bit of luster in fashion circles, as models and photographers are air-kissing the beach goodbye to shoot catalogs in cheaper locations like South Africa and Spain. In addition, increasingly mainstream tourism has driven many gay residents – traditionally, some of the area's most lively supporters – north to Fort Lauderdale and beyond. Whether the beach can bounce back one more time remains to be seen.

# Architecture

I t's arguable that **architecture** vies with warm weather and wild nightlife as the prime draw for visitors to Miami. The style the city is best known for is undoubtedly Art Deco, which grew out of the 1925 *L'Exposition des Arts Décoratifs et Industriels Modernes*, a major exhibition in Paris that showcased designs employing modern, industrial production methods. Originally called Style Moderne, or Modernistic – the term Art Deco wasn't coined until well after its birth – the sleek, long-limbed designs became popular for furniture, clothing, fabrics and, soon after, buildings, being both simple to design and cheap to construct.

## Art Deco's beginnings in Miami

It took the disastrous hurricane that swept through the city in 1926 to bring this style to Miami. As a result of the hurricane's devastation, large amounts of land were suddenly clear – especially in Miami Beach – and on much of it, buildings in the cost-efficient, popular Art Deco style were erected. For the earliest of these, the style was heavily influenced by archeologist Howard Carter's discovery of the Egyptian pharaoh Tutankhamen's long-buried tomb in 1922. The opulent golden treasures from this royal time capsule were soon sent on headline-grabbing tours around the world, and fashion and design immediately incorporated the geometric, zigzagging Egyptian shapes, as did Art Deco.

During this time, Art Deco buildings were heavily decorated with ornamental panels that were often filled with symbolic images, much like the reliefs in Egyptian tombs. The difference was in subject matter: reliefs on so-called **Tropical** – or **Miami** – **Deco** buildings often featured palm trees, flamingos, pelicans, sunbursts and other indigenous symbols. Other features which are unique to buildings in the Tropical Deco style include sun-blocking eyebrows above windows and terrazzo floors. These floors – essentially colored concrete laid in geometric designs – are both durable and cool, as they absorb little heat from the sun.

As the glamour of Ancient Egypt receded and the realities of the Great Depression approached, the movement splintered into factions, as Tropical Deco sloughed off its fancy panels and excessive ornamentation, resulting in two new variations. There was **Depression Moderne**, a less decorative relative of its parent, in which ornamental elements were relegated to a building's interior, and **Streamline** – or **Nautical** – **Deco**, which featured rounded corners and "speed lines," intended to convey an impression of movement – and occasionally, even porthole windows and ornamental smokestacks.

## An alternative: Mediterranean Revival

Not everything being built at this time was in the Art Deco style, though: in fact, one third of the buildings in the Art Deco Historic District of South Beach are actually **Mediterranean Revival**, which was a contemporary architectural refuge for those who loathed the simplicity and starkness of Deco's poured concrete. Essentially, this style is Spain by way of California, based as it is on the

Mission architecture of early West Coast settler buildings. It featured terracotta roofs, ornate ironwork and deliberately ramshackle façades, so that a structure would appear well-aged.

## THE CITY BEAUTIFUL MOVEMENT

By 1910, almost one in two people in the United States lived in a city with more than 2500 inhabitants; with this mass urbanization came problems of crime, disease and overcrowding. Reformers like Chicago's Daniel Burnham had for several years been looking at ways to impose the moral order of a village onto these growing cities and so solve such problems: their theories became known as the City Beautiful Movement.

Inspired by the order and harmony of Europe's new Beaux Arts style, these reformers pitched utopian cities in vaguely classical style whose beauty would inspire civic loyalty and upstanding morals in even the most impoverished resident. Burnham initially outlined his blueprint for the perfect city at Chicago's World's Fair in 1893 and kept promoting it until his death in 1912; its buildings uniform, its parks enormous, the city would be crimeless, he said, from a combination of civic duty and plenty of police.

Key features included wide, tree-lined avenues, monumental buildings, ample greenspace, and frequent plazas or fountains. Later additions even included proscriptions about lampposts (which should be attractive as well as functional) and straight roads (which should be broken up by winding streets whenever possible).

This movement so inspired developer George Merrick's utopian megalomania that he set about building Coral Gables in 1925 to these specs; his lone deviation was employing Mediterranean Revival, rather than Beaux Arts, for the architectural framework.

Snobs dismissed such whimsy as a lower-class delight, but Miami's Latino heritage, coupled with a compatible climate, helped popularize the style. One of its biggest fans was Carl Fisher, the father of Miami Beach, who commissioned Española Way, the densest concentration of the style in the city – although the City Beautiful aesthetic (see box below) of George Merrick's Coral Gables owes much to Mediterranean Revival, too.

## Miami Modern

After World War II, America's confidence was refreshed in the glow of victory and economic prosperity. Reflecting this wide-eyed optimism, the buildings of the times – in a style that came to be known as **Miami Modern** (MiMo) – are stamped with that same sense of possibility and fun.

More than all else, designers in the MiMo age were fascinated with speed. Take, for example, tail-finned cars, or sleekly patterned polyester dresses – these designs were inspired not by ocean liners or trains, but by the futuristic jets of wartime and beyond. Many MiMo buildings also feature boomerang and kidney shapes, lending a looping sense of movement, as well as cheeky, unexpected ornamental holes, which play games with the viewer's perspective. There's great use of decorative collage, as well as architectural features like wide eaves, masonry *bris-soleils* (literally, "sunbreakers"), and jalousie windows, with louvered, overlapping glass panels, used expressly to create shade. Architects like the late Morris Lapidus and the still-active Norman Giller designed enormous, sweeping buildings, many in central Miami Beach, that dwarfed their Art Deco counterparts further south; Lapidus's philosophy, laid out clearly in the title of his autobiography, was "Too Much is Never Enough."

## The preservation movement

By the 1970s, the optimism that had prompted the MiMo boom had been drained, and the city was facing all manner of urban blight; had it not been for the efforts of one inde-fatigable, transplanted New Yorker, the Art Deco legacy that later helped revive the city might have succumbed to this downturn.

**Barbara Baer Capitman**, then editor of an interiors magazine called *The Designer*, became involved in Miami's efforts to honor America's Bicentennial in 1976. For her contribution, she seized upon the quirky, dilapidated Art Deco buildings of run-down South Beach and, along with five friends, founded the **Miami Design Preservation League**. A powerful, publicity-savvy woman who knew the value of a grand gesture, Capitman protested in person as the wrecking ball bit into the *Senator* hotel on Collins Avenue. She didn't manage to save it, or, indeed, several other hotels nearby, but she eventually helped secure South Beach the honor of being listed on the National Register of Historic Places (though it was still some time before the area cleaned up its crime-ridden image).

And Capitman didn't stop at simply conserving Art Deco: working with her friend, interior designer Leonard Horowitz, she then set about spiffing up the buildings that she'd saved. It was Horowitz who came up with the now-familiar sherbet palette of peaches, lemons and lavenders, to echo the cool tones of the sky, ocean and flowers. Outside the official preservation district, he varied the palette, amp-ing up the colors to neon shades of turquoise and cerise. Originally, most Deco buildings had been much more muted: either white or cream, with their key features picked out in navy or brown – City Hall in Coconut Grove is a rare, remaining example of this original color scheme.

# Preservation today

Although Capitman's crusade was successful, worries remain. Restorations are often tweaked for modern needs, and ambitious developers occasionally try to sneak around regulations, seeking to have buildings declared structurally unsound and in need of demolition. But the preservationist movement marches on; the recently designated **John S. Collins Oceanfront Historic District**, in central Miami Beach, has given MiMo the same elevated status as Deco. In addition, the latest massive hotel to arrive on the waterfront, the *Loews*, was greenlit only after its owners agreed to renovate and run the tiny, adjoining Art Deco hotel, the *St Moritz* – a happy union of commerce and conservation.

# Books

ost **books** that deal with Miami revel in the one thing the city most wants to forget: crime. These hardboiled novels with hardbitten heroes – written by the likes of Elmore Leonard and Edna Buchanan, among others – are distinctive enough to form a subspecies in the thriller genre.

Unfortunately, some of the books listed below are out of print (o/p), though even these should be available at many secondhand bookstores, through online searches, or perhaps at the terrific Fifteenth Street Books in Coral Gables (see p.193).

## History and society

(see p.193).

**T.D. Allman** *Miami*. Although its endless references to *Miami Vice* soon grate on the contemporary reader, Allman's insightful observations now serve as a time capsule of late twentieth century Miami. Worth dipping into for his sensitive analysis of what being from Miami means.

**Kathryne Ashley** *George E. Merrick & Coral Gables, Florida*. Brief, workmanlike account of the founding of Coral Gables that's notable for its checklist of landmarks and first-person accounts of George Merrick.

**Edna Buchanan** *The Corpse Had a Familiar Face* (o/p).

Buchanan was a reporter covering Miami's crime scene for the *Miami Herald* in the 1970s; here, she fuses her own tough life story with the tough cases she follows. Gripping, readable and a gory reminder of Miami's recent past.

**Joan Gill Blank** *Key Biscayne: A History of Miami's Tropical Island and the Cape Florida Lighthouse*. An exhaustive and readable history of one of the city's least celebrated districts. Gill Blank has a fine eye and a wry tone, managing to highlight Key Biscayne's importance in local history while retaining a critical perspective.

**Howard Kleinberg** *Miami Beach: A History* (o/p). This book combines text with archival photographs of Miami Beach, and is a great overview of its beginnings, with pithy, insightful commentary from Kleinberg, a former editor-in-chief of *The Miami News*.

**Morris Lapidus** *Too Much Is Never Enough* (o/p). Lapidus's autobiography is charming, vain and great fun – much like the man himself. The master of

MiMo architecture makes his life story into a lively yarn, but it's the juicy, tangential history of mid-century Miami that really grips.

**Helen Muir** *Miami*. Most consider this the definitive history of the city. However, while it's strong in the early chapters, the book becomes more toothless as it approaches the modern era, where she avoids any event too lively or controversial.

**Helen Muir** *The Biltmore: Beacon for Miami*. Muir's other major work is a well-rendered history of Miami's most famous hotel, the *Biltmore* in Coral Gables.

**Thelma Peters** *Lemon City: Pioneering on Biscayne Bay 1850–1925* (o/p). Thorough, quirky book that focuses on the forgotten settlement of Lemon City (now Little Haiti) to the north of downtown Miami. Readable, if a little scholarly.

**John Rothchild** *Up for Grabs*. Rothchild weaves his own experience of building a hippie-era house into the nasty story of South Florida's shady, postwar

**HISTORY AND SOCIETY**

land boom. He dissects the pioneer psyche of Florida and its settlers, as well as nailing the hard-sell showmanship that developers used to lure the hopeful to Miami and around.

## Fiction

**Edna Buchanan** *Miami, It's Murder*. The first novel by this Pulitzer Prize-winning author stars rebellious, no-nonsense crime reporter (and Cuban-American) Britt Montero. The story's entertaining enough, and zings with local detail, though it's Buchanan's ability to condense all that's good and bad about Miami into casual details that's most impressive.

**Stanley Elkin** *Mrs Ted Bliss*. An award-winning, amusing oddity set in Miami Beach, wherein 82-year-old widow Dorothy Bliss manages to get mixed up with a drug lord and a Hebrew-speaking Native American, all by selling her late husband's car.

**James W. Hall** *Bones of Coral*. A standard mystery, bringing a curious big city paramedic back to his home town of Key West to investigate his father's murder. Worth reading, though, for the cartoonish – but scary – villain Dougie Barnes.

**Vicki Hendricks** *Iguana Love*. This pulpy, raunchy novel is an explicit tale of a woman who leaves her husband and ends up popping steroids and chasing her younger lover. Its ripe sleepiness is signature South Florida, although Hendricks's prose can get tangled at times.

**Carl Hiaasen** Various. Local novelist Hiaasen relentlessly skewers South Florida's failings, and no one should visit Miami without having read one of his whipsmart, funny stories – try *Sick Puppy* or *Skin Tight* for starters. All the novels take breakneck tours around the area: the hero of the plastic-surgery-themed *Skin Tight*, for example, lives in a shack in Stiltsville (see p.93, "Key Biscayne and Virginia Key")

**Carl Hiaasen, Edna Buchanan, and others** *Naked Came the Manatee*. Thirteen of Miami's best-known novelists team up for a caper that centers on the

FICTION

discovery of Fidel Castro's dismembered head. It's a broad, in-jokey satire that's good, if uneven, fun – fans of local crime novels will enjoy a tale that weaves each author's signature hero together into one story.

**David Leddick** *My Worst Date*. The prolific gay author Leddick offers a nimble and arch coming-of-age tale set in the model-centric world of South Beach, where smart, beautiful teenage Hugo shares a hunky lover with his unwitting mother.

**Elmore Leonard** *LaBrava* (o/p). Plenty of Leonard's stories are set in South Florida, but *LaBrava* is one of the best. In it, photographer LaBrava meets a fading Hollywood villainess, who was once his childhood idol; from there, he's drawn into a violent, balletic mess that blurs fiction and reality. Leonard's rangy prose and colloquial style clash well with the surreal world of the trancelike hero.

**Theodore Pratt** *The Barefoot Mailman* (o/p). Novelized account of the Barefoot Mailman service (see p.57, "Central Miami Beach and north"): unremarkable but entertaining, and far better than the awkward film it inspired.

**John Sayles** *Los Gusanos*. Door-stopper novel written by the cult film director that's set in 1981, in the shadow of the Mariel Boatlift, and covers six decades of a family's life in Cuba and the United States – an intriguing, if grueling, patchwork of characters and stories.

## Photography

**Barbara Baer Capitman and Steven Brooke** *Deco Delights* (o/p). The standard work on Miami's Art Deco treasures, written by the woman who championed their preservation. Glossy and fun, but insubstantial.

**Laura Cerwinske and David Kaminsky** *Tropical Deco: Architecture & Design of Old Miami Beach*. A brisk survey of the significant styles and buildings that make up Miami Deco; the photographs are lush, but need updating – the *Delano*, for example, is still shown and discussed in its pre-Schrager state.

**Bill Wisser** *South Beach: America's Riviera, Miami Beach, Florida*. Glossy, glitzy pictorial history of South Beach that's strongest on the resort's origins and the building explosion that produced dozens of Art Deco hotels.

## Travel and current affairs

**Marjory Stoneman Douglas** *The Everglades: River of Grass*. More than fifty years old, this pioneering environmentalist's book galvanized feelings against over-aggressive development, and arguably saved the Everglades. Douglas is almost too engaged with her subject (skip some of the more sentimental passages), but by focusing on the human history of the area she pumps life into what can seem like an inherently empty place.

**Susan Orlean** *The Orchid Thief*. Orlean spotlights the obsessive and spat-ridden world of orchid fanciers in South Florida, following one orchid hunter into the Everglades on his illicit gathering trips. Hypnotized by the world she uncovers, Orlean tells a fascinating, if occasionally flabby, story.

**Maureen Orth** *Vulgar Favors: Andrew Cunanan, Gianni Versace, and the Largest Failed Manhunt in US History*. A gripping account of the life of Andrew Cunanan, the man who murdered Gianni Versace, that bristles with an exhaustive and salacious eye for detail. However, Orth's initial incisiveness is undermined by her own obvious distaste for South Beach and its hedonistic gay culture.

**David Rieff** *Going to Miami: Exiles, Tourists, and Refugees in the New America*. Rieff tackles the contentious subject of immigration in Miami with pompous but maddeningly perceptive observations. Though now somewhat dated (it was published in 1988), it's still a good introduction to Cuban-American issues.

# Miami on Film

iami on **film** is much like Miami in literature: a city of gritty crime and cynical cops. Its seedy glamour has attracted dozens of would-be noir thrillers to shoot here, though the sunnier sides of the city have also been the backdrop for plenty of light sex comedies.

**Ace Ventura, Pet Detective** (Tom Shadyac, 1994). The film that gave birth to Jim Carrey as a comedy phenomenon: he stars as a detective out to recover the Miami Dolphins' kidnapped mascot Snowflake, on the eve of the Superbowl.

**Any Given Sunday** (Oliver Stone, 1999). Al Pacino stars in this disappointing professional football movie from conspiracy master Oliver Stone. Notable for giving Cameron Diaz a rare chance to play against type as the team's fierce, determined owner.

**The Bellboy** (Jerry Lewis, 1960). Shot almost entirely in Miami Beach's *Fontainebleau* hotel, Jerry Lewis stars as the bellhop from Hell in this, his writer-director debut.

**Big Trouble** (Barry Sonnenfeld, 2002). Madcap caper based on humorist Dave Barry's novel of the same name, and featuring a top-quality comic cast including Stanley Tucci, Janeane Garofalo and Rene Russo.

**The Birdcage** (Mike Nichols, 1996). Remake of the French farce *La Cage aux Folles*, this riotous, campy movie stars

Robin Williams as Armand, the man behind South Beach's most successful drag club, and Nathan Lane as Albert, his lover and star. The story corkscrews when Armand's son announces his marriage to the daughter (Calista Flockhart) of ultra-conservative parents. The opening scene is a love letter to Ocean Drive, a single shot that pans in from the sea onto the riot of neon and nightlife.

**Black Sunday** (John Frankenheimer, 1976). A terrorist thriller, where Palestinian extremists plan to blow up Miami's Orange Bowl on Super Bowl Sunday – wiping out 80,000 football fans as well as the President. The climax of the movie offers some amazing aerial views of 1970s Miami.

**Blood and Wine** (Bob Rafelson, 1997). Jack Nicholson plays a wine dealer who teams up with a savvy Cuban nanny (Jennifer Lopez) and a Brit safe-cracker (Michael Caine) in this dark, underrated thriller. The crooks plan to steal a million-dollar necklace and, when it all goes wrong, they head off in pursuit

of their payoff to the Florida Keys.

**The Cocoanuts** (Joseph Santley & Robert Florey, 1929). Set during Florida's real estate boom, the Marx Brothers' first film stars Groucho as an impecunious hotel proprietor attempting to keep his business afloat by auctioning off land (with the usual interference from Chico and Harpo) in Coconut Grove, "the Palm Beach of tomorrow." Groucho expounds on Florida's climate while standing in what is really a sand-filled studio lot.

**Donnie Brasco** (Mike Newell, 1997). Al Pacino and Johnny Depp team up for this crime movie, based on the true story of FBI Special Agent Joseph Pistone, who infiltrates the Mob. The action heads to Miami from New York as Brasco helps the mafia expand a new nightclub operation there.

**Get Shorty** (Barry Sonnenfeld, 1995). Miami makes only a cameo at the beginning of this funny, bitter movie from the novel of the same name by Elmore Leonard. John Travolta stars as Chili Palmer, a local loan shark who heads out to Los Angeles on a debt-collecting mission, but ends up making movies.

**Goldfinger** (Guy Hamilton, 1964). The first Bond movie to make it to Miami – the opulent *Fontainebleau* is the backdrop for the scene at the beginning where we spot Bond sunbathing. However, these scenes were shot on a set in England, and were later edited into the Miami footage.

**The Heartbreak Kid** (Elaine May, 1972). A neurotic Neil Simon-Elaine May gem, where Jewish New Yorker (and new husband) Charles Grodin starts regretting his marriage as soon as the honeymoon drive to Miami begins. A flirty, sexy Cybill Shepherd hitting on him on the beach while his sunburnt wife lies inside doesn't help.

**Illtown** (Nick Gomez, 1995). Tony Danza's a gay mob boss, joined by indie royalty like Michael Rapaport, Lili Taylor and Kevin Corrigan, who play a supporting cast of Miami drug dealers.

**Miami Blues** (George Armitage, 1990). Adapted from the Charles Willeford novel, this hit-and-miss movie stars Alec Baldwin as a just-released sociopath looking to start over – crime-wise, at least – in Miami. He teams up with a college student and prostitute (Jennifer Jason Leigh), and is pursued by a burnt-out homicide detective played by Fred Ward.

**Miami Rhapsody** (David Frankel, 1995). Disappointing comedy of infidelity, starring Sarah Jessica Parker as Gwyn, who has to examine her commitment to a long-term boyfriend while finding out that everyone else in her family – parents included – is unable to stay faithful.

**Moon Over Miami** (Walter Lang, 1941). Bombshell Betty Grable comes gold-digging in Miami in this colorful, old-fashioned musical comedy. She and her on-screen sisters pose as a wealthy young woman and her two maids – a little too successfully, though, as she's soon pursued by two handsome bachelors at the same time.

MIAMI ON FILM

**Porky's** (Bob Clark, 1981). The classic, revolting teenage-boy romp is set in Fort Lauderdale, and is based on a real-life strip bar there.

**Scarface** (Brian De Palma, 1983). A modern masterpiece set in and around Miami during the 1980 Mariel Boatlift, *Scarface* stars a young Al Pacino as a small-time Cuban thug who maneuvers his way up to control Miami's drug cartels. It was filmed all across the city, and is a brutal time capsule of Miami's darker days.

**Some Like It Hot** (Billy Wilder, 1959). Wilder's classic farce begins in 1920s Chicago where Tony Curtis and Jack Lemmon, witnesses to the St Valentine's Day massacre, disguise themselves in drag and hide out in an all-girl jazz band headed for Miami.

**The Specialist** (Luis Llosa, 1994). A priapic, glossy portrait of the city (if a poor film), this stars one of Miami's former high-profile residents, Sylvester Stallone, as an ex-CIA agent hired by Sharon Stone to take revenge on the Miami mobsters

who wiped out her family.

**Striptease** (Andrew Bergman, 1996). Wretched movie version of Carl Hiaasen's riotous novel about a single mom – played by Demi Moore – who turns to stripping to make ends meet before eventually becoming embroiled in a political scandal.

**There's Something About Mary** (Farrelly Brothers, 1998). This modern gross-out classic climaxes in Miami Beach, where geeky Ben Stiller – still smarting from a prom night disaster years before – tracks down the goofy, beautiful love of his life, Mary (Cameron Diaz), and tries to win her again.

**Tony Rome** (Gordon Douglas, 1967). Frank Sinatra and Jill St John star in this gritty tale of pushers, strippers and gold-diggers in 1960s Miami: worth watching as a period piece, not for the plot – there are some witty one-liners, though.

**True Lies** (James Cameron, 1994). Arnold Schwarzenegger plays a CIA agent with a double life, Jamie Lee Curtis co-stars as his trusting wife, and Tom

Arnold wise-cracks in between the explosions. Look for the scene where a portion of Henry Flagler's old railway bridge to Key West is blown up.

**Where the Boys Are** (Henry Levin, 1960). This original spring break movie stars a young George Hamilton and Paula Prentiss as fun-seeking, sun-worshipping teens: it's the movie that put Fort Lauderdale on the map.

**Wild Things** (John McNaughton, 1998). Steamy, noirish thriller with a serpentine plot that entangles sultry schoolgirls Neve Campbell and Denise Richards with their teacher Matt Dillon, as well as an upstanding local cop (Kevin Bacon).

# Index

# F

# G

# H

# I

# roughnews

**Rough Guides' FREE full-colour newsletter**

News, travel issues, music reviews, readers' letters and the latest dispatches from authors on the road

**If you would like to receive roughnews, please send us your name and address:**

Rough Guides, 80 Strand, London, WC2R 0RL, UK

Rough Guides, 4th Floor, 345 Hudson St, New York NY10014, USA

newslettersubs@roughguides.co.uk

## Visit us online
# roughguides.com

**Information on over 25,000 destinations around the world**

- **Read** Rough Guides' trusted travel info
- **Share** journals, photos and travel advice with other readers
- Get exclusive Rough Guide **discounts** and travel **deals**
- Earn membership points every time you contribute to the
  Rough Guide **community** and get **free** books, flights and trips
- Browse thousands of CD reviews and artists in our **music** area

Rough Guide computing & internet series

HEAR THE WORLD ON YOUR COMPUTER

Internet Radio

THE MILLION COPY BESTSELLER

THE ROUGH GUIDE TO THE

Internet

THE WEB VERSION OF

Shopping Online

HOW TO BUY EVERYTHING ON THE INTERNET

click here

PLAN AND BOOK ANY TRIP ONLINE

THE ROUGH GUIDE TO

Travel Online

HOW TO FIND EVERYTHING ON THE NET

*

THE ROUGH GUIDE

Website Directory

THE ROUGH GUIDE TO

Personal Computers

HOW TO CHOOSE AND USE A PC

*lain speaking pocket guides to help you get the most out of your computer and the world wide web*

£6.00/US$9.95. *Website Directory only available in the UK £3.99

# around the world

# in twenty years

London Mini Guide ★ London Restaurants ★ Los Angeles ★ Madeira ★ Madrid ★ Malaysia, Singapore & Brunei ★ Mallorca ★ Malta & Gozo ★ Maui ★ Maya World ★ Melbourne ★ Menorca ★ Mexico ★ Miami & the Florida Keys ★ Montréal ★ Morocco ★ Moscow ★ Nepal ★ New England ★ New Orleans ★ New York City ★ New York Mini Guide ★ New York Restaurants ★ New Zealand ★ Norway ★ Pacific Northwest ★ Paris ★ Paris Mini Guide ★ Peru ★ Poland ★ Portugal ★ Prague ★ Provence & the Côte d'Azur ★ Pyrenees ★ The Rocky Mountains ★ Romania ★ Rome ★ San Francisco ★ San Francisco Restaurants ★ Sardinia ★ Scandinavia ★ Scotland ★ Scottish Highlands & Islands ★ Seattle ★ Sicily ★ Singapore ★ South Africa, Lesotho & Swaziland ★ South India ★ Southeast Asia ★ Southwest USA ★ Spain ★ St Lucia ★ St Petersburg ★ Sweden ★ Switzerland ★ Sydney ★ Syria ★ Tanzania ★ Tenerife and La Gomera ★ Thailand ★ Thailand's Beaches & Islands ★ Tokyo ★ Toronto ★ Travel Health ★ Trinidad & Tobago ★ Tunisia ★ Turkey ★ Tuscany & Umbria ★ USA ★ Vancouver ★ Venice & the Veneto ★ Vienna ★ Vietnam ★ Wales ★ Washington DC ★ West Africa ★ Women Travel ★ Yosemite ★ Zanzibar ★ Zimbabwe

### also look out for our maps, phrasebooks, music guides and reference books

age of historical and cultural issues. Now Rough chronicles series

Rough Guide chronicles series

Chronicles are pocket histories, written by ... illustrated with maps and ... recorded history

**China**
JUSTIN WINTLE

**England**
ROBIN EAGLES

**France**
IAN LITTLEWOOD

**India**
DILIP HIRO

# Dip
*into*
*the*
*past*

**'uniquely accessible pocket histories'** — History Today

*A vital pocket history series for travellers and students alike*

Series price £7.99

# NORTH SOUTH
# TRAVEL
## Great discounts

North South Travel is a small travel agent offering excellent personal service. Like other air ticket retailers, we offer discount fares worldwide. But unlike others, all available profits contribute to grassroots projects in the South through the NST Development Trust Registered Charity No. 1040656.

For **quotes** or queries, contact Brenda Skinner or her helpful staff, Tel/Fax 01245 608 291. Recent **donations** made from the NST Development Trust include support to Djoliba Trust, providing micro-credit to onion growers in the Dogon country in Mali; assistance to displaced people and rural communities in eastern Congo; a grant to Wells For India, which works for clean water in Rajasthan; support to the charity Children of the Andes, working for poverty relief in Colombia; and a grant to the Omari Project which works with drug-dependent young people in Watamu, Kenya.

## Great difference

**Email** brenda@northsouthtravel.co.uk
**Website** www.northsouthtravel.co.uk

ATOL
5401

North South Travel, Moulsham Mill, Parkway, Chelmsford, Essex, CM2 7PX, UK

## Travel Insurance

# ·BACKPACKERS·

**£2m Emergency Medical Expenses**
**Repatriation, 24 Hour Helpline**
A policy designed for the
longer-term or gap year traveller.
Essential cover for up to 12 months
continuous travel.

|  | Ages16-35 |
| --- | --- |
| 1 Month | £22 |
| 2 Months | £41 |
| 3 Months | £59 |
| 6 Months | £109 |
| 9 Months | £155 |
| 1 Year | £189 |

- Worldwide Travel - *incl* USA
- Sports and Activities
- Baggage extension available.

## ·Annual Multi-Trip·

| Europe | £42 |
| --- | --- |
| Worldwide | £58 |
| *per year* | |

Cover for the frequent traveller.
The policy covers unlimited trips
up to 31 days each during a year.
17 days Winter Sports included.

## · Single Trip Cover·

| 10 days | |
| --- | --- |
| Europe | £16.50 |
| Worldwide | £23.00 |

Full cover for individual trips
ideal for holidays & business trips
up to 66 days. Special rates for
Families. Ski cover available.

All prices correct May 2002    Underwritten by CNA Insurance Co (Europe) Ltd.

# 0800 16 35 18

Full details of cover available at:
www.ticdirect.co.uk

TRAVEL INSURANCE CLUB

# Cape Air

**FLYING FOR FLORIDA & THE KEYS**

*Ever seen a pelican stuck in traffic*

Ft. Myers
Naples
Ft. Lauderdale
Key West

800-352-0714 • 508-771-6944 • www.flycapeair.com

# Don't bury your head in the sand!

# Take cover!

## with Rough Guide Travel Insurance

**Worldwide cover, for Rough Guide readers worldwide**

UK Freefone **0800 015 09 06**
US Freefone **1 866 220 5588**
Worldwide **(+44) 1243 621 046**
Check the web at
**www.roughguides.com/insurance**

**ROUGH GUIDES**

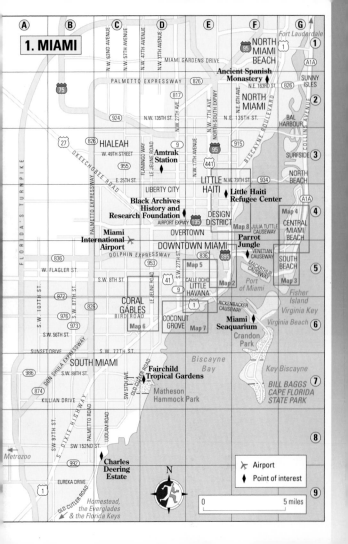

# 1. MIAMI

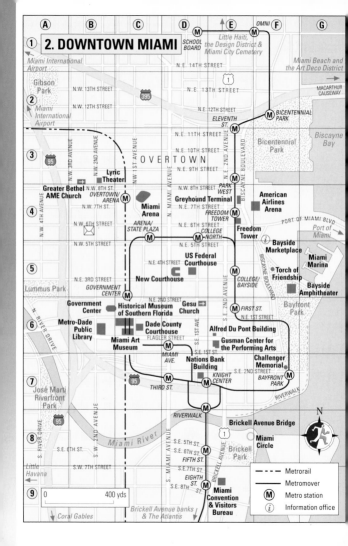

# 2. DOWNTOWN MIAMI

- A
- B
- C
- D
- E
- F
- G

1

2

3

4

5

6

7

8

9

**OMNI**

SCHOOL BOARD

Little Haiti, the Design District & Miami City Cemetery

Miami Beach and the Art Deco District

Miami International Airport

N.E. 14TH STREET

Gibson Park

N.W. 13TH STREET

N.E. 13TH STREET

MACARTHUR CAUSEWAY

Miami International Airport

N.W. 12TH STREET

N.E. 12TH STREET

395

BICENTENNIAL PARK

ELEVENTH ST.

N.E. 11TH STREET

Bicentennial Park

Biscayne Bay

N.E. 10TH STREET

95

N.W. 3RD AVENUE

N.W. 2ND AVENUE

N.W. 1ST AVENUE

OVERTOWN

N.E. 9TH STREET

BISCAYNE BOULEVARD

N.E. 2ND AVENUE

Lyric Theater

N.W. 8TH ST.

N.E. 8TH STREET

PARK WEST

American Airlines Arena

Greater Bethel AME Church

N.W. 7TH STREET

OVERTOWN/ ARENA

Miami Arena

Greyhound Terminal

N.E. 7TH STREET

FREEDOM TOWER

PORT OF MIAMI BLVD

N.W. 4TH AVENUE

N.W. 6TH STREET

N.E. 6TH STREET

Freedom Tower

Port of Miami

ARENA/ STATE PLAZA

COLLEGE NORTH

Bayside Marketplace

i

N.W. 5TH STREET

N.E. 5TH STREET

Miami Marina

US Federal Courthouse

N.E. 4TH STREET

COLLEGE/ BAYSIDE

Torch of Friendship

Bayside Amphitheater

Lummus Park

New Courthouse

N.E. 3RD STREET

BISCAYNE BOULEVARD

GOVERNMENT CENTER

N.E. 2ND STREET

Bayfront Park

S. RIVER DRIVE

Government Center

Historical Museum of Southern Florida

Gesu Church

FIRST ST.

N.E. 1ST STREET

Metro-Dade Public Library

Dade County Courthouse

N.E. 1ST AVENUE

Alfred Du Pont Building

Miami Art Museum

FLAGLER STREET

Gusman Center for the Performing Arts

MIAMI AVE.

Jose Marti Riverfront Park

Nations Bank Building

Challenger Memorial

S.E. 1ST ST.

95

S.E. 2ND STREET

BAYFRONT PARK

THIRD ST.

KNIGHT CENTER

S. RIVER DRIVE

S.W. 2ND AVENUE

RIVERWALK

RIVERWALK

Brickell Avenue Bridge

Miami River

Miami Circle

Little Havana

S.E. 6TH ST.

S.E. 5TH ST.

Brickell Park

BRICKELL AVENUE

S.W. 7TH STREET

FIFTH ST.

1

S.E. 7TH ST.

EIGHTH ST.

S.E. 8TH ST.

Miami Convention & Visitors Bureau

Coral Gables

0        400 yds

Brickell Avenue banks & The Atlantis

N

- - - - Metrorail
——— Metromover
Ⓜ Metro station
ⓘ Information office

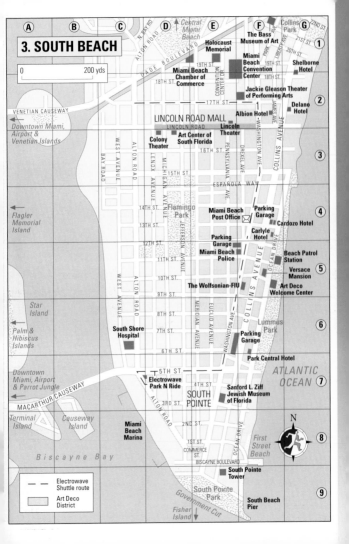

# 3. SOUTH BEACH

A   B   C   D   E   F   G

| 0 | 200 yds |

Central Miami Beach

N BAY RD

ALTON ROAD

DADE BOULEVARD

COLLINS Park

21ST ST.

2ND ST.

The Bass Museum of Art

Holocaust Memorial

19TH ST.

Miami Beach Convention Center

20TH ST.

Shelborne Hotel

Miami Beach Chamber of Commerce

18TH ST.

19TH ST.

18TH ST.

17TH ST.

Jackie Gleason Theater of Performing Arts

Delano Hotel

LINCOLN ROAD MALL

LINCOLN ROAD

Albion Hotel

Lincoln Theater

VENETIAN CAUSEWAY

Downtown Miami, Airport & Venetian Islands

Colony Theater

Art Center of South Florida

WEST AVENUE

BAY ROAD

ALTON ROAD

LENOX AVENUE

MICHIGAN AVENUE

MERIDIAN AVENUE

PENNSYLVANIA AVE

DREXEL AVE

WASHINGTON AVE

COLLINS AVENUE

16TH ST.

15TH ST.

ESPANOLA AVE

ESPANOLA WAY

14TH ST.

Flamingo Park

13TH ST.

JEFFERSON AVENUE

Miami Beach Post Office

Parking Garage

Cardozo Hotel

Flagler Memorial Island

12TH ST.

11TH ST.

10TH ST.

9TH ST.

Parking Garage

Miami Beach Police

The Wolfsonian-FIU

Carlyle Hotel

OCEAN DRIVE

Beach Patrol Station

Versace Mansion

Art Deco Welcome Center

Star Island

Palm & Hibiscus Islands

8TH ST.

7TH ST.

6TH ST.

South Shore Hospital

EUCLID AVENUE

Lummus Park

Parking Garage

Downtown Miami, Airport & Parrot Jungle

5TH ST.

Electrowave Park N Ride

Park Central Hotel

ATLANTIC OCEAN

MACARTHUR CAUSEWAY

4TH ST.

SOUTH POINTE

3RD ST.

Sanford L. Ziff Jewish Museum of Florida

Terminal Island

Causeway Island

2ND ST.

Miami Beach Marina

1ST ST.

COMMERCE ST.

OCEAN DRIVE

First Street Beach

Biscayne Bay

BISCAYNE BOULEVARD

South Pointe Tower

N

South Pointe Park

Government Cut

South Pointe Pier

South Beach Pier

Fisher Island

| - - - | Electrowave Shuttle route |
| | Art Deco District |

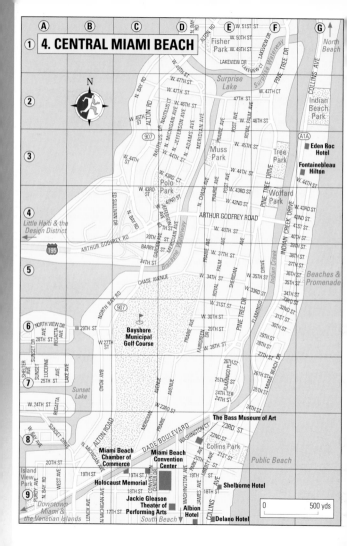

# 5. LITTLE HAVANA AND AROUND

0       400 yds

Orange Bowl Stadium

LATIN QUARTER

Unidos en Casa Elián

Máximo Gómez Park

Brigade 2506 Memorial

Cuban Memorial Boulevard

Woodlawn Cemetery

Riverside Park

Jose Marti Park

Downtown

Museum of Science and Space Transit Planetarium

Villa Vizcaya

Coconut Grove

VIZCAYA

- - - - Metrorail
Ⓜ Metro station

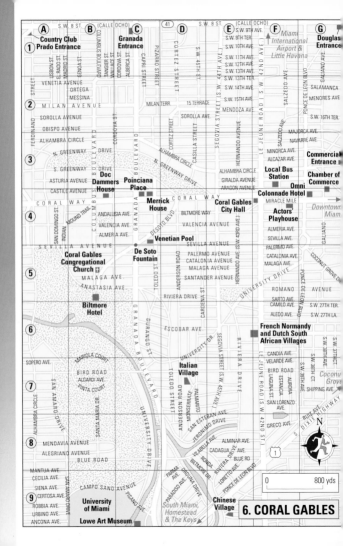

6. CORAL GABLES

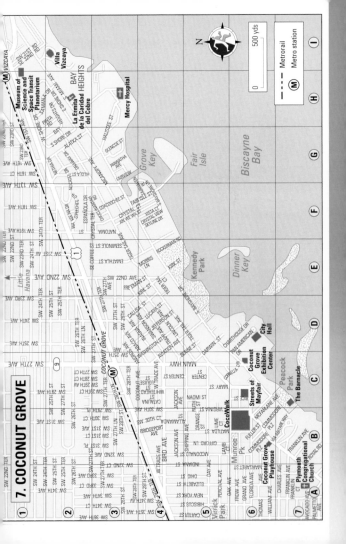

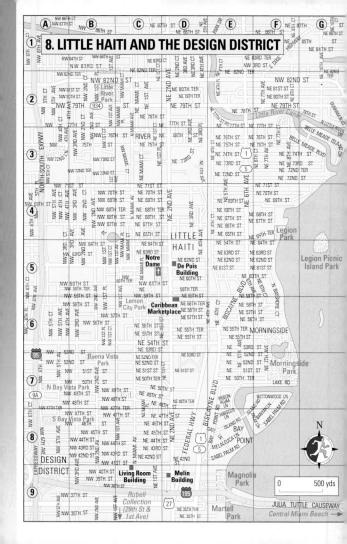

# 8. LITTLE HAITI AND THE DESIGN DISTRICT